ONWARDS FROM OSNABURGS

ONWARDS *from* OSNABURGS

THE RISE & PROGRESS OF A SCOTTISH TEXTILE COMPANY

DON & LOW

OF FORFAR 1792-1992

CHRISTOPHER A. WHATLEY

MAINSTREAM PUBLISHING

EDINBURGH AND LONDON

First published in Great Britain in 1992 by
MAINSTREAM PUBLISHING COMPANY (EDINBURGH) LTD
7 Albany Street
Edinburgh EH1 3UG

ISBN 1 85158 509 5

A catalogue record for this book is available from the British Library

Produced in Edinburgh by Mainstream Publishing Co. Ltd

Printed and bound in Great Britain by
Butler & Tanner Ltd, Frome and London

For
Eilidh and Neil

Contents

Acknowledgments

Without the interest, encouragement and above all the financial support of Don & Low (Holdings) Ltd, the research for this book could not have been carried out, nor would it have been written or published. The group's commitment to business history in general, and their recognition of the value to future generations of a serious account of their own history, is to be commended. Invaluable assistance has been willingly given by certain people who have been or are still connected with the company. These include Ernest Gourlay, Stuart Howie, John Smart, the late Louis Smith, Alister Wilson and Miss Jean Duncan. Mrs Helen Shearer and Mrs Deborah Baer have helped me find documents, made appointments with interviewees and guided me around the offices at St James' during my visits there. In addition to providing me with information and unique insights into the workings of the company, Michael Hill, Addison 'Ed' Stewart and Mr and Mrs Gavin Don have been extremely generous with their hospitality. Hamish Tough, chairman and managing director of Scott and Fyfe Ltd, was also kind enough to discuss aspects of the recent history of the industry with me, while Professor Peter Grinyer of the University of St Andrews (and a former board member) willingly gave of his time and expertise. Above all, thanks are due to William Low, who instigated the project, his son Barclay Low, currently personnel director at Don's, with whom I have had the pleasure of working during its final stages, and to Alasdair MacCallum, chief executive since 1986, who has shown an interest in my work from the outset, and was responsible for bringing it to fruition.

The company not only provided most of the finance for the book, but also gave my research assistant John Stewart and myself considerable freedom to work our way through Dons' voluminous records. Most of these are now deposited with the University of Dundee, although some more recent material is still at the company's headquarters in St James' Road, Forfar. Access to the company's records on deposit in Dundee, as well as to the invaluable records of the Association of Jute Spinners and Manufacturers, has been facilitated by Mrs Joan Auld, the university's archivist, who has been instrumental in obtaining many of the photographs which appear in this volume. I am grateful to Linda Ramsay for cleaning and preparing a massive plan of St James' Works for photographing, although sadly this could not be incorporated in the publication. The diagrams were prepared by Carolyn Bain, of the University of Dundee's Central Media Services. Enid Gauldie kindly allowed me to see transcripts of Buist family papers in her possession.

Help has also been obtained from Forfar Public Library, the Local History department in Dundee Central Library, the Scottish Record Office and the Library of the University of St Andrews. Two local archivists, Iain Flett in Dundee and Fiona Scharlau in Montrose, have been extremely generous with their time in assisting me in my enquiries. I am grateful to Mrs Mary Drysdale and her sister Mrs Brora Butterworth for talking to me about their late father, Frank Buist, and for going to a great deal of trouble to make Buist family material in their possession available, and to others who had connections with the firm for corresponding with me, notably John Watson, who is related by marriage to the Buists, and John and Louise Hurst, who provided information on James Strickland Oliver, Mrs Hurst's late father.

I am grateful to my colleagues in the Department of Scottish History at the University of St Andrews, especially Professor Christopher Smout and Dr Bill Knox for their encouragement and, in the former's case, for practical support in easing somewhat my teaching load in session 1989–90. Thanks too are due to the Research Committee of the Faculties of Arts and Divinity at St Andrews for a small grant which enabled me to complete the first draft of the book, which dealt with the period up to 1986.

Sincere thanks are due to Kerry Withers for undertaking the mammoth task of re-typing the text in a form suitable for publication. My father, Allan Whatley, willingly agreed to undertake the laborious task of compiling the index. Not for the first time I am grateful to him for putting aside his retirement pursuits to come to my aid in this way. Patricia Gibb has provided invaluable assistance with the technical aspects of the book's production. Her enthusiastic support for and interest in the subject sustained me during those periods when my energies were flagging. Claire Watts, Janene Reid and Judy Diamond at Mainstream have been a tower of professional strength.

Finally, I wish to express my thanks to John Stewart, who acted as my research assistant in the initial stages of this project. Owing to the fact that I had other commitments during part of his period in post, I was not always able to provide him with as much support and guidance as I would have wished. He coped well, however, and provided me with clear transcriptions from the company's records as well as his own interpretations of events which proved invaluable during the writing-up stage of the first draft of the book in the spring and early summer of 1990. The final responsibility for what is now contained within the covers of the book, however, is mine.

Christopher Whatley
January 1992

Foreword

This book describes 200 years of human endeavour in a textile company.

It is at one level a factual account of historical events which will be technically interesting to people in both business and academic life. At another level it is a human story of joys and sorrows, wisdom and foolishness, success and failure, confidence and anxiety to which we who work for the company can easily relate. We cannot but be grateful to the determined, courageous and resourceful men and women who, over two centuries, have dealt with the opportunities of their day and passed on to each successive generation a company which has grown to become a leader in its field in the United Kingdom.

What of the future? Our recently revised mission statement sets out our aim to be the industrial textile supplier that customers choose because of the competitive advantage our products and services provide.

Our success will be built on a spirit of partnership and respect both within and without the company, coupled with the very best training that we can provide to all who work for Don & Low.

Alasdair N. MacCallum
Chief Executive

Introduction

The linen and jute industries of east central Scotland, which for the best part of two centuries dominated Dundee and outlying towns such as Arbroath, Brechin, Kirriemuir and, of course, Forfar, have not attracted their fair share of historical attention. It is true that important studies have appeared over the years, notably A. J. Durie's *The Scottish Linen Industry in the Eighteenth Century* (1979), and *The Dundee Textile Industry 1850–1914* by Bruce Lenman, Enid Gauldie and Charlotte Lythe (1969). Others have followed, such as William Walker's history of textile trade unionism in Dundee, *Juteopolis: Dundee and its textile workers 1885–1923* (1979), and Mark Watson's industrial archaeological survey, *Jute and Flax Mills in Dundee* (1990).

Much remains to be done, however, and it is almost certainly no exaggeration to say that the coarse linen, jute and, more recently, polypropylene industries of Dundee and Angus have between them created one of the largest collections of unused business records in the country. Many of these records have been deposited by individual firms, yet none has formed the basis of anything like a substantial publication.

Although the business lives of some individuals have been the subject of serious enquiry, no comprehensive study of entrepreneurship in the coarse textile region has been undertaken, and indeed, despite the fact that some firms have had short histories written for private consumption, to date no professionally written, full-length account of any of the region's linen and jute companies has appeared in print.

This book attempts to go some way towards filling that gap. Its primary function is to inform and act as a record of the history of Don & Low Ltd from its foundation some two centuries ago until the present day. As the publication marks the company's bicentenary the book also has a celebratory purpose. It is not, however, a piece of hagiography; hopefully readers will feel that the book has been written with sufficient critical rigour. However, while professional historians may glean something from its pages, the book will have failed in its purpose if it cannot be read and enjoyed by a wider audience. For this reason jargon and esoteric technical terms have been avoided, and wider historical concerns are introduced only where these have helped to illuminate some aspect of the company's history. Readers wishing to explore further will be able to do so by following up the footnotes, which have been provided largely with this in mind. Others may simply ignore them.

Dons are presently one of the largest extruders and weavers of polypropylene tape in Europe. In 1986, when the company became a wholly-owned subsidiary of Shell UK Ltd, its total net assets were £15.8 million and, in the financial year ending May 1985, pre-tax profits were over £4.5 million; even in the depths of the recession in 1990, pre-tax profits were still a highly respectable £4.6 million.

The company's roots, however, stretch far back into the coarse textile industry's past when annual income from yarn and cloth dealings totalled hundreds rather than millions of pounds.

It is impossible to put an exact date on the company's foundation and therefore ascertain precisely the historically correct year for its bicentennial celebration. One candidate is 1788, the year in which William Don returned to Forfar from Dundee and established the business from which the present company is descended. As will be seen, however, both William's father, Gilbert, and his uncle, Andrew Binny, had been involved in the textile trade prior to 1788, and so it is perfectly reasonable for the company to lay claim to even greater antiquity.

Within the company it has long been believed that the official foundation date was 1794 when, according to tradition, a partnership was established by William and John Don. Yet the recent rediscovery of the company's earliest surviving record, a copy letter-book covering the period 1794–1801, does not support this view. There is nothing at all to suggest that any new formal arrangement was made in 1794, and even if there had been, it would not exclude the possibility that the brothers had been in business together previous to this date. Almost certainly William Don and his uncle had been working together, for a letter from William dated 26 December 1795 refers to their having done business with a Glasgow firm, Buchanan, Stiven & Co for 'a very considerable time past'. He is unlikely to have meant a year.

The year 1992 has been fixed on for a variety of reasons: in 1790 Gilbert Don died and, as will be seen later, the early 1790s marked the beginning of William Don's independent career as a successful flax and linen merchant. Gilbert Don's efforts notwithstanding, William must be considered as the firm's founder. Much more recently, in 1991, Dons finally shut down their jute weaving operation; 1992 thus marks the beginning of a new era at the commencement of which the company has wholly committed itself to the manufacture and utilisation of man-made fibres. This year also heralds the opening of the Single European Market. It is an appropriate time to look back – and forward.

The company's surviving records have provided most of the raw material for this book, and, while these are extensive, they are not complete. Where they are invaluable is that they go back, in one form or another, to the early 1790s. The Buist family papers – mainly still in private hands – take us back even earlier. Although the collection of Dons' letter-books, minute-books, accounts, price lists, cloth samples, photographs and plans is a rich one, there are partial gaps for some of the potentially most interesting periods in the company's history, notably for the six decades from *c.*1842 until 1904, when the jute industry enjoyed its finest years. It was rare too, to find a lengthy period for which an overlapping series of records survived, a minute-book and a set of output or sales figures, for example. Long runs of figures for production are hard to find. Inevitably then, and especially as two centuries are covered in this book, the story is sometimes patchy and uneven and, at times, frustratingly uncertain.

For the period within living memory such shortcomings could sometimes be overcome by conducting interviews with current or ex-directors, senior employees and others who were familiar with the principal actors. Understandably, those involved did not judge it prudent to authorise publication of remarks which were made in confidence. Nevertheless, the account published here is a full and reasonably frank one, and while some sensitive matters have been written about accordingly (there seems no point in causing gratuitous hurt or offence), little of significance has knowingly been left out.

It is a story within which certain key themes emerge, the most notable of which is a virtually unbroken tradition of concern for the quality of the company's products as one means of overcoming the locational drawback of their Forfar base. Product innovation has featured strongly, while good relations with customers usually formed part of the equation. In earlier times the company's leaders found it beneficial to distance themselves from Dundee goods. The company still strives to distinguish itself from its major rivals there. Good labour relations have been essential too, although regrettably the constraints of time and space have meant that less attention has been paid to the company's workers than their contribution merits.

There were times when the company's leading figures had their backs against the wall, occasions when all seemed lost. Good fortune undoubtedly played its part in ensuring that such setbacks were overcome. So too did some remarkable businessmen.

Chapter One

The Context: Dons and the Scottish Coarse Textile Industry, *c.*1700–1992

Linen had been manufactured in Scotland long before the end of the eighteenth century, when William Don (d.1817) laid the foundations of the present company from his Forfar base. Rapid extension had taken place in the seventeenth century, notably in and around Glasgow, and by the 1690s as many as 1.8 million ells of linen cloth may have been going south from Scotland into England, compared with as few as 18,000 ells one hundred years earlier.[1] Even so, it was during the 1700s that flax-spinning and linen-weaving flourished to the extent that linen became the country's 'staple' industry and, apart from agriculture, Scotland's largest employer of labour. Growth continued into the nineteenth century, though more slowly, and linen was superseded by jute as Scotland's leading coarse textile manufacture.

The company's place in the textile industry is best understood within the wider context of the history of the production of, and markets for, coarse linen cloth, jute and, more recently, polypropylene. During the course of the eighteenth century the Scottish linen industry was divided along two fairly distinct paths, although there were points at which they overlapped; in the west, especially in the vicinity of Glasgow and Paisley, competition from Irish and Dutch producers of fine linen after the Union of 1707 drove manufacturers and merchants into new product areas, such as lawns and gauzes. Ultimately this led to the establishment of the renowned Paisley silk industry, while from the late 1770s, linen manufacture elsewhere in the west was replaced by cotton, which, by and large, failed to establish itself to the east and north of Perth.

In the east, however, little attempt was made to compete in the finer end of the trade, and instead attention was paid to ways of expanding sales of coarse linen, which had been made in towns such as Dundee at least as early as the sixteenth century. As a result, over time the three counties of Angus (Forfarshire), Perthshire and Fife came to dominate the Scottish coarse linen industry and, after the establishment of cotton in the west, the linen industry as a whole. Thus in 1760, 57 per cent of Scotland's stamped linen yardage was coming from the counties of Angus, Perth and Fife; by 1820 this had grown to 88 per cent.[2] Most came from Angus, which in 1728 accounted for 27 per cent of the linen stamped in Scotland, in 1790 48 per cent and by 1820, 62 per cent. These proportions would be lower if they were calculated on the basis of the value rather than the yardage of stamped cloth, as coarse linen tended to be worth less than the finer linens.

Within the coarse linen region, however, a pronounced degree of local specialisation occurred. By the end of the eighteenth century, for example, Arbroath had become Scotland's leading producer of canvas, but a glutted market after 1783 encouraged some manufacturers there to embark on the production of coloured and white threads. The linen trade, however, was dominated by 'osnaburgs', some of which were made in all the textile-producing towns in Angus, with the possible exception of Coupar Angus.

Forfar specialised in the production of osnaburgs. This type of cloth had first been made in Scotland in the late 1730s, perhaps by the firm of Wallace, Gardyne and Company of Arbroath, although James Donaldson, a Perthshire manufacturer, has also been credited with the first serious efforts to make it in Scotland.[3] He may have been one of the beneficiaries of George Murison of Montrose's efforts in October 1738 to obtain samples of various sorts of foreign linen, which were provided by the Board of Trustees on condition that he show them to 'any other Manufacturer that intends to imitate them'. Amongst the package sent north were 'osnaburgs'.

This was a loosely woven, coarse lint or tow-based low-grade unbleached linen cloth which had originally been made in Osnabrück, Germany. It was extremely popular in the rapidly expanding colonial markets of the West Indies and North America. Its introduction to the coarse linen area, whether in

Arbroath, Perthshire or indeed Montrose, was evidently extremely successful, for around 1745 the manufacture of osnaburgs had spread to Forfar. Prior to that the only cloth made in Forfar was a few yard-wides called 'Scrims'.[4] Interestingly, a modern form of scrim was to become Dons' staple product for a time after the Second World War.

Previously heavily dependent for its prosperity on leather and shoemaking, Forfar's economy was transformed as the linen trade expanded – although even in the mid-nineteenth century, 'highland brogues' were still being made in the town. With the introduction of osnaburgs, in the space of four or five years the number of looms more than doubled, from 60 to 140, while by the mid-1790s there were between 400 and 500. Indeed so rapid had been the rise in the numbers of weavers working in Forfar during the late 1740s and 1750s that in 1758 the weavers incorporation in Forfar decided to abandon its practice of providing public dinners on the grounds that it could no longer afford to bear their cost.[5] It was during this period of expansion in Forfar that Gilbert Don, father of William, the company's founder, appears to have first entered the linen trade, as a small flax-merchant and hackler, who it must be assumed purchased either locally grown flax or flax imported into Dundee from the Baltic ports of Riga and Archangel, as well as Holland, before preparing and distributing it to the growing army of Forfarshire's outworking female hand spinners.

Without any of the falls of running water which were sought elsewhere in Angus to power flax-spinning machinery, it was impossible to produce yarn in this way within Forfar itself. Significantly, flax-spinning machinery – which first appeared in Scotland in 1787 – was adapted for the purpose of making yarns suitable for osnaburg manufacture in 1790 at Brigton mill in Kinnettles parish, which bordered Forfar.[6] Forfar concentrated on weaving and by the end of the second decade of the nineteenth century Forfar weavers were putting out more osnaburgs than any of the other Angus towns – the average annual figure of 2.6 million yards between 1819 and 1822 being greater than Dundee's 2.1 million. Dundee's speciality at this stage was the more traditional 'brown' linen, which was also made in Forfar, though in much smaller quantities.[7] It was fitting that for a time in the early nineteenth century, the premises of Robert Don, William's brother and successor in the business, were located in Forfar's Osnaburg Street.

The expansion of coarse linen production in Scotland was facilitated by a number of factors. In spite of the difficulties which the fine linen trade faced after 1707, there are indications that there was an active demand from London for coarse unbleached linens. Linen which was of consistently good quality throughout its length was at a premium.[8] As will be seen later, satisfying this requirement was to be a major factor in the early success of William Don – although long before his entry to the business, Forfar merchants had established close links with London, from whence cloth from the town was shipped across the Atlantic.[9]

Efforts were made to improve the quality of the Scottish product, however. These culminated in the establishment of the Board of Trustees in 1727. Pressed for by the 'Honourable Society of Improvers in the Knowledge of Agriculture', which included several of Scotland's leading landowners amongst its members, inspired by the Irish Board of Trustees which had been set up in 1711 to improve standards there, and instituted by a government which was concerned about the political dangers of the disaffection which poverty and underemployment amongst the lower classes might bring, the Board played a major part in transforming the Scottish linen industry.[10]

Within ten years of the Board's foundation, there was a doubling of the quantity of linen stamped, that which met the approval of the Board's stampmasters or inspectors of linen cloth. Thereafter, although there were setbacks, as in the mid-1750s, the early 1770s and on several occasions during the Napoleonic Wars, the industry continued to expand, with output rising from 7.8 million yards per annum between 1748–52 to 26.6 million yards between 1813–17.[11] It is important to note that rarely was expansion sustained for more than five consecutive years. The typical pattern was of 'two or three years of advance, followed by one or two of no gain or even retreat'.[12] These were critical times for linen merchants such as the Dons.

The Board of Trustees' contribution was not confined to the appointment of stampmasters, although theoretically and often in practice these men, who were stationed in most of the weaving towns and villages of any importance, could exercise considerable power – by cutting up unmarketable cloth and giving it to charity, for instance. Efforts were made, by regulation, instruction and the payment of premiums, to improve the quality and quantity of flax grown in Scotland, and to raise the standard of preparation, spinning, weaving, and above all, bleaching.[13] Vital as far as Forfar was concerned, was the role which the Board played in encouraging the trade in osnaburgs, both by sounding out the viability of the market in the colonial Plantations by consulting knowledgeable dealers in London and Glasgow, and offering prizes, partly money and partly looms, to those who turned their hand successfully to this grade of cloth in the counties of Angus, Perth and the Mearns.

Even more important for the coarse linen trade were the bounties which were payable on exports from 1742. Under the terms of the Bounty Act of 1742, a bounty of ½d per yard was paid for colonial exports of cloth under 6d a yard in value, and one penny if between 6d and 12d. The terms were made more generous in 1745 in order to encourage the industry further. The effect of the bounties, which were not withdrawn until 1832, was to make it easier for Scots to sell their low-value coarse linen to the Plantations, where, it appears, most Forfar cloth was ultimately sent. Indeed, by the 1790s something like 90 per cent of the linen exported from Scotland was being shipped to North America and the West Indies. How much the trade in osnaburgs came to depend on the bounties can be seen when these were temporarily removed between 1754 and 1756 and the British Linen Company's demand for osnaburgs in the Dundee district was cut by half.[14]

Flax-spinning and linen-weaving were labour intensive operations. And fortunately, though less so than Ireland, eighteenth-century Scotland was reasonably well endowed as far as the supply of labour was concerned. Women and children could be drawn into the labour market to engage in domestic spinning, which was often carried on part-time. One contemporary reckoned that in the mid-1750s something like four-fifths of Scotland's adult females were engaged for some part of their time in spinning.[15] Increasingly, it was to become a full-time but poorly paid occupation. Weaving in the first half of that century was in a somewhat different position, in that weaver incorporations in the burghs were able to restrict the expansion of the trade by insisting on five-year apprenticeships followed by periods of work as a journeyman and the payment of entry fees. Such an incorporation, of forty weavers, had existed in Forfar prior to the introduction of osnaburgs.[16]

Anxious to increase the supply of weavers as well as to reduce wages, the Board of Trustees was instrumental in breaking the restrictive power of the incorporations in 1751. This almost certainly contributed to the sharp rise in the numbers of hand-loom weavers in Forfar, where the town's population almost doubled between 1755 and 1792. Young men were said to be attracted by the ease with which they could learn the trade – this could be accomplished in a year or two – and earn wages which were sufficient to enable them to support a family and consequently marry at a younger age than other artisans.[17] An additional feature of the parish of Forfar was the existence in the landward part of 'small possessions' of land, 'as will maintain a cow or two, and sometimes a horse', which were rented by weavers who combined their manufacturing operations with subsistence agriculture. This created classic conditions for the emergence of 'proto-industry', wherein merchant-manufacturers were relieved from the burden of paying wages for full-time labour, as well as from the costs of fitting up looms, which were often owned by the weavers themselves.[18]

In other respects though, Forfar was less favourably placed; manufacturers there were said to suffer from two 'great drawbacks' – the scarcity of fuel (coal had to be imported from the collieries of Fife, the Lothians and Tyneside) and 'the distance from a sea-port, Dundee being the nearest'.[19] The former delayed the introduction of steam-powered industry, and both were factors which, from the time of William Don onwards, exercised the minds and entrepreneurial skills of successive generations of the company's leaders who had to overcome this locational disadvantage.

Fluctuations continued to mark the linen trade in the nineteenth century, which opened with a series of depressions, in 1801, 1803, 1809–11 and 1816, although the underlying trend was still upwards. A century later, in 1907, linen output in Scotland was 103 million yards, three times the 1822 level. Marked increases in output occurred during periods of war. The Crimean War (1854–6), the American Civil War (1861–5) and the

Franco-Prussian War (1870–1) were the three most important, although even before the first of these Forfar's population had again doubled, from 4,756 in 1790 to 9,587 in 1841, at which time there were some 3,000 individuals employed in weaving. For the Dons, like so may of Dundee's textile princes, it was during and especially immediately after the American Civil War and to a lesser extent the Franco-Prussian War that the greatest gains of the Victorian era were made.[20]

Although firms such as Baxter Brothers in Dundee and Dons continued to produce linen throughout the 1800s, there was a noticeable shift towards jute production beginning in Dundee from the 1830s onwards, in which virtually every flax-spinning and linen-weaving business in Tayside region eventually became involved. And although Dundee dominated the jute trade, in 1911 Forfar's 3.6 per cent of those employed in jute in Tayside made it the second largest employer of jute workers in the region. Like Dundee, Forfar had a particularly heavy concentration of female textile workers: in this regard it was again second only to 'Juteopolis'.[21]

Jute was a coarser and more brittle fibre than flax. Although there is some disagreement about why jute supplanted linen when it did, a number of factors clearly played important roles: jute was cheaper than flax, supplies of which were liable to interruption; the market for coarse linens was becoming increasingly competitive so that substantial benefits would result if a suitable lower-cost raw material could be found and used – especially for bags and sacks as world trade expanded. Although jute was no substitute for the fine linens of Belfast and Leeds, it could be used as an adulterant or even replace some types of coarse linen. More specifically as far as Dundee was concerned, since it was difficult to spin, both water and whale oil had to be sprinkled on to the jute to soften the fibres during the preparatory 'batching' process – and fortuitously, Dundee had a sizeable whaling trade which in the 1830s was looking for new outlets for its oil. Manufacturers were able to draw for their labour supplies on rural immigrants from the surrounding counties – and Ireland, which provided a deep pool of cheap female labour which was familiar with the textile trade. Whatever the ranking of these factors though, jute overtook linen as Dundee's 'staple' during the mid-1850s.[22] To last the course in linen was a considerable achievement; in 1861 it was estimated that of all the mills in and around Dundee, three-quarters had suffered bankruptcy at one time or another.

Despite this, jute was not universally popular amongst the Tayside textile manufacturers. Even in the early years of the twentieth century for example, Baxter Brothers of Dundee remained proud of the quality of their 100 per cent linen and were extremely hostile to competitors who tried to undercut them by mixing their fibres with tow or jute yarn. Yet even for Baxters, the immediate future lay in jute, which they began to manufacture around 1867[23]; at the end of the century only three or four firms which specialised in flax remained in Dundee.[24] The Dons, however, first used jute in the mid-1840s (when Baxters had considered it), although it was not until the beginning of the twentieth century that they began to weave jute cloth in significant quantities in Forfar. The indications are that they moved into jute-spinning some time during the 1860s, after they had amalgamated (in 1865) with the Dundee-based merchant and flax-spinner Alexander Jafferson Buist, then based at Old Ward Mill, and whose business links with the Dons went back to the early 1800s. In 1826, for instance, Robert Don had supplied Alexander Jafferson, Buist's uncle, with osnaburgs which, with his partner John Barclay, owner of several whaling vessels at Montrose, he was sending to Honduras.[25]

Both coarse linen and jute were subject to increasing competition in the later decades of the nineteenth century. Profit levels generally were far below those achieved in the balmy years of the 1860s and early 1870s. Thus Don Brothers, Buist & Co continued to make profits after the Franco-Prussian War. The peak was reached in 1872, however, and from the end of that decade the numbers of bad years began to mount, with losses being sustained in 1879, 1881, 1886 and 1891. Efforts by manufacturers to cut their costs by reducing wages embittered industrial relations and led to serious strikes. Dons themselves experienced a rare period of serious labour unrest at this time, and in 1889 a strike following a lock-out interrupted production for over seven weeks.

It is clear that it was largely outbreaks of war which continued to illuminate an otherwise gloomy picture, as tariffs overseas rose, notably those erected by the USA, and as Indian and Continental competition became more intense. In the early 1870s there were over seven times as many power-looms for making jute in the UK (and almost all of these were in Dundee and Angus) as in Calcutta; by 1907 there were twice as many in Calcutta as in the whole of the UK. Flax imports into Dundee in 1910 were only just over one-third of their 1850 level; tow perhaps about half.[26] It was not only Dundee which felt the pinch in this respect. Between 1872 and 1901 an estimated 100,000 spindles had been discarded in Ireland, and several mills were demolished or converted to other uses.

While the First World War – and the demand it created for sandbags and other coarse fabrics – did much to relieve the gloom, the inter-war years were even more difficult for both the linen and jute trades. The situation for linen was the more serious of the two, and in the 1920s, for the first time, Dons made more jute than linen, their staple product from the earliest days of the company. They stopped buying flax in 1935.

In jute too, profits were depressed, wages were low and unemployment was high. Many firms went out of business. Even the outbreak of the Second World War brought no immediate respite, and by the end of the hostilities, more than half of the UK's domestic consumption of jute products consisted of Indian-made goods.[27] Imports of flax to Dundee, which in 1938–9 were no lower than they had been in 1910, fell steeply immediately after the war. Linen, which had employed 997 persons in Forfar in 1911, accounted for only 49 in 1951.

Generalisations which point to a period of unbroken decline in linen and jute are misleading, however. While the long-established linen industry almost disappeared from Forfar (as it did from Blairgowrie and Kirriemuir), in Dundee its importance rose, from an employer of 1,260 people in 1911 to 1,730 in 1951.[28] During the 1950s imports of flax to Dundee, which had fallen from 1860 onwards, began to rise again, while output of canvas rose sharply at the turn of the 1960s, at a time when the price of flax was relatively low. And although a downturn followed, flax-spinners such as Baxter Brothers (then part of Low and Bonar Ltd by whom they were acquired in 1924) continued to find markets for several varieties of canvas.[29]

As far as jute was concerned there was a sharp decline in demand for the product for its traditional end-uses, particularly in bagging and linoleum backing. Even so, while output of jute yarn in the UK peaked in 1955 (followed by cloth in 1956), it was not until the late 1960s that the industry began to enter what looked like terminal decline. Until then, jute had found a use as a backing material for tufted carpets produced both in the UK and Europe, which did much to compensate for the loss of its former markets.[30] Jute manufacturing, however, has not disappeared altogether, and raw jute is still imported, albeit in much smaller quantities than in the industry's hey-day, and is spun and woven by a handful of firms in Tayside.

Neither in the jute nor in the linen industries then was the post-war period one of unmitigated disaster. A relatively small number of the companies which had formed the backbone of Tayside's traditional textile industry managed to survive and flourish in spite of increased competition from Asia as well as the growth of a jute industry in East Pakistan (Bangladesh from 1971), the main jute-growing area which was favoured by wage levels which were even lower than those paid in India. In Dundee and the surrounding district significant productivity gains were achieved as workers were better trained and redeployed on new and more efficient machinery.

Jute Control, introduced by the government as a wartime measure in 1939, was the main reason why some of the former jute producers survived. It provided a significant but diminishing degree of order and protection for the industry until 1969. Behind this tariff wall, however, several companies, including Dons, diversified their product range, and during the second half of the 1960s, by which time protection was rapidly being phased out, turned with varying degrees of enthusiasm to the spinning and weaving of polypropylene. As jute declined, so the number of firms fell by over 50 per cent between 1967 and 1977. Some disappeared altogether, while others were acquired or merged into bigger concerns. Don Brothers, Buist & Co Ltd were very much part of this process, and in 1960 they formed what was to be a crucial association with Low Brothers (Dundee) Ltd, a firm of Dundee jute-merchants. Two years later J. & J. Smart Ltd of Brechin was taken over. Other acquisitions and regroupings followed. Although jute continued to be woven until 1991, the group's main interest was in polypropylene and by the early 1980s Dons had become the largest polypropylene textile extrusion and weaving firm in the UK and the second largest in Europe.

As polypropylene is a by-product of refining crude oil, it was almost inevitable that a number of those companies which were spinning and weaving the fibre would be drawn more closely towards the petroleum and chemical companies which supplied them with their raw material, and in June 1986 the group was bought by Shell UK Ltd, a subsidiary of the Royal Dutch Petroleum Company, and from 1987 traded under the name of Don & Low (Holdings) Ltd.

The rest of this book will describe and account for the rise and progress, and sometimes simply the survival, of a business enterprise which dates back to the beginnings of the industrial revolution in Scotland. It is not simply a company's history though. The precursors of Don & Low Ltd not only acted upon the economic backcloth of the Scottish coarse textile industry which this chapter has described: the metaphor may be crude, but it is entirely accurate to say that they played their part in spinning and weaving it too. Nowhere is this more true than in Forfar itself, initially and now once more the company's headquarters. From the time of William Don, the fortunes of the firm and of Forfar have been inextricably linked.

Chapter One: The Context

1 T. C. Smout, *Scottish Trade on the Eve of the Union, 1660–1707* (Edinburgh and London, 1963), p233.
2 A. Durie, *The Scottish Linen Industry in the Eighteenth Century* (Edinburgh, 1979), p25.
3 Ibid, p51.
4 *The [Old] Statistical Account of Scotland, Vol XIII, Angus* (Wakefield, 1976 ed) p283.
5 Montrose Public Library, 'Acts and Statutes of the Weavers Craft Within the Burgh of Forfar, 1627–1836, 8 December 1758.
6 E. Gauldie, *The Dundee Textile Industry, 1790–1885*, (Edinburgh, 1969), pxx.
7 Scottish Record Office, Board of Trustees Papers, NG1/15/1 & 2, Figures showing linen stamped in Forfarshire, 1819–22.
8 Perth Archives, Perth Burgh Records, B59/34/25, George Yeaman to Perth Town Council, March 1712.
9 *Pococke's Tours in Scotland*, Scottish History Society, Edinburgh (1887), pp217–8.
10 See Durie, *Linen Industry*, pp162–4; R. H. Campbell, *Scotland Since 1707* (Oxford, 1965), p58.
11 Durie, *Linen Industry*, p22.
12 Ibid, pp22–3.
13 Ibid, pp55–9.
14 Ibid, p131.
15 Ibid, p159.
16 *OSA, XIII*. p253.
17 Ibid, pp253–4.
18 See F. F. Mendels, 'Proto-industrialisation: The First Phase of the Industrialisation Process', *Journal of Economic History*, XXXII (1972).
19 *Commercial Directory of Ireland, Scotland and the Four Most Northern Counties of England* (Ridgefield, 1820), p394.
20 B. Lenman, *et al*, *Dundee and its Textile Industry, 1850–1914* (Dundee 1969), pp30–1.
21 A. Carstairs, *The Tayside Industrial Population, 1911–1951* (Dundee, 1974), p33.
22 For recent accounts of the emergence of jute in Dundee, see E. Gauldie, 'The Dundee Jute Industry', in J. Butt and K. Ponting (eds) *Scottish Textile History* (Aberdeen, 1987), pp112–25; C. A. Whatley, 'The Making of Juteopolis and how it was', in C. A. Whatley (ed), *The Remaking of Juteopolis* (Dundee, 1992), pp7–22.
23 A. J. Cooke (ed), *Baxters of Dundee* (Dundee, 1980), p21.
24 *City and Royal Burgh of Dundee, Survey and Plan, 1952* (Dundee, 1952), p116.
25 John Barclay to Alexander Jafferson, 13 September 1826. From transcriptions of Buist family papers in the possession of Enid Gauldie.
26 J. M. Jackson (ed), *The Third Statistical Account of Scotland; The City of Dundee* (Arbroath, 1979), p106.
27 Ibid, p135.
28 Carstairs, *Industrial Population*, p37.
29 Jackson, *City of Dundee*, pp138–9.
30 W. Stewart Howe, *The Dundee Textiles Industry, 1960–77; Decline and Diversification* (Aberdeen, 1982), pp24–64.

Chapter Two

Origins and Foundations: The Dons and the Binnys

The originators of the present company were the Dons of Forfar, who appear to have been descendants of John Don of Dalbog, near Edzell, who lived from around 1660 until 1710. He was credited with fathering 21 children by at least two women. Perhaps because of this uncertainty, apparently only nine of the births were registered. His sons, born in the last two decades of the seventeenth century, migrated southwards and established themselves in Forfar.[1]

Opening the door: Gilbert Don

The son of one of John's children was Gilbert Don (1741–90), who was almost certainly the first of the family to become involved in the linen trade. Unfortunately, virtually nothing in the way of documentary evidence concerning his career has survived and so what can be reported is consequently vague. Although it is not clear when or how he first became involved in textiles, according to one source Gilbert Don was engaged in the flax trade as a hackler by the 1760s, when linen sales were experiencing rapid growth after the bounties on exports of coarse linens had been restored in 1756.[2] Don was almost certainly a small merchant, buying up some of the 'great quantity' of flax which was grown by local farmers at this time, dressing or preparing it, and giving it out to domestic hand-spinners who spun the yarn for the hand-loom weavers. A single piece of evidence – from 1795 – suggests that he may have been trading under the name of Gilbert Don & Co.

William Don (d. 1817), the company's founding father who died in debt but nevertheless established the Dons as important linen merchants and manufacturers in Forfar

It is highly likely that his activities in the trade were further inspired – perhaps even assisted by – his father-in-law, William Binny, the Board of Trustees' stampmaster for Forfar from 1756 until 1788. Notably, both the Dons and the Binnys were members of Forfar's tight-knit Episcopalian congregation. 'Penal Laws' passed in 1718, 1746 and 1748 against Scottish Episcopalians in the aftermath of the Jacobite Risings of 1715 and 1745 effectively barred more than five of them from worshipping together, and drove those who continued to adhere to the faith underground. Certain civil rights were also compromised.[3]

Episcopalianism remained strong in Forfar despite this. Amongst its adherents were several important Forfarshire landowning and mercantile families, such as the Carse Grays, the Carnegys of Lour, the Farquhars of Pitscandly and the Sturrocks, to whom one of Gilbert's four sons, Robert, was later to become related through marriage. Significantly, both the Carnegys and the Sturrocks were in linen too, the former as merchants and the latter as manufacturers, with Mr John Sturrock the younger being credited as the first man in the Forfar district 'who struck out the idea of employing hands, and manufacturing on a larger scale than then obtained of each man working only his own web'. Whatever the substance of this claim, there is no doubt that Gilbert's marriage to Isabel Binny strengthened his connections in the local linen trade. He preceded his sons William and Robert in forming a marriage alliance which was to prove advantageous in business terms. Commencing with William Don's secretaryship of the local Episcopalian congregation in the 1790s (the Penal Laws were repealed in 1792 after the Episcopalians declared their loyalty to the Hanoverians), another long-standing family tradition was established in that each successive generation of Dons was to play a prominent role in the affairs of the Episcopalian Church in Forfar.

At some stage, Gilbert Don became the proprietor of the modest estate of Bankhead in Forfar, at the south end of which he erected a brewery, a means of spreading his business interests in a venture which could be established for around £300.[4] It was a sound location for such an undertaking: the local population was rising fast, while Forfar itself was surrounded by the productive arable lands of Strathmore, from which great quantities of grain had been exported from the seventeenth century. He also had a house or premises near the cross in Forfar, which he was evidently in the process of rebuilding in 1783.[5] When he died in 1790, Gilbert Don left his sons with going concerns in three areas of business: brewing, linen and, to a lesser extent, land. William, the eldest son, took over his father's linen interests. He was also the senior partner in the brewery, in which two of his younger brothers, John and David, also had an interest – this business was in fact run under the name of John Don & Co.

Laying the Foundations: William Don, banker and insurance agent

When Gilbert's eldest son, William, took over his father's flax interests in 1790, he was well prepared to do so, and indeed to develop them further. 'Bred to the business, even from the loom', from around 1783 to 1785 he had served an apprenticeship with a Forfar linen manufacturer, to learn what he later referred to as the 'practical part' of the trade.[6] This was followed by three years with William Alison & Son, a firm of merchants who were based in Dundee's Overgate. In 1788 he was invited to return to Forfar to assist his uncle, Andrew Binny, who had in the same year been appointed by the Board of Trustees to succeed his father as their stampmaster in Forfar.

William Don's return to Forfar was not the prelude to a business life which was to be dominated solely by linen – in fact, until his death in 1817 much of his prodigious energy was channelled into insurance and banking. As will be seen though, while William spread his interests – and risks – widely, there was much overlap between his banking and linen activities. Indeed, so important was Don's involvement in banking that the contribution which he made to the firm's development cannot be fully understood without a fairly full account of this aspect of his business life.

Don's entry into the world of insurance occurred at around the same time that he returned from Dundee, when he secured a post as the Forfar agent of the Dundee Assurance Company.[7] Formed in 1783, the company provided cover against losses by fire and for at least ten years had a monopoly in the field. It was evidently the Dundee Assurance Company which was referred to by the Revd. Robert Small, in his *Statistical Account* entry for Dundee, compiled in 1792–3, where he wrote of the town's single insurance company, 'whose property is supposed to amount to half a million; and by whom assurances are already made to the value of £800,000'.[8] Its success in Forfar under the guidance of William Don was no less impressive, with Don claiming in 1809, after 21 years work on the company's behalf, that 'tho' there are three offices here, namely Sun Fire, Aberdeen and Fife . . . I have under cover a great part of this town and neighbourhood.'[9] Indeed, in the same year, Don turned down offers of agencies for both the Hercules and the North British insurance companies.

One reason for the company's success appears to have been the relatively low rates charged, with 'Common Insurance' costing 2s per cent, plus 3s per cent duty. Such rates would have been attractive to the growing numbers of weavers in Forfar and its vicinity, with whom Don was becoming increasingly familiar. His insurance work also strengthened his connections with members of the local landed classes, such as a Mr Clark, whose three properties at Woodside and Hospitalfield near Arbroath, and Linthill, were valued at £11,664, or Andrew Dalgairns, whose properties in Ingliston and Sandyford were valued at £4,360.[10] These values, of course, were approximate, but they were by no means necessarily below the real worth of the property and other assets. In the case of the Douglas's 'House of Brigton' the valuation of £4,500 which was eventually put on the property and its furnishings and the owner's possessions, included £400 for clothes and jewellery, and £100 for books. This was rather more than the real worth of the articles in question, but William was happy to satisfy the family's vanity. In a letter to David Blair, the Assurance Company's cashier, Don advised him to:

> just write the policy as near to the Lady's ideas as possible, taking care at the same time to generalise the Plate and Jewels, Household furniture and wearing apparel etc as near the Prospectuses of our Puffing neighbours as may be.[11]

Don's ability as an insurance agent, which it must be assumed was evident at an early date, and his wide range of contacts in and around Forfar may have impressed the directors of the Dundee Banking Company, who were keen to open a branch in Forfar, as in other Angus towns.[12] Anxious that the credit-worthiness of their customers should be known to them and as it was prudent for them to be familiar with local business conditions, it was usual for the Scottish provincial banks to extend their operations to satellite towns, such as Forfar, where the economic base was similar to that of the head office town, in this case, Dundee.[13] An additional advantage was Forfar's reputation of being a good risk financially. The local minister went as far as claiming that 'there is no town in Angus where they find fewer bankruptcies and more punctual payments'.[14]

At this comparatively early stage in his career it is questionable whether Don himself had all of the attributes which were said to be sought in potential bank agents, who, ideally, were:

> tried men of business, who have proved, by their manner of conducting their own affairs, their capability of successfully transacting whatever may be confided to them.[15]

His uncle easily fitted this description and there can be little doubt that the first steps in Don's banking career were greatly assisted by his being Andrew Binny's nephew, although it seems likely that Don's recent succession to his father's Bankhead estate would have lessened any doubts the bank may have had about his financial standing. Indeed, in order to secure his post with the bank, Don had to sign a bond to them for £6,000, with twenty people acting as sureties.

There is no doubt that between them Binny and Don satisfied the bank's requirements. Binny, of course, was the local stampmaster, as his father had been before him. With their experience in the linen trade, both Binny and Don were used to dealing with a complex network of credit transactions and in short, were already familiar with one of the main functions of the banker. One of the local agent's most important tasks was to boost the bank's note circulation, which could be facilitated by their widening circle of business connections, which ranged from small-scale domestic spinners and weavers, through the ranks of the local mercantile and landed classes to merchants in Dundee and further afield. As bank directors were inclined to

Bankhead as it was in the late 1980s. It was purchased by Gilbert Don and later became the home of William Don and successive members of the Don family

appoint as agents the men of the 'highest integrity',[16] it must also be assumed that both had established reputations for honest dealing which may have been underpinned by their close adherence to the Episcopalian Church. Thus after a six-month search for suitable personnel, both Binny and Don were appointed as the Forfar agents of the Dundee Banking Company, with business commencing on 4 August 1791. Don stayed with the company until 1817, apart from a spell between 1801 and 1809, when he joined the Dundee New Bank.[17]

While both men were pleased to obtain their appointments, in the longer term it was William Don who derived much greater benefit from his banking activities than his uncle, who withdrew in 1802. Don gained substantially from the influence it gave him in the town and the use he could make of the bank's facilities for promoting his other business ventures.

The bank's note issue was principally extended by encouraging local merchants and traders to use the Dundee Banking

Company's paper through the operation of cash accounts and, more importantly, by discounting bills. Cash accounts, however, tended to remain the responsibility of the head office, although with his local knowledge it is probable that Don had some say in setting the limits of such accounts in the first place.

Where the provincial banks' agents had a greater element of discretion was in extending credit – and thereby issuing the bank's notes – by discounting bills. Bills were basically notes giving the value of the transaction between the buyer of the goods and the seller of them. The buyer signed the seller's bill, thereby undertaking to pay the amount due at a given future date, usually three months, and returned the bill to him. The time between the acknowledgment and the date of payment of the bill provided the buyer with an opportunity to sell the goods he had obtained and so raise the money to pay what he owed. If the seller wanted his money before the bill was due for payment, he could sell it to a bank, who gave him cash minus charges and interest, usually 5 per cent, the discount. At the end of the three months the bank presented the bill to the buyer and expected to receive full payment for it. If the bill was not paid within three days it was 'protested', followed by 'diligence', a legal procedure to recover the debt.[18] It was either by sanctioning or restricting their agents' business in bills that banks exerted the greatest control over their local economies.

In practice it appears that cash credits were used mainly to finance wage payments and small running expenses, whereas bill discounting provided finance for production and sales.[19] Agents of the Dundee Banking Company such as Don were paid by commission – 0.1 per cent of all interest received on cash accounts and varying amounts on bills discounted – 0.25 per cent on local bills discounted where they guaranteed the whole amount for example.[20] London bills gave 0.35 per cent, with the agent guaranteeing half of the amount. Evidently Don was more heavily involved with local bills, remarking in September 1799 that 'every bill I discount is at my own risk, and that risk sometimes makes my blood run cold'.[21]

His discomfort was not eased by the tendency of his friends and relations to strain the bank's patience. Whatever the benefits of his close ties with Forfar's landed élite, they were not without their tribulations. In 1809 Don wrote to George Dempster, son of the Dundee Banking Company's founder, giving him the names of a number of people who were in debt to the bank, which he claimed he had previously withheld 'from motives of delicacy'. They included General David Hunter of Burnside, William Douglas of Brigton, Charles Gray of Carsegray, Colonel Fotheringham and 'others of lesser note'.[22] The first three were all related to William through his marriage to Mary Ann Hunter: General Hunter was his father-in-law, Douglas was his wife's uncle, while Gray had married into the Hunter family.

In 1814 William once again found himself under pressure to call in debts owed by his father-in-law and Douglas of Brigton. The former, General Hunter of Burnside, had been in the practice of using accommodation bills, whereby a number of parties agreed to sign bills to each other at different times in order to raise sums in ready cash. Banks sought to avoid these bills as they were not usually supported by any concrete trade transactions and might prove difficult to retire, if indeed they could be retired at all. By November 1814 Hunter had run up a debt of over £1,838 by this means.[23] At what was a time of general economic uncertainty, Don was ordered by the bank to take steps to reduce Hunter's deficit. After offering him a means of paying off part of his debt, Don wrote to him in a tone not usually adopted by a man when addressing his wife's father, pointing out that while at some personal cost he had uncomplainingly assisted Hunter for some time, 'it is right I warn you that if the accommodation I offer while I have it in my power . . . be not accepted of . . . I will almost certainly do that which I have hitherto most anxiously avoided doing . . . namely, ultimate diligence to recover the money which I and the Bank have been too long out of.'[24]

His approach to Douglas of Brigton was rather different. Douglas was one of the proprietors of what had been the very first water-powered flax mill for spinning coarse threads in Scotland, the Douglastown Spinning Company, which was apparently making heavy losses, partly due to mismanagement, during the final years of William Douglas's life.[25] Rather than have Douglas owe the bank a large sum of money, Don split the amount owed between himself and the Dundee Banking Company, so that in December 1814 Don reckoned that the bank was owed £777 2s 11d and himself slightly more than £976.[26]

It is impossible to be sure why Don took this step, although it is quite likely that Douglastown provided some of the yarn used by the weavers from whom he purchased cloth; concern for the 'honour' of the company in general and Douglas in particular appears to have played some part though.[27] This was not out of character, for Don frequently found it hard to resist the appeals of his family and friends for credit, doing what he once described as 'standing in the gap for others'. And although he could admit that 'my errors are many', but not wilful, he did not open accounts or grant requests for credit willy-nilly, claiming in 1810 that while he could not 'pretend to trace every note that comes from the Office', he thought he knew 'pretty well the nature of every man's business who had been in the practice of doing it here for many years'.[28] At the same time, however, Don does seem to have been convinced in a more general sense of the advantages to Forfar's economy of a more generous credit system. As a banker he was extremely liberal, deliberately so, although as has been seen above, this could cause him considerable anguish. 'I am too accommodating,' he admitted in a letter to one of the directors in 1811. 'Your late Agent would do nothing,' he went on, 'yet, I am blamed for doing too much. I confess my disposition leads me to the latter course.'[29] Often harried by the bank to chase up overdue bills or to close dormant cash accounts – 'I never see a Director now that I do not expect to be found fault with one way or another' – Don frequently found himself exasperated as he attempted to match the competing pulls on the bank agent, to 'provide for his own safety and satisfy the country at one and the same time'.[30]

It was a difficult tightrope to walk, but one which Don recognised was both in his own and his customers' interests to cross. A bankrupt concern was a drain on his own funds as he had to meet any bills which were due, while a struggling debtor at least provided him with some hope of a return.[31] Until 1815, however, when he reported his first banking loss (of no more than £150) owing to the failure of a P. Murray, Don's expansive strategy appears to have been successful. As will be seen later though, from around that time he became burdened with growing difficulties in his banking affairs as well as with his other business interests.

Don's understanding of the periodic problems of merchants such as Laird & Co was firmly based on his own experience in the linen trade. His position as bank agent, however, gave him access to both credit and cash which others would have found much more difficult to come by, though his practice of utilising the banking system in his own interests was not always done with the sanction of head office. In 1803, for instance, at a time when the Dundee New Bank had restricted its branches at Forfar and Brechin to discounts of £500 a week,[32] it was found that Don and other agents of the bank had been using money lying in deposit accounts to discount their own bills. As a result, an instruction was issued that 'all transactions must be for the behoof of the bank'.[33] As will be seen, this was not the only time or way that Don used his position as a bank agent to support his expanding interests in linen.

The Rise of William Don, Linen Merchant

Although at the end of the eighteenth century William Don remarked that banking was the 'great stake' he had, linen dealing became an increasingly important part of his activities, so much so that by 1811 he described it as 'the chief part' of his business.[34] As has already been seen, it was this trade for which he had been trained, on a path which had in large part been prepared by his father and uncle.

When he first became involved in linen on his own account in the late 1780s, Don was clearly not prepared to devote all his time to it. A variety of factors meant that the linen trade was extremely unstable. On the supply side there was the state of the flax crop, which if poor, could raise raw material prices to uneconomic levels. There was also 'an inherent tendency to overproduction' in an industry in which numerous small producers were involved.[35] Market demand, in America and the West Indies as well as at home, was notoriously volatile. Thus William Don's decision to embark on a career in finance must be considered a prudent one. At the same time, it was probably also essential for him to seek openings outside linen, for although his father had long been engaged in that trade, there is no evidence to suggest that his involvement was substantial. The Binnys, however, members of whose family had business interests in India, had been involved in dealing in linen with London houses on their own account, although unfortunately no idea can currently be obtained of the scale of this trade. From the end of the 1780s William Don began to sell finished pieces of linen cloth to customers in Dundee, Glasgow – and London.

Don's career as a linen merchant roughly coincided with the period which commenced with the French Revolution and ended with the defeat of Napoleon Bonaparte in 1815. For the Scottish linen trade, it was a time of severe fluctuations: output in 1803, for instance, was one-third less than the previous year. Yet over the period as a whole, total cloth production rose from around 20 million yards at the turn of the 1790s to an annual average of 26.6 million yards between 1813 and 1817.

Wartime demand for certain types of linen cloth, including those with which Don dealt, was intense, leading William to write anxiously in May 1810, after hearing a rumour that peace was imminent, 'I neither wish it nor believe it'.[36] In December 1813 there is more than a hint of annoyance in his report that 'Our market advanced in price till rumour of peace flattened it again'.[37] It would have been remarkable if someone who had been a colonel in the 3rd Forfarshire Volunteers had not been delighted to learn of Napoleon's first abdication in 1814, but even so the merchant in Don could not fail to reflect that this would 'make our trade dull for a while'.[38]

During the course of the war the industry in Scotland continued to concentrate in the east, on coarse linen and in larger enterprises, at least where spinning was concerned. Hand-loom weaving tended to be much more widely dispersed: 'the greater part of all Scottish linen is manufactured by poor weavers who have not a shilling of capital', one contemporary remarked in 1814.[39] As far as can be ascertained, the rate of growth of the industry in Forfarshire was considerably faster than that for Scotland as a whole, with output virtually doubling from around 8.8 million yards in 1790 to 16.3 million in 1820. William, along with his brother Robert, both shared in and contributed to this increase, although figures relating to the quantities of cloth the Dons dealt with are frustratingly thin on the ground, thus making it hard to be precise about the scale of their contribution. Sharp year-by-year fluctuations in the level of their business further complicates the task. Expansion though is certainly suggested by the fact that between 1807 and 1810, the Don brothers purchased on average 1,219 pieces of cloth a year, a 35 per cent increase on the 1806 figure of 906 pieces.[40] In good times the value of their cloth purchases could be substantial. In the period from January 1808 to March 1809 they sold over £19,500 worth of cloth to their biggest London customer, Cowleys.[41] Estimates suggest that Dons' total purchases may have amounted to the equivalent of around one-fifth of the cloth sold in Forfar.

Owing to the instability of the trade which the war intensified, there were numerous business failures, notably between 1809 and 1811. William Don, however, managed both to expand and develop his linen interests and survive, at least until 1817. The part which good fortune played in his career should not be overlooked. So great had the expansion of linen-weaving in Forfar been after the middle of the eighteenth century that following the death in 1788 of William Binny, the town's stampmaster, the Board of Trustees was urged by some local weavers to appoint two stampmasters to replace him.[42] Although it was considered that unlike Dundee, Forfar could support only one office, Andrew Binny required an assistant, and it was his nephew William Don whom he invited to join him. Unfortunately, no details have survived about the nature of the business relationship between Binny and Don. Thus, on the basis of the available evidence it is only possible to surmise that Binny devoted himself to the job of inspecting and stamping cloth, while Don used the opportunity presented by his appointment as Binny's assistant to develop his private interests. Unlike William Don, Binny was a (prominent) member of Forfar's weaver incorporation, and he thereby eased Don's route into the world of Forfar's master weavers with whom, of course, many of his dealings took place.

Although William Don was almost certainly guided in the early years by Binny, in terms of the day-to-day operation of the linen trade he seems to have been on his own, at least for the first fifteen years or so. Like many of the entrepreneurs in the first phases of Britain's industrial revolution, Don played several roles, from managing director through financier, sales manager and quality controller, to transport manager and clerk.[43] Around 1805 he was joined by his younger brother Robert. Like William, Robert Don (1782–1857) had also been well prepared for a career in linen. His marriage to Isabella Sturrock, the daughter of John Sturrock, Laird of Pitreuchie and a man of 'ample means' who also had interests in cloth manufacturing, strengthened the Don family's connection with the trade – as did Robert's appointment in 1807, following in his brother's footsteps, as assistant to Andrew Binny, who was still Forfar's stampmaster. In this position, Robert was better able to fulfil his function as William's cloth-buying agent. Robert's other contribution appears to have been to involve himself and William more directly in manufacturing cloth. This is suggested by his admission in September 1808 as a master and a freeman of the weaver incorporation in Forfar.[44] William played no part in this organisation, and indeed, was never admitted to the craft. On the other hand, although Robert was described in the minute-book as a 'merchant', it was made clear that he had served an apprenticeship as a weaver.

Osnaburgs, strelitz and sheetings

A major factor in William Don's success in the linen trade in Forfar was that by and large he was able to supply his main customers with well-made coarse linen cloth, principally osnaburgs. Sometime early in the nineteenth century he had participated in the development of a speciality cloth, 'strelitz' osnaburg, another name which may have originated in Germany (Mecklenburg-Strelitz was the home state of King George III's queen, Charlotte), and had earlier been given to a planned village near Coupar Angus.

While the exact circumstances of the adoption of the name is uncertain, the nature of the cloth is clear. 'Strelitz' differed from common and 'drest' osnaburg cloth in being wider (27 inches rather than 25) and made from better quality yarns. Like common and 'drest' osnaburg, strelitz could be designated either 'lint' or 'tow', depending on the length and coarseness of the flax fibres which had been used in the yarn. Whichever of these was used, it could be sold for something like a penny more per yard. There were times, however, when the differential was much greater, as in October 1810 when common tow fetched only 5d per yard, compared to strelitz which could still find buyers at 10d.[45] This type of cloth, Don was convinced, would establish the reputation of both Forfar and his own company, and by distinguishing it from that of the neighbouring towns, he could carve out a secure, and more financially rewarding, niche in the market. And this he appears to have done, confidently asserting in 1815 that the 'Fabrics . . . made in Forfar [are] of the first qualities and almost all the respectable West Indies Houses prefer them to any other.'[46]

A matter of major importance to William Don was that Forfar cloth should not be confused with cloth made in Dundee, of which he was consistently scornful. Inasmuch as it was possible, he concealed from Dundee manufacturers the differences between his cloth and theirs, writing to his main London buyer in 1813 that were Dundee's merchants to see the kind of goods he was sending to London, 'it would tend to render them quite dissatisfied with the sorts they are at present perfectly well pleased with'.[47] So disdainful did he feel about the critical faculties of Dundee's cloth buyers that when he was unable to obtain orders from London, Don occasionally made use of the numerous hawkers who appeared at Forfar's twice-weekly cloth markets, to 'pass on a few of the inferior sorts [of cloth]' to Dundee.[48]

Plain osnaburgs and strelitz were not the only types of cloth in which William Don dealt. Over time, the returns which could be obtained from sales of all grades of osnaburg fell, thereby encouraging dealers to look for more lucrative varieties of cloth. Between 1805 and 1807, 1.7 million yards of linen – with a total value of just over £81,000 – were sold in Forfar, giving an average of 11d per yard. By 1816–18, when the town's linen output (three-quarters of which was osnaburgs) had risen by around a third to 2.6 million yards, the total sales value had risen by only 22 per cent, which pushed the return per yard down to an average of 9½d. The average for the four years 1819–1822 was even lower, at 8d per yard.[49] Accordingly, sheetings, traditionally Arbroath's speciality, began to interest the Don brothers as these could normally be sold at higher prices than osnaburgs. British 'duck' was an even more expensive material, which at peak periods of wartime demand could fetch as much as 1s 3d and in 1812, as much as 1s 7d a yard. Woven with bleached or whitened yarn, it is hardly surprising that William Don considered it to be superior 'to any' that had been made in Forfar.[50] He found it difficult to organise the production of this type of cloth, however, and was never as successful in either of these lines, which he turned to somewhat later in his career, as he was in the lower end of the market.

The quality, quantity and price of linen cloth was heavily dependent upon the supply and quality of flax. Although flax had been raised in the countryside around Forfar earlier in the century, by William Don's time most flax was being imported from Russia, shipped either to London, Dundee, Montrose or Leith, and in smaller quantities to other ports on Scotland's east coast.

Following in their father's footsteps, William and Robert were both involved for a time in importing flax to the district. William, for instance, was a partner in a 'flax and tallow concern' with Charles Adam of Dundee until some time in the early 1800s.[51] This was a very uncertain business, and during the French wars prices fluctuated violently within the space of even a few days. On one occasion when demand collapsed William was left with £2,600 of flax which he had bought from John Airth, Provost of Arbroath, who had as the market roared 'picked up every cwt' of the best quality while in London.[52] As cloth merchants, it was in yarn rather than flax that the Dons were directly interested.

Spinners and weavers

With their reputation very much dependent upon their ability to provide their customers with good-quality cloth, it was vital that the weavers from whom William and his brother purchased cloth should be able to obtain sufficient quantities of well-spun yarn. Yet the yarn market was inherently unstable. One difficulty was that spinners could be tempted by a price rise to turn to other lines, thus reducing the supplies of the types of yarn the Dons wanted. William also found it hard to persuade weavers to experiment with new yarns: 'You cannot conceive the toil and trouble we have in introducing anything,' he wrote exasperatedly in September 1811, at a time when he was trying to supply a London customer with a quantity of lucrative Duck.

One reason for this was that he had little effective control over the supply of yarn. On one occasion he managed to persuade two local manufacturers, John Butchart and David

Yeaman, who between them had twenty looms, to weave some duck for him. However, mistakes made in bleaching the yarns and the subsequent shortfall in supply raised the price of a spindle from 5s to 8s. Don could scarcely control his anger at the situation in which he found himself, and wrote to the main supplier of the requisite yarns, William Sandeman:

> I have been for a good while back amused by some of our manufacturers as to the quantity to be delivered of British Duck and I had pledged myself for more than I can now get . . . I have induced others to try the trade . . . they cannot get the yarn from you . . . their hands are mainly idle. This is a hardship on them and they are apt to throw the blame on me diverting them from their own steady trade.[53]

The weavers' conservatism was perfectly understandable. Their 'steady trade' was in osnaburgs and they were unwilling to turn to heavier and broader sheetings; they 'will not work sheetings', William Don noted, when 'the OS trade' was buoyant. Only when conditions deteriorated could he draw them away from it.[54] At the same time the hand-loom weavers from whom the Dons purchased cloth, whose income depended in large part on the price at which they could obtain yarn, were understandably tempted when yarn prices were high to use less or inferior material, or indeed to stop weaving altogether. Don was acutely aware of these problems, and of what the optimum conditions were if the hand-loom weavers were to work well – ample yarn had to be available at low prices relative to what they could obtain for weaving varieties of saleable cloth, with which they were already familiar. Thus, in September 1812, after several months of depressed strelitz prices (and a restricted supply of yarn) which had evidently persuaded the weavers that they would be better off working their plots of land, William was relieved to report that the market was rising. As a result, he hoped, 'the corn would soon be cut down and the prices if they continue would induce many hands to return again to their looms'.[55]

It was the difficulties which the Dons faced regarding the supply of yarn which almost certainly explains Robert Don's move in 1810 into a partnership with James Laird, a Forfar 'manufacturer', to build and equip a spinning mill at Murthill, a site some four miles to the north of Forfar, on the South Esk river. Although it is not clear when production began, the mill was certainly in operation by 1814, when William Don confidently informed a customer that in a short time he would send 'Tow better than you have seen yet . . . My brother spins the better part of the best yarns and we know of course where the best cloth is'.[56]

Reference has already been made to the fact that William and Robert's uncle Andrew Binny was Forfar's stampmaster and that they had both worked closely with him. In order to achieve the high quality of cloth upon which the Dons built their reputation, this connection was of critical importance. For one thing, as weavers and 'manufacturers' (who employed a number of weavers) had to bring their cloth into the stamp office for stamping before it could be sold, the stampmaster and his assistants had early and first-hand knowledge of who was bringing the best cloth to market. There was a conviction (born in part of self-interest on the part of the Dons and some other Forfarshire linen merchants) that it was advantageous for a stampmaster to be a person of some substance and experience, preferably obtained from direct involvement in the linen trade; this was the view of one of Dundee's stampmasters, David Blair, a close acquaintance of William Don who was strongly opposed to any suggestion that stampmasters should be prohibited from dealing in linen. This, he argued, would:

> destroy the respectability of the Office . . . and throw into the hands of needy men, the mere companions of the weavers, of whom they would not stand in awe and whose poverty is sometimes a temptation to give improper indulgences to the weavers.[57]

This was said to have occurred at the neighbouring stamp office at Letham where, in 1804, Blair had 'reason to believe that the Weavers have only to carry [the stampmaster] to a public house to obtain whatever they want'.[58] Standards also seem to have been lower in Aberdeen and Arbroath, where the stampmasters were alleged to have been prepared to pass cloth in which inferior Indian sunn hemp had been used instead of Baltic hemp.[59] A reduction in standards was, of course, beneficial to those manufacturers and merchants such as the Londoner John

Maberley, of Maberley & Co, who was concerned more with quantity than quality and who resented the refusal of stampmasters such as Blair to pass adulterated or substandard cloth.[60] Had this occurred in Forfar, it would have been a major blow to the Dons. As buyers of quality cloth, it was vital to their interests that the stampmasters in Forfar and its vicinity passed only top-quality workmanship.

For the Dons then, the post-1807 imprint of the Forfar stamp office, 'Binny & [Robert] Don', on a bale of cloth was a matter of the greatest importance in establishing and maintaining their reputation. Cloth so marked, William noted in 1811 – with some justification – was 'called for in London'.[61] This stamp was applied to all cloth sold from Forfar, whoever wove it, and consequently it was normally the only name – other than the merchant who sold it – which buyers would come across. As long as the reputation of Forfar was high, so too would be that of any cloth from Forfar which the Dons sold. The Don brothers' concern about standards is likely to have inspired Robert's interest, in 1809, in being elected to the committee of master weavers in Forfar which advised the Deacon and Boxmaster about how the trade should be run.

That the general standard of Forfar cloth should be high was, however, the minimum requirement: 'the best qualities I mark with a private stamp', William Don noted smugly,[62] and much of the cloth which evidently met with the approval of the Board of Trustees was not considered good enough by Don; in a six-week period during February and March 1812 for example, of 528 pieces of stamped strelitz lint, only about half were judged to be suitable for Cowleys, his main London customer.[63]

The connection with the stamp office and the experience which he gained when working there was also useful to William Don for other reasons, not least that he was made aware of the means which the weavers used to defraud both the stampmaster and cloth-merchants. One such means was the practice of stretching the webs before bringing them in for stamping as standard goods. This 'nefarious' practice had been commonplace during William's time as Binny's assistant, and he was able to warn Robert about it, advising him to stamp it as short of the claimed width, 'for assuredly it will come back sooner or later to its original breadth'.

Another problem was the occasional attempts which weavers made to forge the stampmaster's mark or stamp. Such an offence was committed by Alexander Waterstone, a Forfar master weaver of some thirty years' standing, in October 1813. Waterstone, the father of five children, was alleged to have fraudulently stamped four webs, each of which was shorter than the 146 yards they were supposed to have been. The cloth, however, was of fairly good quality throughout. The crime, described by Robert Don as only a 'threepence halfpenny matter', was apparently committed by Waterstone in order to avoid paying the stampmaster's dues. The Board of Trustees in Edinburgh deemed it to be a rather more serious matter, and they ordered a prosecution. Don proposed that Waterstone would be punished by having to forfeit the cloth and give an undertaking 'never more to manufacture a web on his own Act, under penalties', which, in effect, would have removed from him his master's status but retained an able weaver in the district. As it was, the affair cost Waterstone his reputation and the opportunity to work in the locality, Robert Don reporting that 'the business is already whispered about and his character is gone forever . . . The Asylum may be the poor Culprit's last resort'.[64] The news that Peter Rankin, the Sheriff Substitute of Forfar, was to commence proceedings against him was evidently sufficient to cause Waterstone to abscond, leaving behind him an outraged Sheriff Substitute who hoped and wished, 'that the culprit will not have the folly to stay in the county, nor ever to make his appearance in Forfar again'.[65]

Open breaches of this sort and confrontations between the weaving fraternity of Forfar and its neighbourhood and the Dons were rare, despite the reputation the Forfar weavers had in the 1780s and 1790s for being 'inflammatory' and a 'set of scoundrels'. Tensions, of course, did exist. The problem was basically that the weavers from whom William and Robert Don bought cloth, whether they worked principally for 'manufacturers' or on their own, were to some degree independent men (and to a lesser extent, women, growing numbers of whom turned to weaving as opportunities for hand-spinning diminished). As was pointed out in Chapter One, many still had a foothold in the land, and with several cloth-buying merchants active in the region, they had some freedom to determine what yarns they purchased and what type of cloth they wove. The number of weavers involved was substantial, and presented the Dons with major organisational challenges. Thus between May 1805 and February 1811 William and Robert bought cloth from almost 250 different individuals. Such circumstances made it difficult for any merchant to exercise a significant degree of control over the weavers. Twice a year they simply abandoned their looms altogether, for ten days or so during the early summer to cut peat and for a week in August or September to lift potatoes.[66] Their 'gamboling' at New Year created another gap in production.

At other times, when the returns from weaving were low, either because yarn prices were high or cloth prices depressed, they turned to agricultural work. Cloth-dealers such as William Don were faced with something of a paradox: on the one hand it was essential in the increasingly competitive linen trade that the costs of weaving be kept low, whilst on the other hand low wages discouraged the weavers from paying as much attention to the quality of their work as Don would have wished, and, if their wages fell too low relative to agricultural wage rates, labour became scarce – for there were times, such as at the end of 1811, when yarn and cloth prices were so depressed that the weavers had 'not a shilling' for their work[67] and were better paid as agricultural labourers. Don was sympathetic to the weavers' plight. If the yarn was in short supply (as it was between 1809 and 1811, largely because Dutch and Riga lintseed were almost unobtainable) its price rose, and while that situation prevailed 'the weavers have literally nothing for their labour, they cannot stand it,' he observed. Better offers too from rival firms could deprive Don of sufficient weavers, who made it their business to know where the best deals were to be struck. Thus, with demand for British duck rising in November 1811, and after having waited impatiently for some time for looms to empty, it was with some difficulty that Don obtained just two bales.

Yet in the instance just referred to, the weavers were taking full advantage of one of the rare periods in the nineteenth century when the market turned in their favour. This had led William Don to write to his main London customer that he had 'had another fight with the manuf[acturers] of B. Duck', who wanted an advance in their price, although some of them were 'not adhering strictly to the Fabric'.[68] Ever anxious to distance himself from substandard cloth, he added that he had rejected seven pieces, although he was resigned to the fact that they would 'reach the London market throu' another channel'.[69] Quality control was difficult even after the Murthill mill had begun to produce uniform yarns, as the weavers could still buy whatever yarn they thought would do best. Thus in 1814 they caused William Don some anxiety as they would only buy osnaburg yarns, in spite of his attempts to get them to make up an order he had for sheetings. Yet on this occasion the market soon fell and the weavers' gamble failed. 'Conceiving the demand would continue and that anything would sell,' Don reported, 'the weavers filled their hands with miserably ill-coloured trash of yarn', which he noted with some satisfaction, would take them some time to dispose of.[70]

Customers – and Cowleys

It was clearly in Don's interest, if he was to expand his linen business, to secure a pool of manufacturers and weavers upon whom he could depend. In order to do so William needed first of all to convince them that he would purchase their cloth on a regular basis. This he did by developing a close association with a limited number of London merchants, by far and away the most important of which was the firm of Cowley & Son. During the 1790s a considerable part of William Don's linen-dealing was conducted in what he evidently considered to be a highly unsatisfactory manner, with some consignments of linen being sent directly to the West Indies. This, while being not only an extremely risky business, also stretched his credit to the limit and thereby considerably weakened his capacity to continue trading. Thus in February 1797 for instance, he had received an order from Cowleys which he was simply unable to fulfil, as he could not raise the funds which would have allowed him to accommodate their six-month discount bill.[71] The drawbacks of consigning goods direct to the West Indies can be seen even more clearly in 1799, when he sent the relatively small consignment of six bales to Alexander Angus in Kingston, Jamaica, which, he complained, 'locks up part of my property for eight or nine months'.[72] Don had still not received payment by January

1801 despite his willingness to take 'produce' in the form of rum and sugar in place of cash.

Rather than dealing directly with customers overseas then, William preferred to do most of his business with Glasgow and London merchants. From around 1807, however, until the autumn of 1815, he did virtually no business with Glasgow, preferring instead to cultivate his connection with Cowleys. They had been amongst his earliest customers and, like the Glasgow house with which he dealt most frequently, Buchanan, Stiven & Co, may have been introduced to him by Andrew Binny. However the relationship began, it is clear that by 1799 Don had so impressed the Londoners that they invited him to join with them in a trading partnership which they hoped would double the quantity of linen being shipped south. William declined their offer both on the grounds of 'pressure of business' (probably a reference to the liquidity problems created by his dealings with Alexander Angus), and prudence: 'altho' I had the wherewithal,' he wrote, 'I am in doubt as to the propriety of involving myself deeper in speculation.'[73]

In spite of this rebuttal, Cowleys (who now became Cowley, Son & Sancton) continued to trade with Don. For Cowleys the advantage was that he could provide them with the very highest quality coarse linens. On one occasion in 1800 they had purchased some 25-inch cloth from Dundee, but it turned out to be less satisfactory than had appeared at first sight, 'being glazed at the end of each piece, which smooths it out'. When Cowleys put the cloth through a calendar the glaze had melted and the cloth had shrunk. William Don, in comparison, prided himself on the standard of his merchandise. After the cloth was purchased in the Forfarshire markets he personally arranged the bales prior to their carriage to Dundee where they were packed, taking scrupulous care to sort the pieces into even qualities and colours. The goods he sent, he boasted, 'shall be what the[y] are designated':

> No Tow in Lint Bales, nor Lint in Tow. The Stamp shall be on the outside and the outside shall be a fair representation of the inside, the goods shall be perfectly selected, if you see one piece of the Bale you may trust the rest is as good.[74]

It was not until 1811, due to illness, that they received a shipment from Don which he had not sorted personally.[75]

In addition, there was an element of exclusivity about the trade: 'none can in the London market match you as to quality', he assured Cowleys.[76] The importance of this is revealed in a letter he wrote to George Lindsay of John & George Lindsay & Co of London, to whom Don had been introduced in the summer of 1809. Although William agreed to send them three bales of strelitz, he was mindful that such a step could cause offence:

> I mean to ship the goods at Arbroath because I do not want to excite the curiosity of ither [*sic*] of your friends or my own at Dundee, and I could likewise wish the same to pass at London without observation for tho' I am conscious that I can still do all the business of my old friends Cowley & Co, and at the same time do you justice in the execution of any orders you may be pleased to entrust me with, yet I know they do not like to see me sending goods to London to any other house in town similar to their own.[77]

Don's caution was firmly based on the appreciation he had of the significance of Cowleys' orders for his own success: 'I am quite sensible [that] the interest of your good House is my interest', he wrote to them in 1815.[78] This is difficult to quantify, but figures which survive from 1810–12 show that over the two years from May 1810, Don sent Cowleys some 241 bales of linen, at an average cost of £80 5s per bale. The total value of the cloth was therefore some £19,338. William's commission, which was 2.5 per cent, would have produced an annual average income of £408 from this customer alone.

Cowleys' orders were remarkably regular in a trade which was notable for its unpredictability – indeed, following an unexpected six-week absence of orders from Cowleys in 1809 William Don concluded that 'my trade is up', which led him to begin dealing with the Lindsays. Prior to this, from January 1808 to March 1809, Cowleys had purchased cloth from the Dons virtually every month.[79] Regular orders, of course, helped the Dons maintain good relations with the weavers, who, if they produced cloth of the requisite quality, could depend on William and Robert to take it off their hands.[80] As William was fairly confident that Cowleys would take any cloth he purchased, he could afford to indulge in what otherwise would have been the risky step of buying in a 'backward market'. By 'relieving' the manufacturers of their goods during such times, 'and giving nearly value for them', Don reflected, he acquired 'command of the market, and ensures me at all times of a preference, on equal terms'. The good relations which this built up between Don and the weavers was extremely important when it came to fighting off competition from other large trading houses such as Courtneys, Smithson & Parker and Maberley & Co, each of whom at various times attempted to establish a presence in the Tayside area.

It was not all plain sailing, however, and there were times when Don had to try hard to persuade Cowleys to take anything at all. Sometimes, for instance, he would simply dispatch cloth in the hope they would be interested in it by the time it arrived in London. In 1814, after Cowleys had slashed their weekly order for strelitz, Don attempted to persuade them to reconsider, by playing what he was convinced was his trump card: 'I would advise you to take a few Bales tho' it were only to keep our customers together and prevent our quality from ever touching the Dundee market.'[81]

It took more than regular orders for the Dons to maintain the dominant position they had achieved in the local market by 1813: William Don was highly appreciative of the fact that Cowleys paid promptly for their cloth. This, allied to his role as a bank agent, gave him a further advantage when he was dealing with the weavers – for what they preferred from buyers were cash payments for their cloth.

Don did his best to satisfy this preference: 'it had been and still is my uniform practice to buy and pay money down directly,' he wrote in 1810, when he also reported that 'we can buy [strelitz] here at anything for Money'.[82] And Don was able to pay in cash much more easily than most of his competitors. As was seen earlier on, he was not averse to making full use of the access he had to his bank customers' cash accounts. Furthermore, William's position as bank agent meant that he could cash bills of exchange immediately without going to Dundee or Edinburgh, and thereby continue to buy cloth without interruption. And while Cowleys were unhappy that he did so, on at least two occasions Don obtained sums of money – £600 and £800 in 1811 and 1812 respectively – by drawing from their account with him before he had consigned any cloth.[83] The usual practice was to draw on their account only after the cloth had been dispatched. With his access to short-term credit Don was able to run the risk of buying in advance of orders from London, usually when prices were low, and so obtain the double benefit of the gratitude of the weavers and the profits which he obtained when the market for his goods recovered.

Another means of ensuring steady supplies of the requisite cloth was to employ weavers directly, and as has been indicated already, there is some evidence that prior to the end of the Napoleonic Wars William and Robert Don had acquired a small stock of looms of their own, which they appear to have supplied to manufacturers who worked for them. By so doing they could pay close attention to the production process and indeed late in 1814 they had introduced 'improved machinery'[84] which was reportedly 'going on well', although not to the uniform delight of their weavers, one of whom had 'not the patience for it'.[85]

Spreading the net

The Don brothers' influence over the weaving community was spreading in other, much less direct ways. A large number of Forfar's weavers, for example, were recruited into the 3rd Forfarshire Volunteers, of which William was a lieutenant-colonel and from *c.*1804–8, a colonel. In one sense the participation of the weavers was detrimental to his business interests, there being 'no cloth at market', when they were on duty.[86] On the other hand paternalist relations within the community were strengthened by the respect which was generated from Don's appearance as a military officer and by his prompt payment of the men's wages, the funds for which he later reclaimed from the government.[87] The wages for part-time soldiering were low, however, although on one occasion he was able to relieve the men from the suffering which might have resulted from grain shortages by purchasing fifty bolls of meal from a ship which had arrived at Dundee, and distributing it amongst the weavers in lieu of wages. The form of the gesture, he recorded, was 'credit given until the pay amount to the quantity each may receive'.[88]

Don's local esteem must also have been enhanced by his efforts from early in 1814 to raise funds for his friend David Blair's 'laudable scheme for the relief of the most unfortunate men', namely the building of the Dundee Lunatic Asylum.[89] In order to support this much-needed venture (Forfar's unfortunates having no rightful access to Montrose asylum for instance), Don was able to obtain contributions from the town's Episcopalian Church, members of the Binny family in India, as well as Cowley, Son & Sancton.[90] Not all of his efforts at social reform met with such a warm response though: his ambitious plans to provide English, arithmetic and mathematics, and languages schools in Forfar in three separate buildings had to be substantially modified owing to the indifference and sometimes outright hostility of some of the parish's heritors.[91]

TRANSPORTATION: THE ROAD TO DUNDEE

Quality and a command of the manufacture of strelitz cloth in Forfar and its vicinity were not enough to guarantee Don's success as a linen trader. It was a cut-throat business and essentially a buyer's market in which profit margins were extremely tight. In December 1812 for instance, Dundee prices were a quarter of a penny lower than in Forfar, which was judged to be quite enough to deter purchasers from looking beyond Dundee.[92]

Even in the best of times, as Forfar is situated some 15 miles inland from Dundee from where most of the Dons' cloth was sent either for sale or shipment to his London and Glasgow customers, William and Robert Don were at a considerable disadvantage. To compete therefore, they were forced to bear the costs of transporting their cloth from Forfar to the coast.

In order to demonstrate to customers that his inland location would cause them no inconvenience, William Don was prepared to go to quite extraordinary lengths. Relatively early in his career as a linen-merchant, for instance, at the start of 1795, a severe frost had been followed by a snowstorm which had made the road to Dundee impassable, thus preventing delivery of twelve bales of cloth to a Glasgow customer. Don reassured them on 21 February that he would 'cause the road to be cut before the carts on Monday whatever the expense may be'.[93] By

25 February he was able to inform John Cowley in London that the job had been done, in a quite spectacular fashion: 'I . . . levied 60 men at 2/- a head to cut the road before the carts which was effected, I and Mr Mann of this place at their head.'[94]

Don's care and attention to this matter should certainly have impressed his customers – even though Buchanan, Stiven & Co had not received the last of their bales until the end of March, owing to a short-lived embargo on vessels leaving Dundee. Any benefits William obtained from his exertions were certainly not immediate, though: the twelve Glasgow bales were later invoiced for £501.18s.6d, for which Don obtained a commission of 2½ per cent, or £12 11s. Of this he had paid out at least £6 on clearing the road and another £6 when he had attempted to send some of the cloth by cart to Perth in a vain attempt to get it to Glasgow by the overland route.[95] His own profit on this occasion was therefore virtually nothing.

The road to Dundee continued to present the Dons with problems: the 15-mile trip could take a whole day. That 'infernal Road' is how William described it in 1814, adding that 'Horses are killed and carts are broken, and it is the business of no-one to mend it, or which is the same thing, nobody makes it their business.'[96] If they could do little about the road's condition, the Dons could at least make sure that they made the best use of it they could. This was achieved in part by their acquisition of their own fleet of carts, which they had done some time prior to 1809. This, of course, gave them a degree of independence and made it possible to respond to the needs of customers by allowing William Don to promise that goods would be able to 'catch the first ship that sails from Dundee'. As London-bound ships sailed only once or twice a week depending on the season, a missed embarkation could mean up to a week's delay.

Perhaps with the aim of exerting some influence over the shippers, William became a minor shareholder in the Dundee & Perth Shipping Co (later the Dundee, Perth & London Shipping Co). Largely because its vessels sailed regularly, Don preferred to do business with the D&P. Its chief rival, the Tay Shipping Co, in Don's view, conducted its affairs in an unbusinesslike fashion, failing to provide receipts for bales sent for shipment for instance, and not making it clear when their vessels would sail. If his customers insisted that their bales be sent by the Tay Co, he could still deliver, though, 'being my own carrier'.

Nevertheless, it was only reluctantly that he made use of the Tay Shipping Co's services, and then only after considerable prompting from Cowleys – indeed, he had simply ignored John Cowley's initial suggestion that he should send some bales by the Tay company. Further pressure in 1814 forced his hand however, although in January 1815 he had still not relinquished his connection with the D&P, reporting to Cowleys that bales from the 'pick of the week's buying', which he 'could not think' of offering in the Dundee market, had been sent to both shipping companies, 'that the risk might be divided'.

A further step which Don took in order to get round the problem of matching deliveries in Dundee with sailing times was to take some warehouse space in Dundee where he could store cloth. The carts brought other advantages; with them, William and Robert were able to attend markets and visit weavers in the outlying districts. Best 'drest tow osnaburgs' were 'chiefly made in the country', and with the carts they could buy cloth and take it back to Forfar there and then. The ability to get around the countryside quickly to obtain cloth when it was wanted could be of the greatest importance – such as in 1812 when William had beaten a clerk from Maberley & Co in getting to Brechin, leaving his rival only the cloth for which he had no use.[97]

Chapter Two: Origins and Foundations

1 W. G. Don, *Memoirs of the Don Family in Angus* (London, 1897), p25, p49.
2 *Forfar Herald*, 11 June 1886.
3 R. W. Dill, *Episcopacy in Forfar* (Forfar, 1911), pp14–27.
4 I. L. Donnachie, *A History of the Brewing Industry in Scotland* (Edinburgh, 1979), pp80–1.
5 Forfar Town Council Minutes, 23 April 1783.
6 Department of Modern History, University of Dundee (hereafter DMHUD) card index, William Don to Henry Hardy & Co, 21 December 1795.
7 DUA, MS 100/1/2/1, Letter-Book, 1809–14, William Don to Nicol Allan, 12 April 1809; William Don to Walker Thomson & Co, 17 November 1809.
8 *OSA*, XIII, p167.
9 Dundee University Archives (hereafter DUA), MS 100/1/2/1, Letter Book, 1809–1814, William Don to Walker Thomson & Co, 17 November 1809.
10 DUA, MS 100/1/2/1, Letter Book, 1809–1814, William Don to David Blair, 12 February 1813.
11 Ibid, William Don to David Blair, 1 June 1813.
12 C. W. Munn, *The Scottish Provincial Banking Companies, 1747–1864* (Edinburgh, 1981), p45.
13 Ibid, p176.
14 *OSA*, XIII, p258.
15 T. Joplin, *An Essay on Banking in England and Scotland* (London, 1827), p24.
16 C W Boase, *A Century of Banking in Dundee* (Edinburgh, 1867), pp226–7.
17 The Dundee New Bank was founded in 1802 to take over and continue the business of the Dundee Commercial Banking Company, founded in 1792.
18 Munn, *Scottish Provincial Banking*, p121–2.
19 Ibid.
20 Boase, *Banking in Dundee*, p183.
21 DMHUD, card index, William Don to John Cowley, 27 September 1799.
22 DUA, MS 100/1/2/1, Letter Book, 1809–1814, William Don to George Dempster, 20 March 1809.
23 DUA, MS 100/1/2/2, Letter Book, 1814–1817.
24 Ibid, William Don to General David Hunter, 10 November 1814.
25 Gauldie, *Dundee Textile Industry*, pxx.
26 DUA, MS 100/1/2/2, Letter Book, 1814–1817, William Don to James Fife, 7 December 1814.
27 Ibid, William Don to James Fife, 18 November 1814.
28 DUA, MS 100/1/2/1, Letter Book, 1809–1814, William Don to William Wilson, 31 December 1810.
29 Ibid, William Don to David Blair, 1 May 1811.
30 Ibid.
31 DUA, MS 100/1/2/2, Letter Book, 1814–1817, William Don to James Laird & Co, October 1815.
32 Munn, *Scottish Provincial Banking*, p180.
33 Ibid.
34 DUA, MS 100/1/2/1. Letter Book, 1809–1814, William Don to Cowley, Son & Sancton, 15 June 1811.
35 Durie, *Linen Industry*, p24.
36 DUA, MS 100/1/2/1, Letter Book, 1809–1814, William Don to David Christie, 3 May 1810.
37 Ibid, William Don to Cowley, Son & Sancton, 15 June 1811.
38 Ibid, William Don to John & George Lindsay, 16 April 1814.
39 Quoted in Gauldie, 'Dundee Jute', p117.
40 DUA, MS 100/1/5/1, Cloth Buying Book, 1805–1811.
41 DUA, MS 100/1/2/1, Letter Book, 1809–1814, account with William Don, March 1809.
42 SRO, Board of Trustees Papers, NG1/1/26, p193.

43 See P. L. Payne, *British Entrepreneurship in the Nineteenth Century* (London, 1984), pp13–16.
44 Montrose Public Library, 'Acts and Statutes of the Weavers Corporation Within the Burgh of Forfar, 1627–'836', 23 September 1808.
45 DUA, MS 100/1/2/1, Letter Book, 1809–1814, William Don to Robert Bogle & Co, 20 October 1810.
46 DUA, MS 100/1/2/2, Letter Book, 1814–1817, William Don to A. & W. Smart, 7 August 1815.
47 DUA, MS 100/1/2/1, Letter Book, 1809–1814, William Don to Cowley, Son & Sancton, 6 February 1813.
48 DUA, MS 100/1/2/2, Letter Book, 1814–1817, William Don to Cowley, Son & Sancton, 28 April 1814.
49 SRO, Board of Trustees Papers, NG1/15/2, Accounts, 1819–1822.
50 DUA, MS 100/1/2/1, Letter Book, 1809–1814, William Don to Cowley, Son & Sancton, 18 January 1812.
51 DMHUD, card index, William Don to John Cowley, 27 September 1799.
52 DUA, MS 100/1/2/1, Letter Book, 1809–1814, William Don to John Scott, 25 July 1810.
53 Ibid, William Don to William Sandeman, 30 October 1811.
54 DUA, MS 100/1/2/2, Letter Book, 1814–1817, William Don to Cowley, Son & Sancton, 13 August 1814.
55 DUA, MS 100/1/2/1, Letter Book, 1809–1814, William Don to John & George Lindsay, 19 September 1812.
56 DUA, MS 100/1/2/2, Letter Book, 1814–1817, William Don to George Lindsay, 4 August 1814.
57 Ibid, David Blair to William Arbuthnott, 4 March 1816.
58 SRO, Board of Trustees Papers, NG1/2/5, p49.
59 Gauldie, 'Dundee Jute Industry', p117.
60 Ibid.
61 DVA, MS 100/1/2/1, Letter Book, 1809–1814, William Don to Cowley, Son & Sanction, 9 November 1811.
62 DUA, MS 100/1/2/2, Letter Book, 1814–1817, William Don to Robert Bogle & Co, 4 December 1816.
63 DUA, MS 100/1/2/1, Letter Book, 1809–1814, William Don to Cowley, Son & Sancton, 31 March 1812.
64 Ibid, Robert Don to David Blair, January 1814.
65 Ibid.
66 See, for example, DMHUD card index, William Don, May 1796; or DUA MS 100/1/2/1, Letter Book, 1809–1814, William Don to Cowley, Son & Sancton, 29 June 1811.
67 Ibid, 7 December 1811.
68 Ibid, 23 November 1811.
69 Ibid.
70 DUA, MS 100/1/2/2, Letter Book, 1814–1817, William Don to Cowley, Son & Sancton, 23 November 1811.
71 DMHUD, card index, William Don to John Cowley, 2 February 1797.
72 Ibid, 27 September 1799.
73 Ibid.
74 DUA, MS 100/1/2/2, Letter Book, 1814–1817, William Don to John Macfarlane, 2 November 1816.
75 DUA, MS 100/1/2/1, Letter Book, 1809–1814, William Don to Cowley, Son & Sancton, 15 June 1811.
76 DUA, MS 100/1/2/2, Letter Book, 1814–1817, William Don to Cowley, Son & Sancton, 15 October 1814.
77 DUA, MS 100/1/2/1, Letter Book, 1809–1814, William Don to George Lindsay, 1 July 1809.
78 DUA, MS 100/1/2/2, Letter Book, 1814–1817, William Don to John Cowley, 5 July 1815.
79 DUA, MS 100/1/2/1, Letter Book, 1809–1814, account, March 1809.
80 Ibid, William Don to Cowley, Son & Sancton, 31 March 1812.
81 Ibid, William Don to Cowley, Son & Sancton, 29 October 1814.

82 DUA, MS 100/1/2/1, Letter Book, 1809–1814, William Don to Cowley, Son & Sancton, 8 December 1810.
83 Ibid, see letters of 29 May 1811, p158; 1 February 1812; 20 June 1812.
84 DUA, MS 100/1/2/2, Letter Book, 1814–1817, William Don to Bruce Younger, 17 October 1814.
85 Ibid, William Don to David Blair, 7 November 1814.
86 DUA, MS 100/1/2/1, Letter Book, 1809–1814, William Don to John & George Lindsay, 14 August 1813.
87 Ibid, William Don to George Shee, April 1814.
88 DMHUD, card index, William Don to Provost Ritchie, nd.
89 DUA, MS 100/1/2/2, Letter Book, 1814–1817, William Don to David Blair, 7 November 1814.
90 Ibid, William Don, to Cowley & Sancton, 28 December 1816.
91 Ibid, William Don to Charles Greenhill, 6 May 1815.
92 DUA, MS 100/1/2/1, Letter Book, 1809–1814, William Don to John & George Lindsay, 3 December 1812.
93 DMHUD, card index, William Don to Buchanan, Stiven & Co, 21 February 1795.
94 Ibid, William Don to John Cowley, 25 February 1795.
95 Ibid, William Don to Buchanan, Stiven & Co, 14, 23 March 1795.
96 DUA, MS 100/1/2/2, Letter Book, 1814–1817, William Don to David Blair, 29 October 1814.
97 DUA, MS 100/1/2/1, Letter Book, 1809–1814, William Don to Cowley Son & Sancton, 25 April 1812. For a recent account of Dundee's shipping trade see G. Jackson and K. Kinnear, *The Trade and Shipping of Dundee, 1780–1850* (Dundee, 1991).

Chapter Three

1815–17: Difficulties – and William's Death

The end of the wars with France in 1815 had a devastating effect on the Forfar linen industry in general and William Don in particular. At the beginning of 1816 he asked rhetorically: 'Are things not at the lowest yet? Cloth and corn surely are.'[1] Yet cloth had even further to fall. Towards the end of the year William noted that 'These are shocking times' – linen prices were 'one penny per yard lower' than he had ever known them, 'tho' Thirty years in the Trade'.[2] As the reference to corn suggests though, Don's business interests – and troubles – were not confined to linen. Even so, it had become his primary business interest.

Linen

With the ending of hostilities, war-induced demand for linen collapsed. So too did the pattern of regular orders from Cowleys in London, although the fact that their interest was cooling rapidly was not immediately clear to Don. Indeed, shortly after the cessation of hostilities, he was evidently heartened by the discovery that Courtneys, who had from 1812 taken most of the British duck sold in Kirkcaldy and Forfar, had been conducting a 'losing trade'. With Courtneys tottering, Don wrote to Cowleys, urging them to provide him with orders and thereby secure part of the market:

> . . . our people conceived the trade was up and were willing to give me [a number of pieces] at anything . . . If you could

> promise a continuation, Courtney should not get one piece from this neighbourhood, I could command the market as I do with strelitz.[3]

Yet despite his purchase of cloth at a full penny less than Courtneys were able to buy it, Cowleys were not in a position to support Don in his ambitions.

By the autumn of 1815 William Don noted that other goods were 'lower priced than they can be made and our manufacturers are falling like ninepins'.[4] The fall in cloth prices appears to have reawakened the interest of some Glasgow and west of Scotland houses based in Angus. It was a move which was not entirely unexpected since for several years Don had been sending current price lists to some leading Glasgow houses such as Dennistoun, Buchanan & Co and Robert Bogle & Co.

The renewal of trading links with Glasgow and the west was a mixed blessing. An order from John Harvey of Castle Semple for 6,500 yards of the 'best strelitz lint', to be sent either to Greenock or Port Glasgow, was undoubtedly welcome. Its arrival, however, provoked Don to write to Cowleys a heart-felt plea not to turn their backs on the strelitz trade which they had built up together: 'I regret excessively to see the pink of our goods both Lint & Tow falling into other hands.'[5] Cowleys' only order at the time was for 'some sheetings & out of the way articles', but no strelitz.

A further blow for Don was the loss through retirement of his long-time acquaintance, John Cowley, who left his business to his son Samuel, with whom William did not have the same personal ties. Hints that the post-war linen trade might be less favourable than it had been, also came from two other directions: first, in a move which was made to prohibit stampmasters from dealing in linen in their own office, which, had it been successful, would have weakened Robert's position; and secondly, a proposal, made by Kirkman Finlay, Glasgow's MP whose constituents were in cotton rather than linen, to lift the transit duties on German linen, 'a measure pregnant with the most baneful consequences to the Linen trade of this country and Ireland'.[6] Although neither of these threats materialised, they were pointers to the future, when linen would cease to benefit from the privilege of state support which it had enjoyed since 1727.

Other orders came from the houses mentioned above, with Dennistoun, Buchanan & Co sending Don £1,000 in October 1815 to 'invest' for them.[7] Hard times necessitated new trading methods in order to maintain some sort of cash flow, however. From as far back as the mid-1790s, Don had acted principally as a commission agent rather than sending consignments to London and elsewhere on a speculative basis. This was to change. From April 1816 Don commenced business with John MacFarlane, an agent based in Glasgow, who sold cloth on the spot for cash, at a 5 per cent discount, with 3 per cent going to the vendor. It was not a business of which Don was proud, and he confessed that he was only sending MacFarlane 'the refuse of old stock'.[8] Bales designated 'Best', 'Very Best' and 'Extra' had usually gone to London, whereas those called simply 'Good' or 'Very Good' were more often than not destined for Glasgow (and Dundee). At least sales could be obtained in Glasgow though, and indeed in 1816 British duck could obtain there ½d more than in London.

Sales were not easily achieved. With Cowleys out of the market for long periods, Don had to look to cloth dealers and merchants who were based in Scotland, and in August 1816, for example, he sent some samples of linen to Mackie & MacKay in Aberdeen, assuring them that strelitz was now preferred to 'drest' tow and common lint in America. As far as strelitz was concerned though – the market for which only the previous year he had boasted he was in full command of, with no one being able to buy it on better terms than himself – Don was now under great pressure as its price collapsed to around 6d and 7d for tow and lint respectively. In December 1816 he had to concede to Robert Bogle & Co that he knew 'well enough that you can buy Strelitz in Glasgow as low as the prices are here'. As an inducement to them 'to go from home', Don offered Bogle & Co a free yard of cloth for every ten, effectively a ten per cent discount.[9] Even had he been successful in his attempt to capture a share of the duck market it would have been to no avail: at the end of 1816 its price had fallen by 25 per cent to 12d a yard; by 1817 it was made in Forfar only when ordered in advance.

As demand declined and prices dropped, weavers' wages fell. By January 1816 they had dipped to 10d a day, and in March that year stood at only 4s a week for those working 'indoors' on their own looms, or 6s in the case of 'outdoor' weavers, under contract to a manufacturer. The result was that the workforce dispersed as many weavers drifted off to obtain what agricultural work was available. Even by the end of the year things had not improved, with wages standing at around 7s for ten days' labour at the loom.[10] As was usual in such circumstances the quality of the work which was put out deteriorated, thus making Don's task of selling cloth even more difficult.

Banking Difficulties

Even before the end of the Napoleonic wars in June 1815, there were signs that William Don, who had hitherto managed to enjoy a career in banking unscathed by serious losses, was running out of luck. What he described as 'wild speculation' had led in February to the failure of William Murray, with debts reputed to be in the region of £20,000.[11] In June the London house of Smithson & Parker fell, with dire consequences for several Dundee merchants who had been supplying them: 'This business,' Don wrote, 'will put a stop to anybody shipping goods who can't retire the Bills should they come back . . . I hear my friend Mr Alison [a Dundee stampmaster] is in £15,000, Cargill & Fleming £7,000.'[12] Others involved were John Baxter and William Sandeman. Don, who was by no means a tight-fisted bank agent, was appalled at some of the sums involved: 'Would you not wonder,' he wrote incredulously in June 1815, 'how these people find the credit?'[13]

For a short time, Don's position looked reasonably secure and he was able, for instance, to persuade Cowleys to take some bales of cloth off Smithson's hands, once it became clear that they would be unable to pay him. As he had already discounted a bill on the strength of this sale, his action ensured that the bank would not incur a bad debt.[14]

Yet as conditions worsened during 1816 and the first months of 1817, Don found himself in increasing difficulties. Although few details have survived, it appears that Don's previous liberality in his lending policies back-fired as it became clear that his debtors would be unable to repay him. The virtual cessation of orders from Cowleys was a savage blow, leaving him with virtually no financial flexibility. In the end, according to one estimate, he had over £30,000 in 'deficiencies and defalcations' written against him. This sum included £4,403 which he had lent on behalf of the bank to James Laird & Co, the flax-dressers and mill-spinning concern in which his brother Robert was a partner.[15] Accordingly, William Don's period as agent of the Dundee Banking Company drew to a close in January or early February 1817. The adverse effect of this on the way he conducted his linen dealings was immediate, although it may have been compounded by the general precariousness of Don's financial position by this time. Whereas previously he had been able to purchase cloth without an advance of money from his main customers, he wrote to William McClarey in Glasgow to explain that it was not possible for him to continue to purchase cloth unless he had cash in hand with which to pay the weavers, who demanded payment within four to seven days of disposing of their cloth. Having no funds of his own, Don suggested that McClarey open an account with the agent of the Dundee New Bank, and give him the authority to advance sums to Don when required.[16]

Brewing and Land Improvement

The darkening clouds which surrounded William Don in the aftermath of the Napoleonic wars were not solely due to the misfortunes which he faced in linen-dealing and banking. As was noted earlier, Gilbert Don had left his sons a brewery, of which William had become the senior partner. His younger brothers John and David were also both actively involved in the business, which concentrated in the production of porter, which had originally been imported from London 'in great quantities', according to the Revd. John Bruce in his *Statistical Account* report. With Forfar's population growing fast, and being located within an established grain-growing region, it made a great deal of sense for the Don brothers to extend their father's brewing operations, and by the early nineteenth century they appear to have made significant inroads into the local market.

Of the greatest importance to the brewer was the price of barley, the purchase of which was considered to be the province of John Don, whose ability in this regard evidently impressed William. 'I do not see that you can do better than make use of

[John's] judgement' in the purchase of grain, he wrote to one potential customer, in a letter which again emphasises the importance which the Dons attached to their intimate and detailed knowledge of the area and their consequent ability to strike a shrewd bargain: 'We lie in the very heart of the best corn country and know every individual Farm and Farmer in it.' Their customers too must have been well known to them, for until July 1812, when she retired from the business, Mary Ann Don, William's wife, had been the proprietrix of an ale and spirit house.[17]

From around 1811, however, there are suggestions that the Dons' brewing venture was less successful than it had been formerly. Ominously, it was agreed that no strong ale should be brewed, as demand was virtually non-existent.[18] And despite the inflationary pressures of the war years, the selling price of a hogshead of the type of porter made by John Don & Co, which competed with 'small beer', was £3 5s in 1815 compared to the £3 10s which had been obtained earlier. Rising barley prices, which were set by the Dundee market, made brewing unprofitable. Thus in 1812, with the price of barley standing at above 35 shillings per boll, the Dons simply stopped buying – and for three years restricted their brewing for public sale, 'only keeping together our private customers'.[19]

In 1815 yet another threat appeared, when the Dons found themselves faced with an Exchequer court trial, at which the legality of the method they used to cool their worts was challenged. The brewing industry was subject to high taxation, with around half of a brewer's costs taking the form of excise duty.[20] From early in the eighteenth century the brewing process had been closely monitored by unwelcome excise officers. The traditional method of brewing, which involved gradually cooling the 'worts' (a mixture of hot water and grist from ground barley) in the open air, prior to their being put through the washback for fermentation, was easily followed by the excisemen. The Dons, however, had begun to cool their worts with a water-cooled 'worm' or spiral pipe, as used by distillers, thereby making it possible to control the cooling time – and brew throughout the year. The excise officers argued that they were prevented from checking the brewing process at a vital stage and claimed £200 in compensation for, as William

Don put it, 'playing our Pipes at the Brewery to the tune of "Coolers" in our own way instead of "Auld Lang Syne" in theirs'.[21]

Much to Don's delight, however, the jury found in his favour, and he called on his friends to join him in celebrating his delivery 'from the hands of the most iniquitous oppression open trade ever suffered . . . according to law and by sallary [*sic*] the Barons of Exchequer'.[22] The case also brought Don some welcome notoriety, and a request to send Archduke John of Austria a plan of his cooling apparatus, even though, as was soon discovered, an 'invention' similar to theirs had been patented by two men in England in 1790.[23] Yet the cost of the trial was high, both in terms of William Don's energy and expense, and the longer term result was the appointment by the Excise Board of a full-time 'watcher' at the brewery, an action which once more raised Don's wrath and indeed that of the whole 'indignant' town of Forfar. Despite this, popular sympathy which derived from the widespread hostility which was felt towards the 'gaugers' (excisemen) could do nothing to relieve Don from the difficulties into which his involvement in brewing and further ambitions as a general merchant and farmer had led him by 1815.

Although John Don had been the main buyer for the brewery, William had also been tempted to deal in barley and other grains. Having observed the rising trend in cereal prices 'for upwards of Twenty years', and anticipating that this would continue, he embarked in 1809 on yet another business venture, this time as land improver, farmer and miller. One of his first steps was to erect a windmill on the northern edge of his own estate of Bankhead on the outskirts of Forfar. Even making do with an old post from the town's Hill Quarry, the total cost of the windmill and its accompanying barn and offices was £522, which he borrowed at 5 per cent interest.[24] As Bankhead itself was simply too small for commercial farming, Don leased a piece of waterlogged ground from the town council at Whytemyre.[25] He was to pay an annual rental of £25 for the first two years, then two guineas for each acre for the following 25 years. In return Don obtained £200 from the burgh towards the drainage costs (which were anticipated to be £300) of land which he calculated would yield some seven bolls of grain per acre each year.[26]

Windmill tower, Bankhead, Forfar, erected by William Don in 1809 as part of his venture into cereals

Whytemyre, the area of waterlogged ground to the north of Forfar which William Don tried in vain to cultivate profitably after 1809

Don cannot be accused of having gone into this venture with his eyes closed: 'The farming trade is not all harvest, especially at the starting,' he informed his friend David Blair.[27] Indeed, he leased the land fully expecting that it would take him three or four years to drain and prepare 50 of the 70 acres which he hoped eventually to be able to cultivate.[28] His inexperience in land management and farming, however, left him unprepared for the immensity of the problems which did arise.

Indeed almost from the outset the scheme looked doomed. The stocking costs, of just over £338, for livestock and implements, were predictable. The cost of drainage, however, proved to be twice what Don had expected, while much of the land turned out to be 'good for nothing' until the soil was mixed with what was brought from other parts of Whytemyre.[29] Neither the labour nor the transport costs had been allowed for, nor were the extra sums which he had needed in order to construct some small bridges over the watercourses at Whytemyre. Don's efforts to recoup some of these additional outlays brought little reward. In 1814, for example, he experimented with Poland oats instead of potato oats, as they could be harvested earlier, 'a great consideration with me,' he wrote, meaning presumably that he could get them to market earlier than the traditional variety.[30] He did manage to sell 224 bolls, although his total output in 1814 was lower than it had been in the previous two years. In 1815 he had tried growing wheat, which sold for a higher price than oats, but he only managed to harvest 30 bolls.[31] Only in one year, 1811, did he manage to make a profit, and that was of just £51 14s. And only in one year too, did his crop yield reach the anticipated seven bolls per acre. His crop losses for 1814 and 1815 came in each year to over £200.[32]

What Don could not have predicted was that far from rising, as he had expected, cereal prices fell; in 1816 he noted disconsolately that 'for the past three years the price of Grain has fallen more than one half upon average'.[33] Indeed in the previous year, 1815, when there had been a sharp fall, it was fortunate that he was able to utilise the credit facilities which were available to him through his agency of the Dundee Banking Company, although even here it was necessary for him to write to the bank's cashier to ensure that credit facilities were still available to him:

> My own account may be heavy for a while and if it should be occasionally overdrawn, I trust the Directors will not object until I get a little empty handed. I have much Barley bought and much Oats to sell, and they must know I can go nowhere else for relief.[34]

Matters did not improve, despite his hopes that changes in the Corn Laws would bring some relief and in June 1816 William Don was left with no alternative but to petition the Magistrates and Town Council of Forfar for an abatement in the terms of his rent. His plea was based on the claim that he was 'in advance no less than £1,300 9s 3d'.[35]

The end of the era of William Don

Mounting pressures from all sides with no relief in sight finally broke William Don, and at the beginning of March 1817 he wrote to Cowley & Sancton to announce 'with much sorrow' that 'from bad health and the severe pressure of the times' he had been forced to put his affairs 'under trust for the behoof of my creditors'.[36] Three weeks later he was dead.

In spite of William Don's large debts, for the rest of the Don family all was by no means lost. Shortly before his death William established a co-partnery with his brothers Robert, John and David, to carry on the linen business under the name of Don & Co.[37] Although the company was effectively in the hands of Robert (who, of course, had been employed as William's chief buyer), assisted for a time by David Don, who assumed some general management duties, provision for William's widow Mary Ann Don had been made by enabling her to succeed her late husband as a partner in the company and obtain a share of any profits.

William Don died an exhausted man, and as will be seen, in spite of his success in the linen trade up until 1815, considerable effort was needed to ensure the future of Don & Co. Yet the new partners were able to build from a base laid by William (and to a lesser extent Robert, and possibly John, about whom virtually no documentary evidence has survived), in terms of the reputation of the Dons, both in the locality as buyers, and further afield as sellers of linen cloth. William's influence within the community was substantial and he was held in high esteem by the weaving fraternity. As a banker he had played a central role in financing the expansion of business activity in Forfar. His influence on the firm, especially as regards the trading links he had developed and the business methods he employed, was to be felt long after his departure.

Chapter Three: Difficulties

1 DUA, MS 100/1/2/2, Letter Book, 1814–1817, William Don to David Blair, 27 January 1816.
2 Ibid, William Don to Mackie & MacKay, 31 August 1816.
3 Ibid, William Don to Cowley, Son & Sancton, 6 June 1815.
4 Ibid, William Don to Cowley Son & Sancton, 5 August 1815.
5 Ibid, William Don to Cowley Son & Sancton, 11 November 1816.
6 Ibid, William Don to David Blair, 22 April 1816.
7 Ibid, William Don to Dennistoun, Buchanan & Co, 21 October 1815.
8 Ibid, William Don to Robert Stirling, 2 December 1816.
9 Ibid, William Don to Robert Bogle & Co, 21 December 1816.
10 Ibid, William Don to Robert Bogle & Co, 14 December 1816.
11 Ibid, William Don to John & George Lindsay, 25 February 1815.
12 Ibid, William Don to John Airth, 30 May 1815.
13 Ibid, William Don to Cowley, Son & Sancton, 6 June 1815.
14 Ibid, William Don to Cowley, Son & Sancton, 3 June 1815.
15 A. Reid, *The Royal Burgh of Forfar: a local history* (Paisley, 1902), p240.
16 DMHUD, card index, William Don to William McClarey, 24 February 1817.
17 Ibid, William Don to Supervisor of Excise, Forfar, 24 July 1812.
18 Ibid, William Don to Miss Drummond, 19 April 1811.
19 Ibid, William Don to Charles Wedderburn, 30 June 1812.
20 Donnachie, *Brewing Industry*, p20.
21 DUA, MS 100/1/2/2, Letter Book, 1814–1817, William Don to John Airth, 28 June 1815.
22 Ibid, William Don to David Jobson, 6 December 1815.
23 Ibid, William Don to David Christie, 30 November 1815.
24 Ibid, William Don's Statement of Expenditure, June 1816.
25 Ibid, William Don's Petition to Forfar Town Council, June 1816.
26 Ibid.
27 DUA, MS 100/1/2/1, Letter Book, 1809–1814, William Don to David Blair, 30 August 1813.
28 DUA, MS 100/1/2/2, Letter Book, 1814–17, William Don's Petition.
29 Ibid.
30 DUA, MS 100/1/2/1, Letter Book, 1908–1814, William Don to David Blair, 17 March 1814.
31 DUA, MS 100/1/2/2, Letter Book, 1814–1817, William Don's Expenditure.
32 Ibid.
33 Ibid, William Don's Petition.
34 DUA, MS 100/1/2/2, Letter Book, 1814–1817, William Don to David Jobson, 1 May 1815.
35 Ibid, William Don's Petition.
36 DMHUD, card index, William Don to Cowley & Sancton, 5 March 1817.
37 Ibid.

Chapter Four

The Era of Robert Don, *c.*1817–45

William Don had had a wide range of business interests. By contrast, Robert Don, who soon became the dominant partner in the newly created firm of Don & Co, concentrated his attentions almost wholly on linen cloth. Nearer the end of his business career he began to market yarn as well. Ultimately he became the sole active partner, as David Don was apparently only involved in the company's affairs for a year or two. To a large extent Robert's concentration upon textiles was necessary. For the future of the linen business which William Don had created, upon which the fortunes of Robert and to a lesser degree his brothers depended, was by no means guaranteed in the years immediately following William's death. Although the markets for cloth picked up later in 1817 after the post-war trough, Robert was faced with two immediate problems. Firstly, in April 1817 James Laird & Co failed, with outstanding debts of over £6,443, while in addition to his share of these, Don also had personal debts of £618, and total assets, including his house and furnishings, of only £470 19s 3d. Secondly, Don & Co were without the advantage which William had had until the final months of his life, namely that of relatively easy access to cash credit through his ability to discount most bills virtually at his convenience.

In the new circumstances in which they found themselves, Don & Co had to go gingerly through a formal application procedure to the banks, hoping that their requests would be met sympathetically. Thus in August 1817 they wrote to David Jobson, cashier of the Dundee Banking Company, about two bills they had from Cowley & Sancton and J. & G. Lindsay for

£208 and £200 respectively, informing him that they needed the cash for the following Wednesday. Both 'drafts' were for cloth sent to London. Unless they could cash them locally, they would have to meet the expense 'of sending . . . drafts to Edinburgh to be negotiated', which, they complained, 'cuts deep into our Commission and we have therefore a wish to get our bills passed in Forfar if at all practicable'. In future, they hoped, 'you will pass our London bills on these two houses when we shall have occasion to present them'.[1]

Circulating capital then, which was the life-blood of a successful and expanding mercantile concern, was in short supply and constrained the firm's activities in the years immediately after 1817 as Robert Don fought to re-establish his creditworthiness. Unfortunately, the company's need for liquidity came at an extremely sensitive time for the Scottish provincial banks, with a greater number closing than opening between 1815 and 1825.[2] The short-lived foray of the Aberdeen-based firm of Maberley & Co into banking in 1818 did nothing to help matters, as it reduced from 45 to 20 days the time allowed on bills of exchange drawn on Dons' London customers.[3]

At the same time within the linen trade itself, the company was being subjected to considerable pressure from both Maberley & Co and another Aberdeen-based company, Leys, Masson & Co. Both had made inroads into the Brechin district and late in 1818 Leys, Masson & Co were doing their best to engage 200 Forfar weavers in an effort to extend further the control which they had of the linen industry of the north-east.[4] With a large bleachfield, upon which some £16,000 had been laid out between 1805 and 1815, they were anxious to obtain further supplies of 'green' or unbleached cloth, precisely the type of cloth which Don & Co were primarily interested in at this stage.[5]

In the circumstances, it was essential for Robert Don to try to maintain good relations with the customers William had cultivated. Regular orders, even for relatively modest quantities of cloth, a bale a week for example, 'might prevent others from interfering with us'.[6] At the end of July 1818 Cowley & Sancton, who were now back in the market, were assured that 'since you began to buy we have not allowed a single piece of 25 porters to get into the hands of [any] one except one of our neighbours.'[7] Even when they were not buying, Cowleys were informed by

Don, 'we have often prevented the best from reaching the Dundee market so far as our means would allow us.' Cowleys' monopoly of the quality cloth market was thus secured if they continued to deal with Don & Co. Robert Don was painfully aware that without their custom he would be unable to persuade the best weavers in the vicinity to remain loyal to him and that they would instead succumb to the temptation to turn to what he called his 'neighbours'. Around 1820 Don was only one of fifteen 'green' cloth manufacturers in Forfar.

Although Cowley & Sancton continued to be an important customer into the early 1820s, the London firm's purchases of cloth were no longer as regular as they had once been. It was therefore important for Robert to find additional purchasers upon whom Don & Co could depend. The problem the company faced is clearly revealed in a letter written to Cowleys in 1818:

> We have . . . two bales which we can send you if you wish them indeed if we had spare money we would not allow a [piece] of such quality to escape us . . . it is a great advantage to be always in the market less or more. The small capital we have is generally laid out in that way . . . but this is too often exhausted.[8]

In consequence, Robert Don had to be rather more cautious in his dealings in the local cloth market than William appears to have been. Stock building, which William Don had sometimes done, was a risky business which Robert only undertook reluctantly. Don & Co, one potential customer was informed in July 1817, only purchased after orders had been given so that they rarely had 'any stock of goods beside them wanting a sale'.[9] It was only during depressed conditions, such as those which prevailed during 1841 and 1842, that Don appears to have had sizeable quantities of unsold cloth on hand.

There were, of course, other challenges to be met and problems to overcome, which will be discussed below. Worth mentioning at this point, however, is the fact that in 1832 the bounties on exports of coarse linen were finally withdrawn. The Dons were not alone in having to face this loss, but they had to find their own means of compensating for what was considered to be an extremely valuable subsidy for the Scottish coarse linen industry.[10] In Dundee, the threat of the removal of the bounty had caused some spinners to look again at the possibility of using jute, which was a considerably cheaper though lower grade raw material than either flax or hemp. It was not a fibre which Robert Don was anxious to use, and in fact the company managed to survive without employing any jute yarn until 1844.

By 1845, when Robert Don ceased to take an active part in the company's affairs, some notable changes had taken place, although not to the extent that it was unrecognisable from the organisation which William Don had left in 1817. Much more so than previously, the company (the name of which at some point during the period was changed to Robert Don & Co) had become merchant-manufacturers, rather than the commission merchants which they had principally been earlier. Another striking change was the degree of centralisation which occurred, paving the way for the next major departure in the company's history, namely the foundation of St James' Works in Forfar, which will be discussed in a later chapter. Here, however, we will explain what had been developing prior to these developments, in the period when Robert Don took over what was a struggling but well-regarded merchanting concern, and left it on the verge of becoming one of the leading coarse textile manufacturing and cloth merchanting firms outside Dundee.

Sales, Markets and Marketing

Between 1817 and 1845 substantial alterations in the pattern of the company's sales took place. In William Don's era, most of the cloth he dispatched was ultimately destined for the Plantations. The West Indies continued to be the company's most important market, but by the middle of the 1840s Robert Don & Co's goods were being dispatched to a much wider range of destinations, notably Latin America, but also Spain, France, North America, South Africa, and nearer to home, Ireland. Of these the most important appear to have been the first two. Dons thus benefited from the export of British capital which was providing much of the finance for the economic development of several Latin American countries.

Changes in Spanish tariffs in 1842 opened up an important new opportunity within Europe, which Don seized – 38 per cent (67 out of 177) of the correspondents whose names appear in a

Portrait believed to be of Robert Don (1782–1857). Reproduced by kind permission of Mr and Mrs Gavin Don, Gardyne Castle, Forfar

letter-book covering 1840–2 commenced their business with the Dons following the relaxation of the Spanish tariffs.[11] As this suggests, the relative importance of the various markets fluctuated over time, as demand altered. This was often linked with the raising and lowering of tariffs. Low prices owing to a downturn in the fortunes of the Forfar and Dundee linen industry, for instance, encouraged merchants to engage in a short-lived trade with France between 1839 and 1843. This was at its most intense during the depressed years of 1841 and 1842, when prices were sufficiently low to overcome the inhibiting effect of the tariff wall. After 1843, however, trade with France was much reduced as a result of the imposition of new French import duties.[12]

For similar reasons there was a brief flurry of interest in 'low goods' from Forfar from New York buyers in 1841.[13] The Dons were not seduced by the prospects which these new outlets appeared to offer, however, and recognised there was little to be gained by investing much effort in what were only temporary openings.

All this indicates that Don & Co had little interest in the domestic market.[14] Yet the company did have some British purchasers. In common with many other firms in the Scottish linen area, the Dons found that the agricultural market provided a useful outlet, especially when harvests were good and demand for bags and sacks was buoyant. This was the case in 1842, when the harvest was better than it had been for some years. Indeed, on this occasion high yields were not confined to Britain and in September, William Gilbert Don (one of Robert's two sons) wrote favourably of the 'good crop all over the world which we doubt not will have a very beneficial effect on our trade generally by the spring.'[15]

In order to secure sales either at home or overseas, Robert Don made it his business to meet his customers' requirements as closely as possible. In January 1841, for instance, in correspondence with Thomas Whyte of Hartley Row, Hampshire, Robert Don listed some of the varieties of cloth which he could supply, but also urged Whyte to send him full details of what he wanted, 'naming the widths & prices' – indeed, he went on, if there was anything 'out of common you think we could make for you . . . We shall be happy to try it if you send us samples.'[16] The company was equally prepared to match their production to the needs of the overseas market. In 1842 W. G. Don boasted that:

> We are in the habit of supplying Merchants with Scotch linens suitable to the Spanish American & other markets which we can make up as Creguelas, Plugastels, Russia, Sheetings, Canamazos, Burlaps, Creas etc as wanted.[17]

In effect what the Dons were doing was adapting their basic lines, osnaburgs, loom dowlas, sheetings and canvas, and then producing them in the widths and colours which met the specific needs of the various markets they served. Thus, for example, loom dowlas, which was a heavy cloth most commonly used for sheets and men's shirts, was also sold as creguelas (in France), plugastels (in Spain and South America) and lavales, depending on the quality, width (from 25″ to 40″) and colour of the cloth. In all there were 28 different varieties of this cloth, although some were more difficult to produce than others, all requiring specially spun and bleached yarns. Sheetings, their main product, were finely differentiated too, being known variously as canamazos, gante crudos, burlaps, imitation Russias, creas, Forfars and flaxens. Canvas appears to have been sold largely under that name, but even so, different widths were offered – 24″, 30″ and 36″. The canvas which the Dons made, like much of the rest of their cloth, was of the best quality. It was unstarched, which Robert Don was convinced gave it an edge in the market. Accordingly, in 1840, he asked one of the company's customers to

> point out to your friends the advantages of unstarched canvas . . . although they do not feel so stiff as those full of starch still they have more durability for they are made of much finer stuff & have more of it.[18]

For this reason Don & Co's canvas was more expensive than its chief rival in South and Central America, namely starched canvas from the North. Nevertheless, demand for it was strong, for use as sails, tarpaulins (which were used in the mines of Mexico and elsewhere), and waggon covers. Another regular item was padding canvas, while at the bottom of the product range was scrim, cheesecloth and upholsteries.[19]

For most of the period under review, sales continued to be organised in the same way as they had been in William Don's day, with Robert relying like most of the rest of the coarse textile merchants and manufacturers in the region at this time on a network of middle-men to search out overseas sales. 'Our trade,' one correspondent was informed in June 1841, 'is principally in supplying exporters in this Country . . . we are not much inclined to consign abroad on our own act.'[20] They were, it was claimed, 'shy' about 'doing anything in the way of consigning' as this would be seen as 'interfering' with their customers' business. This was so especially as far as Latin America was concerned, where most of the company's sales were obtained through the efforts of R. Zwilchenbart & Co of Liverpool. Liverpool and Manchester had joined London as the main locations of the Dons' British merchant exporters, with very little trade being conducted through Glasgow by 1840.

With the addition of Robert's sons John and William to the firm it was possible for the company to make some significant changes in their marketing arrangements. John was born in 1823 and after a period spent at school in Wilton-le-Wear in Durham, his father sent him at the relatively young age of sixteen to an East India house in London, to learn as much as he could about the commercial end of the textile trade, both at home and overseas.[21] Whilst in London he also acted on occasion as the company's representative. Apparently, he was prepared to take responsibility at an early stage – although this was much to his father's displeasure on one occasion in October 1840 when John had countermanded an order from one of the company's London customers, Luck, Bouch & Coath. John's action, Robert told them, had been taken 'without our authority' and he promised to investigate the matter further.[22] John returned to settle in Dundee around 1842, and concentrated his energies on the merchanting side of the company's operation.

John's older brother William Gilbert (b. 1816) had followed in his uncle William's footsteps and gone first into banking, serving an apprenticeship in the Dundee New Bank's office in Forfar (which was taken over by the Dundee Banking Company in 1838), prior to joining his father in 1840. Although in 1842 he had taken on the responsibility of visiting prospective customers in Bristol, Liverpool, London, Manchester and Glasgow, his main concern came to be the manufacturing side of the business, in Forfar. Freed from the day-to-day concerns of management, Robert Don was able to pay more attention to the marketing of cloth.

The impact of the new men on the firm was immediate, especially in the case of W. G. Don. Prior to their arrival the firm had been managed by Robert Don on his own, except for a short period when he had been able to employ an 'assistant'. Without him the business came to a halt; if he was ill, for example, orders were simply not dispatched.[23]

Evidently with the intention of expanding the firm's own merchanting operations, W. G. Don showed a marked willingness to obtain goods wanted by customers which the Dons did not manufacture themselves. Indeed, such undertakings appear sometimes to have brought no immediate benefit to the company, although their preparedness to help was clearly designed to curry favour with potential buyers. In April 1842, for instance, he had informed J. S. Vott of London, who had enquired about the availability of 'ticks' that:

> Ticks for bedding . . . are made in Kirkcaldy about 50 miles from here & if you wished samples of them we could easily procure them for you or get you the names of the makers of them.[24]

Even an enquiry about jute, which Robert would have nothing to do with, was helpfully answered, to the extent that in July 1842 W. G. Don took practical steps to find an agent who would sell raw jute in Dundee for one of their long-standing correspondents, Thomas & Henry Murray.[25]

More significant than this was the fact that the firm began to adopt a much more expansive and aggressive sales policy. In this the Dons' strategy was very much in line with developments in the Dundee textile industry.[26] Reference has already been made to W. G. Don's forays into key English commercial centres – as well as Glasgow – in search of orders. In March 1842 the company began consigning goods abroad on an agency basis, when Robert Don agreed to take on an agency for a Kingston-based company, Porteous, Carson & Co. Two factors combined to persuade the Dons to take the risk of trading directly with Jamaica. First, it was their major market and also a secure one: the company was 'almost always' making osnaburgs, wrote W. G. Don in August 1842.[27] Furthermore, in November 1841, 'an alteration & improvement in the finishing calendar' (which was probably a 'public' calendar rather than their own) gave them reason to believe that their osnaburgs were 'the best goods of the kind we have yet made'.[28] The second factor was almost certainly that as profit margins were squeezed, it was no longer in the company's interest to pay commission on the large quantities of osnaburgs which they sold to middlemen.

The Dons' own output only partly satisfied demand, however, and as a result Robert Don had to persuade other local makers to sell cloth to him. He was prepared to pay sellers two-thirds of the value of their goods, although he preferred to obtain these on deferred terms. For this cloth he received a quarter of Porteous & Carson's commission, which worked out at 2.5 per cent of the gross value of the goods sent for shipment via Liverpool.[29]

An example of the more aggressive sales methods which can be discerned with the arrival of the two brothers is seen in relation to the South African market. With the departure from Dundee for India of J. G. Gordon of Messrs Gordon & Co, the Dons had heard 'from parties connected with our late Friends' that two firms based in Cape Town 'wished to continue correspondence with the Scottish linen district'.[30] Rather than waiting for orders, which would have been the case previously, Don & Co had 'made up a small shipment truss of hessians' and forwarded it to Messrs Scott, Bell & Co of London to send on to one of the two South African firms, William Dobie & Co.[31]

All this is not to suggest that the company had abandoned its earlier preference for doing business with 'wholesale people' where this was possible. When, for example, in April 1842 they began to look to the Irish market and Cork in particular, it was with wholesalers that they wanted to deal.[32] At this stage in the company's development this was perfectly reasonable. Even with a three-man management team there were practical limits as to how much commercial information Robert, William and John could obtain from abroad – unless they spent a great deal of time travelling to ascertain the state of what has been shown to be extremely volatile markets.

Transportation and Shipping

The transportation of the company's goods caused almost as much concern to Robert Don as it had his brother, for, in spite of improvements in transport facilities with deeper harbours, greater numbers of more reliable steamships and the steam locomotive, the Dons' business, as W. G. Don observed in 1842, was of a 'detached nature', being not only thousands of miles distant from their Latin American markets, but also several miles inland from the chief port in the locality, Dundee. In order to overcome this locational disadvantage, Robert Don and his sons still found it necessary to transport goods free of charge to the coast. The company's continuing challenge was to get goods as cheaply as possible to their main merchant-exporters in the cities of Liverpool, London and Manchester, Glasgow and Greenock.

In the 1840s water transport was still the cheapest method of sending bulk goods any distance. It was not until the end of the decade that the first trans-border railway lines were completed.[33] Following the introduction of steam vessels on the sea-route from Dundee to London in 1834, firms such as Robert Don & Co had a choice of sending their goods south either by steam-powered vessels such as the *Dundee* and *Perth*, or using the slower, cheaper and more numerous sailing vessels, or 'traders'.[34] Competition both between different companies and the two modes of transport was such that the cost of sending linen to London was cheaper in 1840 than it had been in 1816, falling from 3s 6d per barrel (of five cubic feet) bulk (pbb) in 1816, to 3s by steamer, and 2s by sail in 1840.[35]

Although the journey by sailing ship was less costly, the company sent all its goods to London by steamship, which was faster and more dependable.[36] From the date of its departure from Dundee, the Dons allowed three months credit, with a 1.5 per cent discount for cash sales.[37] Goods could be sent 'free' of all transportation charges if purchasers paid slightly more for their cloth, 0.125 of a penny per yard in the case of canvas, for example.

For shipping goods on the longer trip to Liverpool, traders were used. The cost of direct shipping, 2s 3d pbb in 1840, was considerably less than that of sending linen through the Forth and Clyde canal and then loading up again at Glasgow and

Greenock for the sea journey to the Mersey.[38] The drawback to this, however, was that the voyage could last ten days, although if necessary the journey time could be (and sometimes was) halved, by sending linen overland to Glasgow, in fleets of carts such as that run by a Mrs Aitken of Perth.[39] It was evidently a course of action which was only taken if the Dons' major customers wanted cloth in a hurry; a less important customer, Booth & Fox, was informed that the overland route was 'more than we can afford'.[40] The Forth and Clyde canal was also used to ship goods to Glasgow, although how frequently is not clear.

LABOUR AND THE ORGANISATION OF PRODUCTION

At the time of William Don's death, the firm owned a few looms of its own, but most of the cloth was woven by weavers who were independent of William and Robert Don, and as has been seen, they were free to purchase their own yarn, after determining which cloth they thought they could most easily sell at a good price. Under this arrangement, of course, it was the weavers who bore the risks of being caught out with the wrong sort of yarn or losing money if cloth prices fell.

The degree of independence which the weavers had should not be exaggerated, however. When the mill at Murthill had been operating, the Dons almost certainly gave out yarn themselves, for the manufacture of tow sheetings. Even after the failure of James Laird & Co they continued to supply some yarn to weavers, and from the early 1820s, it is clear that the Dons were much more active in the yarn market than before, and regularly supplied weavers with the yarns required to make up their orders. Furthermore, it was clearly in the weavers' interests to manufacture the varieties and quality of cloth the Dons wanted, not least because William Don paid promptly, in cash, for what he took from them. And in the final analysis, despite the foothold in the land which many of them managed to maintain, the weavers were heavily dependent for their livelihoods on the state of demand for and price of cloth, the cost of yarn, and the numbers of entrants to the trade. They had little control over any of these factors.

Such influence as the weavers had been able to exert over the hours they worked at the loom and the proportion of time they devoted to leisure, was also considerably weakened as increased numbers, low wages and the absence of alternative full-time employment drove them to their looms whenever a web became available. Even to go off for the harvest was to risk their prospects at the loom, at least during periods when trade was depressed, as in the autumn of 1840, when it was reported that Forfar manufacturers were unwilling to take in 'those hands that are at the Harvest work'.[41] Forfar exhibited the paradox which marked most of the hand-loom weaving trade in Scotland between *c.*1812 and 1840, of falling real wages at the same time as the numbers entering the trade rose.[42] This was to shift considerably the balance of power between firms such as Robert Don & Co and the weaving fraternity.

Elements of the older system did continue to operate throughout Robert Don's era, however. The 'country weavers', upon which he depended for heavier cloths such as loom dowlas, spent a good deal of their time on the land and indeed were often reluctant to resume weaving after the harvest, much to Don's annoyance. Thus in November 1840 he had to explain that an order for cloth would be delayed as most of it was being woven in the country and that 'at the end of the season it is impossible to get [the country weavers] to continue steady at their looms'.[43] The timing of the harvest partly determined when the company could fulfil orders, with one customer in August 1841, for example, being told that the cloth he wanted could be made up 'if we got begun immediately before the harvest commences'.[44] On this occasion, however, the harvest had 'come on faster than was anticipated', so that in September Robert had to tell his correspondent that 'it is doubtful if the hands be got to remain steady at the 40-inch [loom dowlas] & therefore they may be a week longer in being ready.'

Even the weavers who were based in Forfar itself, and who were employed on a much more regular basis, were also inclined to break off from weaving in favour of agricultural work in both spring and autumn. It was a case of necessity. For their labour at the cereal harvest they were paid by the farmers; during the potato harvest on the other hand they were simply gathering in their own crops. Robert Don was unable to persuade them to 'keep in', for good reason: 'almost their entire existence during the winter,' he observed, 'depends upon the potato crop'.[45] The harvest season could stretch over several weeks and it was only in November, when virtually all opportunity for land labour had disappeared, that loom work was fully resumed, with the firm reporting to the customer on 18 November 1841 that 'The 35/40 pors. [creguelas] are being loomed as fast as the hands come in who are fit to weave them.'[46] The pull of temporary work in the fields which was available in the vicinity of Forfar – located as it is within a region of rich arable farmland – remained a feature of the local textile industry until relatively recent times. It may have been a considerable inconvenience to the Dons, but it was always short-lived, generally predictable to within a week or two, depending on the weather, and by providing their weavers with at least some proportion of the means of their own subsistence, Robert Don & Co were spared from the necessity of paying the higher wages the weavers would otherwise require to purchase all their food and other necessities in the marketplace.

Yet in other respects, the links with earlier work patterns were considerably weakened by the early 1840s. The company had become much more directly involved in the weaving process than had been the case 25 years earlier. It is clear, for instance, that Robert Don had become a sizeable employer of weaving labour, although the sort of records which would have made it possible to say how many were involved, and what expense the company had incurred in purchasing looms and sheds in which to house them, have unfortunately not survived. Certainly the weavers could be numbered in hundreds, for in September 1842 it is possible to calculate that the company could fairly readily turn more than 200 weavers to the production of creguelas alone.[47]

Another new departure was the employment of weavers at night-work, at least for short periods, when goods had to be made up in order to catch a vessel at Dundee. In September 1840, for example, Robert Don informed Lees Bros of Manchester that the weavers were 'making up tonight for tomorrow's steamer'.[48] As the cloth woven in Forfar had to be transported to Dundee and then folded and press-packed before being shipped (aboard vessels which often left at 9 a.m.), night-working was sometimes essential if important customers such as Zwilchenbarts of Liverpool were to obtain their goods on time. This was especially so during the winter months, when only one vessel per week left for Merseyside.

At the same time, however, Robert Don & Co continued to rely on considerable numbers of independent weavers, notably those who were adept at weaving varieties and widths of cloth for which demand was uncertain. This was so in the case of loom dowlas for instance, for which orders tended to be slow and irregular, and accordingly, such work was usually given out to the country weavers, who had long specialised in this sort of cloth anyway.

In other words, if demand for a specific variety of cloth was not likely to be sustained, it was judged best to continue to utilise the labour of the part-time weavers. The weaving trade was a variegated one, with skills and looms not being immediately transferable from one variety of cloth to another, thereby denying the firm the benefits which could be obtained if weavers were set to work on long uninterrupted runs. Thus the advantage of securing more regular orders for loom dowlas was observed in 1841, for then the weavers more directly under the firm's control could specialise in its manufacture. Otherwise, if insufficient numbers of country weavers were to be found – and as has been pointed out, there were times of year when they were unavailable – Robert Don was 'forced to make them in Town', with all of the trouble, expense of setting up looms and unsatisfactory work which resulted when he had to 'shift Canamazos weavers on them'.[49] Fitting-up costs were sufficiently high to cause him to turn down orders, as happened in April 1841 when Booth & Fox of Cork, Ireland, wanted a quantity of brown flax sheetings. These were to be 50″ wide, instead of the usual 25″, and Booth & Fox were informed that 'unless we were to get a continuation of [orders] in 45 and 50 inches we would not be at the expense of fitting up a loom for them.'[50] Conversely, another customer, who earlier had unsuccessfully tried to persuade Robert Don to supply a quantity of canvas of a certain width, was informed in November 1840 that this would now be possible, as the company had received

> an order for 1,000 yards of Bleached very best Canvas, 36 inch wide for South America, and as we are fitting up four looms for this order (having the prospect of a continuation) we can now make what you want of this width.[51]

Nevertheless, there were clearly enough substantial orders to persuade Robert Don & Co to extend their manufacturing operations by the direct employment of weavers. There were other reasons too, not the least of which was the need to maintain the company's reputation for good-quality cloth.

As has been stressed, William Don's success in the linen trade owed much to his concern with the quality of the goods he sold. In this he had been aided by the Board of Trustees' practice of inspecting and stamping cloth. In June 1823, however, the stamping system was abolished and the responsibility for the quality of linen was returned to the manufacturers and merchants. Under the old system, cloth-makers were forced into anonymity as it was the names of the stampmasters and possibly the merchant who then sold it further afield which appeared on a piece of cloth. From 1823, however, individual manufacturers could weave their name into their material and, freed from the necessity of seeking the approval of the stamp office, they could sell their cloth directly to a merchant.

This could obviously have had a major and detrimental effect on the Dons, who had hitherto utilised the stamping system to their considerable advantage. Greater care than ever had to be exercised by the company over the quality of cloth the weavers turned out, especially since around 1822, when jute, a much cheaper potential substitute for flax, had first arrived in Dundee.[52] And although the immediate reaction of Dundee's spinners, weavers and merchants to the new fibre was not enthusiastic, appearances were being made in the region by merchant-manufacturers such as John Maberley of Maberley & Co, who were actively searching for ways of introducing and using flax and hemp substitutes.[53] In these circumstances then, it was crucial for Don & Co to maintain strict control over the weavers, or 'makers', as they were usually called. This had been recognised prior to the ending of the stamping system, when Robert wrote that:

> If we [were] to give the Makers the least indulgence and not . . . look after the yarns they buy, we would have nothing but trash to send . . . we always make it a rule to know what the yarns are made from.[54]

In January 1841 though, after a sharp rise in yarn prices (see below), even Robert Don was forced to 'redress the quality' of the firm's goods.[55] Profits could not be made otherwise, and there was simply no sense in continuing to be pernickety about the composition of their coarse linen goods when he could see 'our neighbours getting as much money for inferior makes'.

In better times, watch had to be kept over the quantity of yarn used by the weavers. The Dons insisted that the weavers produced osnaburgs of 25 porters rather than the more common 24, which meant, of course, that more yarn had to be used in a given length of cloth. This was not popular with the weavers who were considered by Robert Don

> not so safe making the 25 porters . . . they grumble upon us very much for making them adhere so strictly to the weight and the quality of the yarns they are made of, which we are determined to do.[56]

They were clearly successful though, as in 1820 Don & Co were sending 26 porter 'superior threaded strelitz tow' to London.[57] Even more importantly, in 1841, by which time jute manufacturing was beginning to take off in Dundee, Robert Don & Co were able to 'guarantee' a London customer of long standing that their canvas was 'entirely free from Jute hemp now so common in Dundee'.[58] It was judged vital at this stage that they were able to give this assurance, for on the east coast of South America, which by the early 1840s had become an important market for Don & Co, 'low sail cloths . . . if known to have jute in them', were 'unsaleable'.[59]

Cloth of a uniform quality was preferred, as it had been in William's day, and this his successors did their best to provide.[60] A further encouragement to Robert Don & Co to engage weavers of their own was the considerable range of varieties and widths of cloth they made, referred to earlier in this chapter. Clearly, it was easier to switch production quickly in order to meet the needs of an important customer if the Dons themselves owned the looms and could instruct weavers to move from one line to another as required, although as has been seen this was not always practicable.

With more direct control over the weaving workforce, the company was now able to shift some of the burden of potential trading losses on to the backs of their increasingly vulnerable weaver employees. Earlier, as has been seen, weavers simply stopped working when, for example, yarn prices were such as to make weaving unremunerative. With weavers directly in their employment, price reductions could in part be achieved by cutting weavers' wages, and ultimately, of course, men and women could simply be laid off. Thus in January 1841, during a period of considerable distress for most Scottish hand-loom weavers, Robert Don felt confident enough to claim that he could get sheetings made 'at any price wanted'.[61] That this was largely at the expense of the weavers can clearly be seen in a letter written in February of the same year, in which Robert expressed some regret that it was 'by reducing the wages of the weaver' he was able to supply creguelas at an unusually low price.[62]

Nevertheless, the direct employment of weavers was not without its problems. The weavers' attachment to agricultural work at certain times of the year has already been noted. More serious were the difficulties the Dons faced over the supply of yarn. Now, of course, the company, rather than the weavers, had to secure and purchase the requisite yarns, with all the risks that this entailed.

Yarn

As beforehand, the availability and price of yarn was the critical determinant of the profitability of weaving, although by adjusting the wages of the weavers directly in the employment of Robert Don & Co, the company did have some control over weaving costs. With no spinning capacity of their own, however, it was in the Dons' interest to achieve some influence over the supply of yarn.

Although they bought their yarns from a number of

spinners, a marked tendency to concentrate their purchases can be identified between 1835 and 1843. By 1843, although Don & Co purchased yarn from 18 different suppliers, four of them accounted for 76 per cent of the total, whereas the same four had provided 36 per cent of the company's requirements in 1839.[63] The leading suppliers – Aberdein, Gordon & Co, Andrew Duncan & Son, Alexander Munro and Alexander Smith – specialised in particular kinds of yarn, although they could each supply a wider variety if required. Duncan & Son, for example, supplied bleached flax and fine tow yarns, while Alexander Smith supplied green or unbleached flax and common tow. The prices of spindles of 14,400 yards varied according to type and appearance, with tow costing anything between 1s 8d to 3s, depending on whether it was 'dark', 'green' or 'fair', as well as its fineness. Robert Don & Co bought substantial quantities, spending an average of just over £275 per month in 1836, rising to just under £600 per month in 1843.[64] They tended to pay in cash if less than £100 was involved, but demanded four months credit for larger amounts.[65] Again, success in obtaining regular orders for cloth was essential if their transactions were to reap the biggest rewards, for without these it was difficult to estimate what quantities of the various sorts and counts of yarn to buy. If coloured yarn was bought and manufactured without an immediate sale in prospect, there was danger that the cloth would lie in store until the following season, by which time it had usually lost some of its colour.

In a trade where profit margins were extremely narrow at the best of times, manufacturers such as the Dons were sensitive to even minor upwards movements in the price of yarn. A 5 per cent increase in August 1840, for example, was one which local manufacturers, according to Robert Don, 'could by no means afford to pay'.[66] By the end of the month the situation had deteriorated to the extent that Robert Don informed Zwilchenbarts that it was 'quite impossible' for them to go on making goods, 'owing to the price of Flax and Yarns', unless they could obtain more for their cloth, which he thought unlikely.[67] It would have taken an advance of more than 10 per cent on heavy cloth to enable manufacturers to purchase more yarn, while heavy canvas was 'not within 12.5 per cent of our even money'.[68]

At the turn of the 1840s the Dons began to experience acute problems over the supply (and price) of yarn. The principal reason for this was that large purchases of Forfarshire yarns were made by outsiders, partly to supply overseas customers, who were no longer so dependent upon cloth from Forfar and other Scottish textile manufacturers, now that they had developed their own cloth-making capacity. Buyers on behalf of French manufacturers were exceptionally active, a situation which some spinners appear to have taken advantage of by demanding higher prices from local manufacturers. As a result, late in October 1840 a yarn boycott was organised, which temporarily at least had some effect, with Robert Don noting happily on 31 October that prices were 'looking down'.[69] The 'great export' of yarns continued, however, and by the middle of the following month, upward pressures on yarn prices returned as government contracts for yarn were placed in the locality.

A critical situation developed in Forfar. Robert Don was of the view that the price of yarn had risen so high that some of his fellow manufacturers would 'not easily get above it'.[70] The crisis deepened in 1841 as the banks, who had been financing the expansion of the textile industry generally, restricted credit both in Dundee and Forfar.[71] In a letter to a customer in April Robert Don explained that manufacturers were being forced to lay off hands and restrict 'their business within their means of paying and receiving cash payments'.[72] As the first 'casualties' were reported, he despaired of what 'the trade of this place is shortly to come to', and could see only unemployment and misery for the weavers. This was in part because cloth prices had collapsed, with flax and tow sheetings at 'lower figures', according to Robert 'than we ever knew them to be'.[73] The situation had not improved over a year later, when cloth prices were rightly described as being 'ruinously low'; osnaburgs, for example, were able to achieve only $2^3/_8$d and $3^{11}/_{12}$d. The only compensation was that at these prices the Dons could still find a market for their cloth in Spain, for example, where it was possible to overcome the tariffs which had been raised to discourage the importation of finished goods.

For the Dons, the first sign that the yarn famine may have been coming to an end was to be seen in June 1842, when Luck, Booth & Coath were informed that enough yarn was available from a 'very needy' seller to make up their order of 60 pieces of cloth reasonably cheaply.[74]

Don & Co then, had survived another major trough in the fortunes of the Scottish linen trade. They had done so partly by temporarily casting aside their concern with quality. There is a suggestion too that while the Dons were not spinning their own yarns, they had begun to prepare some of them.

This was a first step. Robert had learned from the experience, and with the introduction of his sons to the business in Forfar, was able to do something about it. As has been seen, yarns, rather than cloth, had been in demand throughout the bleak first two years of the 1840s. Alert to this fact, in the middle of 1842 W. G. Don was to be found anxiously awaiting news about what he referred to as the 'tariff question'. The tariffs concerned were those imposed by the Spanish government. If they were to be relaxed, he noted, there would be a 'considerable effect' on the yarn trade as merchants rushed to supply a new market.[75] This time, however, the Dons, whose cloth was already reaching Spain, intended to be part of any such move themselves, and began to prepare for it in July after Zwilchenbarts had requested a quantity of linen yarns.[76] In September news of 'an alteration of a favourable nature' began to filter through to Forfar. The change in Spanish tariffs, it was anticipated, would 'place trade upon a better footing with that country than it has yet been'.[77] Don & Co felt, not without justification, that they were in an excellent position to benefit from such a departure; their 'connection with the first spinners of this country', wrote W. G. Don, would enable them to conduct this branch of trade to the 'entire satisfaction' of their customers.[78] Just as the discriminating skills of William and Robert in identifying the best cloth at market had been an important factor in the firm's early success, so in the 1840s their successors were able to boast that their intimate knowledge of the yarn markets enabled them to judge which were the best.[79]

Thus was commenced a new and lucrative development for the company. Almost immediately their yarn purchases increased, more than doubling from just over £3,082 to £7,187 in 1843.[80] A somewhat later run of figures relating to the number of spindles sold shows that this upward trend continued. In 1844 R. Zwilchenbart, in that year their sole customer for yarns, bought 13,200 spindles; in 1845 five firms purchased 43,381 spindles from the Dons. A sharp dip occurred in 1846, but by 1847 the trade had recovered, with 48,266 spindles being sold.[81] Unfortunately, no further figures have survived; what has survived, however, is a tantalising but vague reference in an obituary for John Don which reported that so successful were the Dons in the Spanish yarn trade that 'for a considerable period' they 'virtually controlled' it.[82]

Dyeing and Finishing

When Robert Don succeeded William in the management of Don & Co in 1817, the processes of bleaching, dyeing and finishing of the cloths in which he dealt were carried out by third parties. This continued to be the case throughout Robert Don's era, although as might be expected, he did take great pains to ensure that the bleachers and dyers he employed worked to a high standard.[83] As cloth buyers became more discriminating such attention became even more important, as did the ability of Don & Co to provide customers with a range of colours and finishes which was much wider than had been the case previously, when the cloth had been sent south either bleached or unbleached. It should be noted, however, that apart from the reds and blues which were used for sheetings, the usual colour range of the Dons' cloth was restricted to black, lead, 'drab', slate and green, in keeping with their role as suppliers of what was for the most part, cloth designed for 'industrial' purposes.

Much dyeing was done on Don & Co's behalf by a Mr Wood, whose premises were in Castle Street in Forfar until the autumn of 1841. The advantage of having the cloth dyed (and bleached) in Forfar, it was argued, was that it could be done more cheaply than in London, and just as well.[84] By concentrating their business in the hands of a handful of bleachers and dyers the Dons were able to exert considerable pressure over those who worked for them. Thus in March 1842, for example, they were able to reduce the cost of shipping cloth to Zwilchenbarts, their main Liverpool customer, after having obtained a 'reduction . . . from the bleachfield'.[85] Yet for a firm like Don & Co, which prided itself on the high standard of the cloth and yarn it sent out, there were dangers in such an arrangement. In May 1841

Robert Don had to deal with a complaint from a customer about the quality of the dyed linen he had been sent. Don had to admit that the goods concerned 'were shipped before we saw the Patterns of them at our Packers, so that we could not return them to the Dyer to be done over again.' In his turn, the dyer blamed his foreman, who was alleged to have been drunk when supervising the operation.[86]

Setbacks such as this notwithstanding, the Dons continued to utilise Wood's services, and indeed seem to have provided enough business to encourage him to move to new and bigger premises sometime in 1841. As a result, costs were cut and the options for the Dons widened. Hitherto they could send cloth dyed in 'any colour wanted', declared W. G. Don enthusiastically in a letter to Zwilchenbarts. Improvements in bleaching and dyeing were accompanied by changes in the finishing process, although for some years they continued to make use of the public calendar. As this was also located in Forfar they were able to achieve a far greater degree of control over the finish of their cloth than had been the case when they had sent it to be processed in Dundee. The improvements in the calendaring department were such that by November 1841 Robert Don & Co were in a position to tell customers that their goods could now be made 'more economically as well as better'. All of this gave Robert Don and his two sons a great deal of satisfaction, as can be seen in the claim they made at the end of 1841, that the canvas and osnaburgs which they were then dispatching were 'the best of which we have yet sent'.

Chapter Four: The Era of Robert Don

1 DMHUD, Card Index, David Don to David Jobson, 11 August 1817.
2 Munn, *Scottish Provincial Banking*, p71.
3 DMHUD, Card Index, David Don to Cowley & Sancton, 12 July 1819.
4 Ibid, 28 November 1818.
5 Durie, *Linen Industry*, p104.
6 DMHUD, Card Index, Robert Don to Cowley & Sancton, 3 February 1818.
7 Ibid, 28 July 1818.
8 Ibid, 3 February 1818.
9 Ibid, David Don to H. Harrison & Co, 26 July 1817.
10 Gauldie, 'Dundee Jute', p119.
11 See index compiled for DUA, MS 100/1/2/3, Letter Book, 1840–42.
12 Lenman *et al*, *Textile Industry*, p14.
13 DUA, MS 100/1/2/3, Letter Book, 1840–42, Robert Don to Lloyd & Haynes, 30 January 1841.
14 Ibid, Robert Don to He---son & Co, 28 June 1841.
15 Ibid, W. G. Don to C. Vidal, 6 September 1842.
16 Ibid, Robert Don to Thomas Whyte, 12 January 1841.
17 Ibid, W. G. Don to Schunck, Souchay & Co, 1 March 1842.
18 Ibid, Robert Don to John Hall & Co, 31 December 1840.
19 As will be seen below, by the 1950s scrim had become the company's main product.
20 Ibid, Robert Don to He---son & Co, 28 June 1941.
21 *Forfar Herald*, 11 June 1886.
22 DUA, MS 100/1/2/3, Letter Book, 1840–42, Robert Don to Luck, Bouch & Coath, 17 October 1840.
23 Ibid, Robert Don to R. Zwilchenbart & Co, 27 September 1841.
24 Ibid, W. G. Don to J. S. Vott, 25 April 1842.
25 Ibid, W. G. Don to Thomas & Henry Murray, 21 July 1842.
26 Lenman *et al*, *Textile Industry*, pp13–18.
27 DUA, MS 100/1/2/3, Letter Book, 1840–42, W. G. Don to W. Winn, 18 August 1842.
28 Ibid, W. G. Don to John Hall & Co, 12 November 1841.
29 Ibid, Robert Don to Porteous, Carson & Co, 11 March 1842.
30 Ibid, W. G. Don to W. Dobie & Co, 6 June 1842.
31 Ibid.
32 Ibid, W. G. Don to Booth & Fox, 6 April 1842.
33 A. J. Robertson, *The Origins of the Scottish Railway System 1722–1844* (Edinburgh, 1983), p315.
34 Lenman *et al*, *Textile Industry*, p180; for a recent study see Jackson and Kinnear, *The Trade and Shipping of Dundee*.
35 DUA, MS 100/1/2/1, Letter Book, 1814–17, W. Don to John Harvey, 13 April 1986, DUA MS 100/1/2/3, Letter Book, 1840–42, Robert Don to Thomas & Henry Murray, 8 August 1840.
36 Ibid, Robert Don to Parson, Hurles & Co, 13 July 1841, although for a time after the introduction of steam, sail was actually more reliable.
37 Ibid, Robert Don to R. & J. Barrow, 6 October 1841.
38 Ibid, Robert Don to Thomas & Henry Murray, 8 August 1840.
39 Unfortunately the letter-books are not sufficiently detailed to allow more rigorous analysis of the company's transportation methods.
40 DUA, MS 100/1/2/3, Letter Book, 1840–42, Robert Don to Booth & Fox, 12 November 1841.
41 Ibid, Robert Don to R. Zwilchenbart & Co, 3 October 1840.
42 Murray, *Scottish Handloom Weavers*, p64.
43 DUA, MS 100/1/2/3, Robert Don to R. Zwilchenbart & Co, 24 November 1840.
44 Ibid, 21 August 1841.
45 Ibid, Robert Don to Shapland & Werford, 28 October 1841.
46 Ibid, Robert Don to R. Zwilchenbart & Co, 12 November 1841.
47 Late in 1842 it was claimed that 300 pieces of linen, each 72 yards in length, could be made in a week. If a weaver made as much in a day in 1842 as in 1816, when one

weaver made an average of 14.6 yards per day, it would have required 211 weavers to make up 300 pieces.

48 DUA, MS 100/1/2/3, Letter Book, 1840–42, Robert Don to Lees Brothers & Co, 4 September 1840.
49 Ibid, Robert Don to R. Zwilchenbart & Co, 5 June 1841.
50 Ibid, Robert Don to Booth & Fox, 29 April 1841.
51 Ibid, Robert Don to Baker, Williams & Co, 20 November 1840.
52 Gauldie, 'Dundee Jute', p118.
53 Ibid.
54 DMHUD, Card Index, Robert Don to Cowley & Sancton, 24 July 1821.
55 DUA, MS 100/1/2/3, Letter Book, 1840–42, Robert Don to Davis, Freeman & Co, 7 January 1841.
56 DMHUD, Card Index, Robert Don to Cowley & Sancton, 10 July 1819.
57 Ibid, 29 July 1820.
58 DUA, MS 100, Letter Book, 1840–42, Robert Don to George & John Lindsay, 14 August 1841.
59 Ibid, W. G. Don to R. Zwilchenbart & Co, 2 March 1842.
60 Ibid, Robert Don to Parson, Hurles & Co, 13 July 1841.
61 Ibid, Robert Don to W. & J. Morley, 7 January 1841.
62 Ibid, Robert Don to R. Zwilchenbart & Co, 6 February 1841.
63 See DUA, MS 100/1/3/9, Yarn Order Book, 1835–43.
64 Ibid.
65 Ibid.
66 DUA, MS 100/1/2/3, Letter Book, 1840–42, Robert Don to R. Zwilchenbart & Co, 12 August 1840.
67 Ibid, 26 August 1840.
68 Ibid, Robert Don to W. & J. Morely, 11 September 1840.
69 Ibid, Robert Don to Lloyd & Haynes, 31 October 1840.
70 Ibid, 26 November 1840.
71 Lenman, *et al*, *Textile Industry*, p14.
72 DUA, MS 100/1/2/3, Letter Book, Robert Don to David Duncan, 20 April 1841.
73 Ibid, Robert Don to Parson, Hurles & Co, 28 June 1841.
74 Ibid, W. G. Don to Luck, Bouch & Coath, 15 June 1842.
75 Ibid, 4 May 1842.
76 Ibid, W. G. Don to C. Vidal, 6 September 1842.
77 Ibid.
78 Ibid.
79 Ibid.
80 See DUA, MS 100/1/2/3, Yarn Order Book, 1835–43.
81 See DUA, MS 100/1/8/1 and MS 100 1/8/2, Specification Books, 1844–49.
82 From obituary of John Don, *Dundee Year Book, 1881*.
83 DUA, MS 100/1/2/3, Letter Book, 1840–42, Robert Don to Parson, Hurles & Co, 28 June 1841, refers to the 'great attention' which was paid to bleaching loom dowlas to 'very bright colours'.
84 Ibid, Robert Don to Thomas Whyte, 12 January 1841.
85 Ibid, W. G. Don to R. Zwilchenbart & Co, 1 March 1842.
86 Ibid, Robert Don to Thomas Whyte, 29 May 1841.

William G. Don (1816–86) and John Don (1823–86), the sons of Robert Don who took the company into jute manufacturing on a large scale. With A. J. Buist they established Dons Bros, Buist & Co as one of the coarse textile region's leading companies

CHAPTER FIVE

Expansion: The Halcyon Days and Beyond, *c.*1845–1904

It is much to be regretted that the longest gap in the company's more useful records for the historian is from the mid-1840s until the end of the Victorian era. It was during this period that the Dons, along with members of the Buist family, with whom they became formally allied in 1865, saw the firm through its greatest period of expansion. The business was transformed from one which until 1840 had been virtually a one-man merchanting and manufacturing operation which still owed much to the domestic system, into a large, highly capitalised business undertaking, with major works in both Forfar and Dundee. It was during the middle decades of this period too that large fortunes were made by the partners.

Unlike William Don, who spent the last few weeks of his life evading the clutches of his creditors, or their father Robert, whose assets (apart from the business) at the time of his death were just over £1,494, when John and W. G. Don died (within a month of each other), in June and July 1886 respectively, they had become extremely wealthy men.[1] The net value of the estate of John Don was £138,535, that of W. G. Don, £94,434.[2] Although these sums were less than those being left by members of the great Cox, Baxter and Caird families, they were still considerable fortunes. Furthermore, the Dons had managed to climb high up the ladder of local esteem.[3] In 1864 W. G. Don was elected President of Dundee Chamber of Commerce, to be followed in 1867 by his younger brother, who in his year of office also had the prestigious task of organising the first visit of the British Association to Dundee. Their successors also became

Presidents of the Chamber, Robert Bogle Don in 1899 and John B. Don in 1904. So did their partner's son, J. C. Buist, in 1895. In 1925, R. H. Adamson was elected President. More recently the company provided Presidents in the persons of William Low (1973) and Michael H. J. Hill (1985).[4]

That W. G. Don and John Don had 'arrived', could be seen through their business connections and places of residence. In 1858 W. G. Don had purchased a house, 'St Margaret's', in Broughty Ferry, the Dundee suburb in which were located many of the grand mansion houses of the city's textile magnates. Like his forebears, he played a prominent role in the local Episcopalian church. Both he and John were considerable benefactors of the church in Forfar, with W. G. Don, who was later described as 'a mainstay of the church', donating over half of the £10,000 which was required in the 1870s to build St John's chapel. Their partner from 1865 onwards, A. J. Buist, followed a roughly similar route, having moved to Broughty Ferry in 1856, where he resided at 'Reres Mount'. Unlike the Dons, he was an elder of the Free Church and supported the Unionist rather than the 'Moderate Liberal' cause of his partners. John Don bought Dunnichen House, once 'by far the best house about Forfar', according to one of his neighbours who was enthralled by its refurbished appearance – 'cold water as well as hot through the house . . . beautifully furnished and in good taste, a magnificent bathroom etc'. In the last years of his life, however, John Don preferred to reside in Edinburgh during the winter months.

With the other successful members of Tayside's textile manufacturing and mercantile élite, the Don brothers shared an interest in overseas investment. Both owned large portfolios of stocks and shares in lucrative American railroads for instance, in companies such as the Union Pacific Railroad Co and Pennsylvania Railroad Co as well as the Dundee-based First, Second and Third Scottish American Investment Trusts. Typically too, they were uninterested in developing other local industries. Apart from their own company, their biggest commitment to the local economy was to be found in the shares they had in eleven of Dundee's ships – in which jute was carried into the Tay. Given the importance of their trading links with Spain, it is not surprising that they also held Spanish government bonds.[5]

Although the period was clearly of momentous importance

St John's Episcopalian Church, Forfar. W. G. and John Don were important benefactors of this church. The Don family had a long-established connection with the Episcopalian faith

for the company, it was not without its tribulations. In 1868, in the aftermath of the remarkable prosperity which was enjoyed by Tayside textile firms during and immediately following the American Civil War, a trading loss was recorded. The Franco-Prussian War produced another boom, but further losses followed at intervals thereafter as competition from overseas grew and tariff walls made life increasingly difficult for the Scottish linen and jute trades.

The rest of this chapter describes and explains in greater detail the progress of the company during the period *c.*1845 to 1904, when the status of private limited liability was adopted.

The Changing Structure and Organisation of the Firm

Robert's sons, William Gilbert and John, joined the family business in 1840 and 1842 respectively. It was under their guidance that the company was expanded and altered in the way which has just been outlined, and accordingly the roles they played are deserving of some attention, even though, as has been pointed out, the materials necessary in order to perform such a task are thin on the ground. Contemporaries were in no doubt that it was they who had established what was to become the firm of Don Brothers, Buist & Co as one of Scotland's leading linen and jute businesses.

Very soon after William Gilbert joined his father, he was made a junior partner, and the name of the firm was changed from Robert Don & Co to Robert Don & Son. At some stage between 1843 and 1845 Robert Don appears to have withdrawn from the day-to-day management of the company, although the payment of a 'business allowance' to him of £144 per annum from 1845 until 1852 suggests that he was still active on the firm's behalf.[6] What is quite certain is that by 1845 W. G. and John had taken control of the management of the company, which became known as William & John Don & Co.[7]

This title only applied to the Forfar end of the firm's operations, however. John Don's apprenticeship in London had honed his merchanting skills and evidently whetted his appetite for a bigger share of the region's linen trade than had been commanded by his father, who had concentrated his attentions on Forfar and its immediate vicinity. Very soon after John's return north W. G. Don was able to report that:

> We are now very frequently in the Dundee market. Our facilities for doing a general Linen business in connection with this district are now such as give us many advantages which we did not formerly possess.[8]

Precisely what those advantages were is not clear, although it seems likely that Don was in part referring indirectly to the presence – and ability as a merchant in the linen trade – of his brother John. For by 1847 a Dundee subsidiary had been established, trading under the name of Don Bros & Co, managed by John Don, who was now based in Dundee, at offices in Bain Square. This was strictly a merchanting operation, buying flax (and jute), and dealing in yarn and cloth from

Dundee itself, as well as from Forfar. Thus in 1848 for example, 604 pieces (86,976 yards) of osnaburg was sent from Forfar to Don Bros in Dundee for sale and dispatch.[9]

Apart from the opportunities which closer proximity to Dundee's weekly cloth market provided, it is highly likely that a major inducement to the Dons to move into Dundee was their interest in yarns. Without adequate supplies of running water, Forfar had not been a suitable site for machine-spinning in the eighteenth century. Although the requirement for water meant the first spinning mills were mainly situated in the countryside, the appearance of steam-powered flax-spinning machinery in Dundee around 1792 presaged a drift of spinning mills towards the town. Indeed, even without steam such a move appears already to have been taking place: in 1804 there were an estimated 63 mills (although not all for spinning) on the Dighty water within five miles of Dundee.[10] In the 1820s there was a flurry of mill construction in Dundee, as elsewhere in Forfarshire, but by the end of the 1830s Dundee had become, in terms of horse-power, the leading flax-spinning centre in the British Isles. As early as 1829, 61 per cent of Scotland's flax imports were landed at its docks.[11]

Thus, although the quantity of yarns sold by the Dons had increased markedly following the first deal they had done in this line, with Zwilchenbarts of Liverpool in 1842, it was decided that Dundee rather than Forfar was a better base for this activity. By the end of 1847, by which time large orders for yarn (worth £6,033 between January and October) were also coming from a limited number of houses in London and Manchester, the business was being conducted through Dundee.[12]

St James' Works

With John Don firmly in charge of the firm's affairs in Dundee, W. G. Don could concentrate his attention on the manufacture of cloth in Forfar. Little is known about the fixed assets of the Dons in the earlier part of the nineteenth century. William Don had certainly some sort of warehouse and office in Forfar, where goods were sorted and made up before being sent to Dundee where he also had some packing and warehousing facilities.[13] In 1812 he had extended his offices, at what his brother John had described as 'considerable' expense.[14] It is likely that this expansion took place in Osnaburg Street, from where Robert Don subsequently conducted his business. Most of the linen cloth, however, was evidently made up by weavers in their own homes or in the sheds of their masters.

The Don brothers first purchased land facing on to the old Brechin Road, later to be called St James' Road, in 1845. This was the first of a series of land purchases made between 1845 and 1928 (see Diagram 1), when they expanded and consolidated the St James' Road site, which was, of course, to become the centre of their manufacturing operation and subsequently the company's headquarters. Long before this, however, the area had been associated with local industry. The Dons had conducted some of their business on it as well as in the surrounding parts of the town. The land itself was owned by a surgeon, John Adam, from 1805, and it remained in the possession of Adam and his heirs for the next 40 years or so, at some time during which it was leased to the Dons. Precisely when this commenced is not clear – it may have been when John Adam's son was in Bombay, where he spent much of his early life – but by 1845, when W. G. Don and John Don purchased a section of it (marked I on Diagram 1), 'extensive warehouses etc', together with a counting room had already been built.[15] This was not the only strip of land in the vicinity with which the Dons already had close connections. The long feu they purchased from Alexander Lindsay in 1865 had once been the property of Andrew Binny, younger, the stampmaster.[16] A smaller feu, further to the west, had been purchased by Alexander Mason, 'beetler to Robert Don, merchant', and his weaver son, Alexander (junior), from Robert Sturrock, although the Dons did not manage to obtain possession of this piece of ground until 1912.[17]

Having bought the feu upon which their warehouse and offices were situated, it was not until 1861 that the Don brothers re-entered Forfar's land market. This they did by purchasing (again from the Adam family) a small parcel of land for further office space. Notably, the next major purchase of land was in 1865, a remarkably prosperous year for the region's textile industry owing to the favourable repercussions of the American Civil War. In Dundee this was a time of substantial growth, with warehouses, mills and factories being built or extended

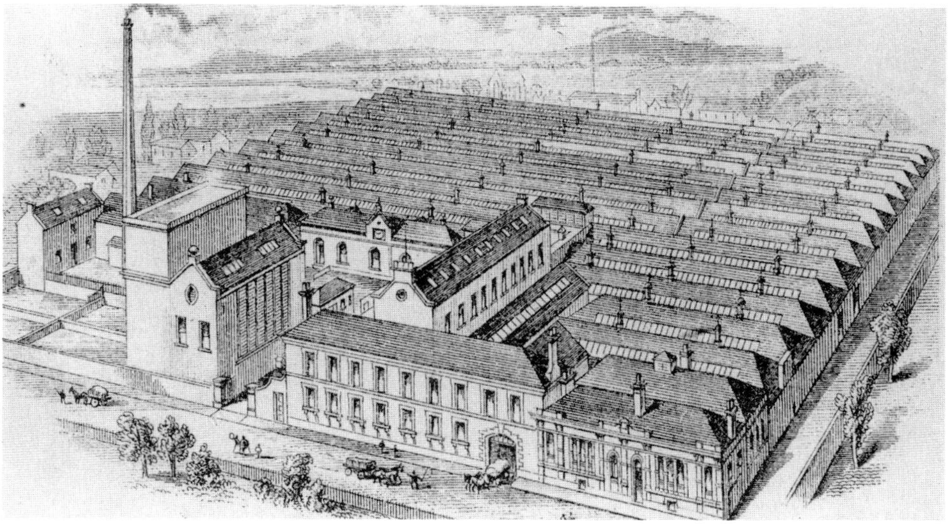

St James' Works, Forfar, c.1888. Note how the works grew up around Robert Don's original warehouse (centre). Some licence has been used by the artist though; the sheds at the top right-hand edge of the picture were never built on what was garden ground and a bowling green

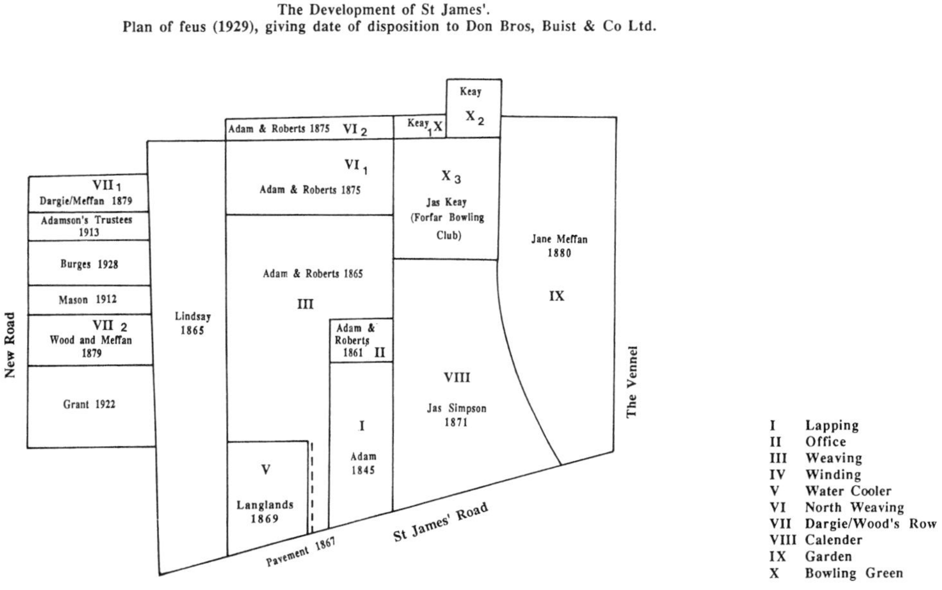

Diagram 1: *The Development of St James'.*
Plan of feus (1929), giving date of disposition to Don Bros, Buist & Co Ltd

throughout the city. The expansion which occurred during this period has been described as 'the greatest in Dundee's history'.[18] For the Dons and Forfar it was a time of even more dramatic change. From 1865 the brothers began to build a permanent manufacturing base on the St James' Road site, thereby revolutionising their system of production. Hitherto they had employed hand-loom weavers, along with perhaps half a dozen power-looms which they had housed in a converted stable in Rosebank Lane, over the road from their office and warehouse.[19] In 1865, however, they began to purchase and utilise power-looms which were housed in custom-built weaving sheds which were constructed on land further to the north of that they had already bought from the Adam family (see Diagram 1).

Up to this time, Forfar had been a hand-loom weaving centre, with some 7,600 people being involved in manufacturing cloth by this means (around 4,500 of whom were weavers, the rest being winders, warpers, etc). The Dons were not the first employers in Forfar to turn to power-loom weaving on a large scale. As Table 5.1 reveals, in 1864 four other firms had established power-loom weaving capacity in Forfar, not long after power-looms had first been used on a large scale in Dundee.[20]

Table 5.1 *Power-loom capacity in Forfar, 1864*

Firm	Engines	hp	Power-looms	Employed
J. & H. Craik & Co	1	30	180	230
John Lowson jnr	1	25	150	200
John Lowson & Son	1	12	108	140
Laird & Co	1	10	100	130

The Dons were not considered worth listing. However, although they were evidently late starters in this respect, they soon caught up with and overtook their local rivals. By 1869, their works at St James' contained 310 power-looms.[21]

Not only weaving was mechanised and centralised, but so too was the winding department, which was housed on land also purchased in 1865, for just over £378, from Alexander Lindsay of Orchardbank.[22] Further purchases followed in 1869 (for land for the water cooler), but mainly in the 1870s, in order

Workers' housing in Lour Road, Forfar, built in 1877. Over the road from St James' Works, this accommodation was provided for foremen and skilled workers. The expansion of St James' at this time necessitated the employment of more foremen in order to control the increasing number of production workers

to build a calendar and to extend the stock of looms. In 1872, after the completion of the calendar, the value of the works was £43,000, compared to £37,000 in 1870. The number of looms had risen to 400.[23]

Trade depression after the Franco-Prussian War halted further expansion. An upturn in 1875 though, evidently encouraged Don Brothers, Buist & Co (which the firm had now become) to increase their capacity and in 1875 the area devoted to weaving sheds was extended northwards to house a further 200 looms by the next year. Despite some concern which was being expressed about over-capacity in the industry, the partners of Don Bros, Buist & Co clearly shared in the optimism which was felt throughout the Scottish coarse textile region that any interruptions to the trade would be temporary and that recovery would follow.[24] Accordingly, by 1880 new offices had been built to the west of their predecessors, the weaving factory had been completed and new engines and boilers introduced, the finishing and packing departments had been enlarged, and seven houses were put up (in what is now Lour Road) to accommodate key employees such as foremen. Over a 13-year period the value of the property, plant and machinery at St James' had more than doubled, to £79,680.[25]

The partnership with A. J. Buist, and Ward Mills

As has just been noted, the changes in the scale and organisation of production at Forfar were a watershed for the Dons, and brought to an end their longstanding links with the putting-out system. Yet the mid-1860s saw even greater investment of capital by the firm in Dundee itself. Power-looms and the other factors of centralised production which were accumulated in Forfar required greater capital resources than were available to the two brothers on their own. To some extent their needs could be met by ploughing back the profits made during the American Civil War, but further development of the firm could only occur by widening its capital base. This was achieved by forming a partnership with Alexander Jafferson Buist, the proprietor of a Dundee spinning mill.

The Don and Buist families had done business in cloth in the 1820s. William Don had been involved with the Revd. John Buist, A. J. Buist's father, in obtaining a loan of £400 for two local landowners as far back as 1816.[26] Of more immediate importance was the fact that A. J. Buist had begun to supply William & John Don & Co with yarn. By the end of the 1840s a small but steady trade had developed, and between January 1848 and July 1852 Buist supplied the Dons with yarn worth over £3,456.[27]

Alexander Jafferson Buist, who had been born at Tannadice manse in 1818, was the youngest of three sons. His eldest brother James Buist (1810–44) had begun his business life as a small merchant, trading prudently (much more cautiously than William Don, for example) from 32 Cowgate, the heart of Dundee's commercial centre, where he had moved from St Andrews Street in 1832. Significantly though, James Buist too was scrupulous about the quality of the flax he imported and the cloth he sold.[28] Although he had begun to send quantities of flax to be machine-spun by a Mr John Buchan in Finhaven in 1837, his direct involvement in yarn production began in 1840 when he purchased one of Dundee's earliest steam-powered spinning

The Revd. John Buist (1754–1845), a remarkably enterprising minister whose estate was valued at £28,000. Descended from tenant-farmers in north Fife, during his life he acquired both land and an inn. He provided financial support for his son James's spinning mill in Dundee. The portrait is reproduced by kind permission of Mrs Brora Butterworth

Portrait, probably of James Jafferson Buist (1810–44). Son of the Revd. John Buist and elder brother of Alexander Jafferson Buist, James was a flax, yarn and cloth merchant in Dundee. With his father's help he purchased what was later to become Ward Mill. The portrait is reproduced by kind permission of Mrs Brora Butterworth

mills (built in 1833) from the bankrupt John Halley. Buist's rise to the rank of mill-spinner was in no small part helped by a substantial loan and guarantees (totalling £7,000) from his enterprising minister father John Buist, son of a tenant-farmer in north Fife, who combined small-scale landownership, private money-lending and the proprietorship of a sizeable inn in Brechin with his pastoral duties. Indeed the Revd. John Buist had set James up in business in the first place, around 1831, although the latter did manage to double his capital by the end of the decade. In 1844 Alexander's sickly brother James Buist died, to be succeeded in business at the four-storey Ward Mill by his brother – and partner after 1837 – Alexander. He was not unprepared for a career in spinning, as after having served an apprenticeship with Shaw, Reid & MacLauchlan, and after his brother's purchase of Ward Mill, he had visited James and William Brown's mills in order to learn something about the mechanics of mill-spinning.[29]

In 1864 Buist's Old Ward Mill was one of Dundee's smaller spinning establishments, with two steam engines of 55 hp driving 2,500 spindles which employed only 240 people.[30] In the mid-1860s, with trade booming and mill and factory building going on all around them, the Dons and A. J. Buist determined to pool their resources and expand their productive capacity. For both it was a logical step. The Dons had been exporting yarns from Dundee for two decades, and could benefit from having their own supply. This would also provide a steady source of yarns for their weavers in Forfar. For A. J. Buist there were the triple benefits of John Don's marketing expertise, W. G. Don's organisational ability, and a secure outlet for at least some part of the production of Ward Mills. Experience showed that those spinners who diversified their interests by moving into the weaving sector tended to do better than the rest. Accordingly, W. G. and John Don, along with A. J. Buist, entered into a co-partnery on 31 May 1865. Their respective stakes were £37,000, £40,000 and £25,500.[31] As this suggests, the balance of power within the triumvirate rested with the Dons, who continued to trade from Forfar under the name of Wm & John Don & Co. Formally though, the Forfar operation became part of the new firm of Don Brothers, Buist & Co. Concerned to ensure that A. J. Buist increased his commitment to the company, in 1872, at

Alexander Jafferson Buist (1818–1901), proprietor of Ward Mill after his brother's death in 1844. Later joined with W.G. and John Don to form the partnership of Don Bros, Buist & Co. The portrait is on loan to Dundee Art Galleries and Museums

which time the Dons' share in the concern had just risen to £60,000 each, it was decided that none of the partners should be allowed to draw more than £5,000 of any profits credited to them 'until such time as the Capital standing at the respective credit of each Partner in the Private Ledger shall amount to the sum of *Sixty Thousand Pounds*.'[32] By 1876 A. J. Buist had raised his stake from £36,500, which it had been in 1872, to the requisite £60,000.

In just over ten years the company's capital value almost doubled, from £102,000 (in 1865) to £200,000 (in 1876).[33] In part this reflected the expansion which was taking place in Forfar. Most of the new investment went to Dundee though, where Don Bros, Buist & Co embarked on the construction of their New Ward Mill, alongside the smaller Old Mill, although most of this seems to have been demolished and rebuilt into a four-storey, 26-bay pedimented block, half of which was a mill, the rest a warehouse.

Work had begun in 1867 on the five-storey building which

fronted Lindsay Street. Iron-framed and with 13 bays, like many of Dundee's mills which were constructed during the short-lived 'golden age' of coarse textile production, it was not entirely functional in its appearance, the confidence and pride of its owners being reflected in this instance in the mill's ornate cast-iron roof and what was proposed to be the centre-piece, a grand Italianate bell-tower. It was yet another indication – indeed a declaration – that Dons had become one of the more successful of the region's textile companies. By 1871, in the aftermath of the Franco-Prussian War, the mill had been fitted up with 7,172 spindles. With the Old Ward Mill, Don Brothers, Buist & Co now had a total spindle capacity of 9,502, which, it was estimated, could spin 50 tons of fibre into 180,000 miles of yarn per week.[34] In terms of mill capacity, however, this was as far as the company ever got in Dundee. Although the New Mill had been planned with 26 bays (and in the firm's advertising material this number is shown in illustrations of the works), the building was never extended to its full length, and until its demolition in 1964, it remained, in effect, half-built.

Between the Old and the New Mills were two preparing sheds, where batching, hackling, carding and drawing were carried out. By 1876, when warehousing facilities had also been built or acquired in the vicinity, the company's Ward Mills were valued at £140,500.[35]

Additional warehouse space was available in their Barrack Street offices. Again, these had been custom built, on the site of Barrack Street Mill and factory, allegedly the smallest in Dundee, which had been built in 1833 and purchased by the company in or just after 1865. The new offices, which again had a strong Italianate influence, were opened in 1871 and completed in 1875.[36]

Further expansion at Forfar and the second co-partnery

Despite the worsening long-term outlook for the linen trade, which some observers noted from the mid-1870s, Dons had enough confidence in the future to expand their manufacturing capacity in Forfar. As will be seen below, by this stage they had begun to manufacture some jute cloth, the volume of which (though not the unit value) was still rising. Ironically, it was the sequestration of the estate of one of their local rivals, John Lowdon, after he had run into business difficulties, which provided them with the opportunity to extend their influence within Forfar. Lowdon's power-loom factory, the Portland Works, was put up for sale in 1880 and acquired by Dons for £10,000.[37] Clearly an important consideration was that this factory, which had been built on the site of one of the Arbroath and Forfar railway's turntables, was situated close to the town's railway station, and appropriately, the factory was renamed Station Works. Even so, in order to make the best of the works' locational advantage, Dons had to lay out some £8,000 for sidings which brought the railway right into their yard and formed a direct connection with the Caledonian Railway Company.[38] Further additions were also made to the stock of looms, which in 1885 totalled 276. With the 670 at St James' Works, this gave the company a grand total of 946. By 1890 Dons had 965 looms.[39]

This, however, did not mark the end of the company's physical expansion. The partners kept a watchful eye over their competitors and moved quickly to obtain at advantageous prices any potentially useful plant and machinery which had belonged to those who had fallen by the wayside. Thus in 1883–4, they

Ward Mills, Dundee, c. 1888. Built between 1867 and 1871, this was one of the most impressive mill frontages in Dundee. Note, however, that the right-hand section was never completed

purchased the site of an old foundry from the sequestrated estate of Munro & Co. Adjacent to the Station Works, at a cost of £8,000 it was turned into a cloth washing and bleaching house, with a yarn warehouse and carting and stabling facilities also being provided on the site.[40] With the establishment of a bleachworks, for the first time in its history the company was able to boast that it had its own facilities for every stage of cloth production, from flax and jute preparation to finishing. The company's next major acquisition, in 1906, was of John Lowson & Son's South Street Works (which became known as Strang Street in 1929) for £10,000, which they had leased from Lowson's at an annual rent of £500 since 1887. This year marked the death of a member of the Lowson family, Andrew, the proprietor of flax mills and a linen factory in Arbroath, and he was discovered to have been far from financially secure in his business affairs, which resulted in the majority of his employees being laid off and, in the longer run, the restructuring of the company.[41]

By 1904, the year of the Dons' incorporation as a private limited company, the valuation of the Forfar operation stood at £152,860,[42] constituted as follows.

Table 5.2 *Value (£) of Buildings, Machinery and Stock at Forfar, 1904*

	Buildings	Machinery	Stock	Total
St James' Rd Works	17,980	49,590	35,700	106,270
Station Works	4,560	12,620	7,660	24,840
Bleachworks	1,490	1,850	6,140	9,480
South St Works	–	800	6,020	6,820

By this time considerable changes had taken place in Dons' ownership and management. The first of these had been necessary in 1885, following W. G. Don's decision to retire, at the age of 70, after 45 years in the business. His departure was not unplanned, and for the previous three years one son of each of the partners had been introduced to the textile firm.

W. G. Don was replaced by his only son, John Birrell Don (1858–1948), an Oxford-educated classicist and lover of literature who inherited £60,000 of his father's £80,000 stake in the company. A handsome man, fastidious in his habits, he was later (reputedly under pressure from his status-conscious wife) to become the owner of Maulesden House, a grand mansion which could proudly compete with the other ostentatious Angus properties of the region's jute barons. An added attraction was that as Maulesden adjoined the railway line, Don could commute daily to Forfar.

The sons of John Don and A. J. Buist, Robert Bogle Don (1853–1917) and John Charles Buist (1852–1944) had smaller shares (£20,000 each) in the new co-partnery, in which their fathers remained the principal partners, with stakes of £70,000 and £63,000 respectively.[43]

The new arrangement lasted only a year, however, as John Don died at the age of 63 in June 1886. Consequently his second son, Gilbert William Don, joined the company. So too did James Wilson Adamson, who was unrelated to either the Dons or the Buists, but who had been part of the management team at least since 1874 and, as in the case of James Carmichael of Baxter Brothers, was evidently considered to be an invaluable asset and deserving of partner status – although his stake, £500 in 1887 and never more than £11,000, was always considerably less than those of the other partners.[44] It is worth noting too that another well-regarded employee was David Allen, who had been involved, probably as manager, at St James' Road Works until his death in 1875, when his heirs had received £8,580 which he was owed by Dons. Prior to that he had been paid a substantial salary of £400 in 1870 and £1,500 in 1871. His best year was 1872, when he received £2,737, rather more than the £2,000 which the partners allowed themselves on this occasion.

By 1887, Don Brothers, Buist & Co had six rather than three partners. First amongst them was A. J. Buist, who was entitled to 37 per cent of the profits. He retired in 1892, however, and with the removal of his assets the company's capital fell to £195,000. With the incorporation and share issue of July 1904 though, this was raised to £245,000. The issue of 10,000 ordinary and 15,000 preference shares made no real difference as far as the direction of the company was concerned, as can be seen from Table 5.3. The ownership of the company was widened slightly, with the inclusion in the ranks of the shareholders of Charles Hill (1850–1931), who had joined Dons as a cashier but been promoted to the post of company secretary in 1904. Although, like Adamson, Hill was unrelated to either of the principal families, he does appear to have had a background in textiles through his father John, who was described as a 'merchant and flaxspinner' in Dundee. Hill later became a director and continued in this role until his retirement in 1929.[45] Although control of the company remained in the same hands, its name changed, in that the designation Wm & John Don & Co was no longer applied to the Forfar end of the operation. Henceforth, the company was simply to be called Don Brothers, Buist & Co Ltd, the headquarters of which were still in Barrack Street, Dundee.

Table 5.3 *Shareholders and shareholdings, Don Brothers, Buist & Co Ltd, 1908*[46]

		Ord.	Pref.
DON	Robert Bogle*	2,200	3,699
	John Birrell*	2,100	4,199
	Gilbert William*	2,000	1,999
	Lucy Flora		1
	Ida Valentine		1
	Emily Mary		1
		(6,300) 66%	(9,900) 66%
BUIST	John Charles*	2,200	4,099
	Isabella		1
		(2,200) 24%	(4,100) 27%
ADAMSON	Robert Hay*	800	600
	James Wilson		400
		(800) 8%	(1,000) 7%
HILL	Charles	200 2%	
		9,500	15,000

*Directors

Profits, Production, Sales and Markets, c.1845–1904

Unfortunately, profit and loss figures from the period when W. G. and John Don were in business on their own have not survived. Nevertheless, a long run of 30 years, from the commencement of Don Bros, Buist & Co, has.

Table 5.4 *Profit (and Loss) Accounts (£): Don Bros, Buist & Co, 1866–96, distinguishing between Dundee and Forfar operations*[47]

YEAR	DUNDEE	FORFAR	TOTAL
1866	15,380	1,526 (8 months)	16,906
1867	5,310	(528)	4,782
1868	(4,498)	(2,996)	(7,494)
1869	6,474	4,053	10,527
1870	7,118	7,560	14,678
1871	14,650	9,382	24,032
1872	32,422	11,365	43,787
1873	23,777	10,027	33,804
1874	15,726	6,440	22,166
1875	8,664	4,095	12,759
1876	16,811	1,948	18,759
1877	6,773	3,300	10,073
1878	6,900	1,019	7,919
1879	(3,731)	391	(3,340)
1880	23,517	8,216	31,733
1881	(18,330)	(2,899)	(21,229)
1882	6,911	1,242	8,153
1883	11,066	4,579	15,645
1884	11,511	826	12,337
1885	5,799	4,178	9,977
1886	1,180	(3,534)	(2,354)
1887	4,618	1,180	5,798
1888	4,997	6,328	11,325
1889	18,142	21,740	39,882
1890	5,643	6,102	11,745
1891	(6,088)	8,425	2,337
1892	11,945	15,522	27,467
1893	7,062	4,475	11,537
1894	2,343	(3,893)	(1,550)
1895	(5,043)	392	(4,651)
1896	2,849	9,001	11,850

The table provides ample justification for the Dons' decision to join forces with A. J. Buist and move into spinning, for until 1887 the greatest part of the firm's profits came from Dundee, where the spinning mills were located. Weaving on the other hand

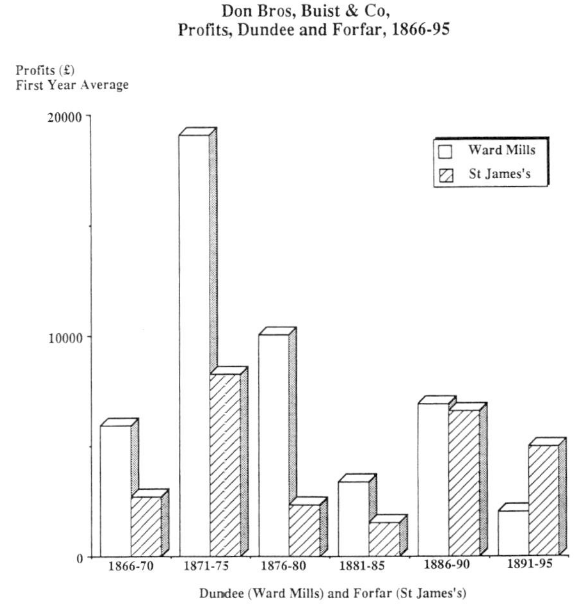

Figure 5.1

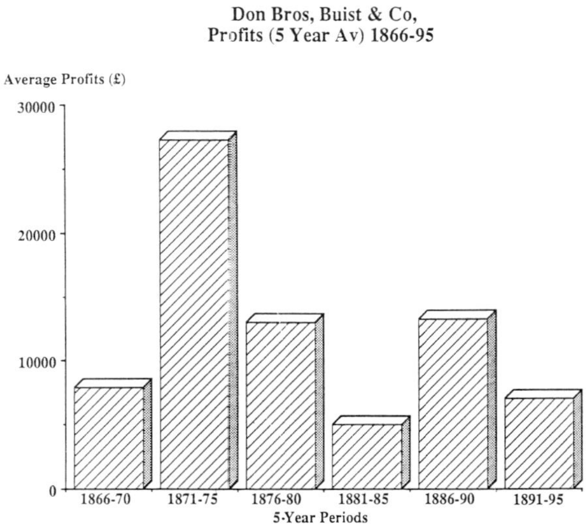

Figure 5.2

made smaller profits (and less spectacular losses) – until after 1887 when it began to overshadow the mills as the main source of the company's profits. This pattern is better seen in Figure 5.1, which is based on average profits over five-year periods. It shows that for the first three quinquennia, Ward Mills greatly overshadowed the contribution to company profitability of the weaving factory in Forfar.

In two respects the experience of Don Brothers, Buist & Co was similar to that of many other textile firms in the area. First, and hardly surprisingly, they felt the effects of the business cycle which was thought to last around ten years.[48] The figures listed above just catch the end of the boom associated with the American Civil War, in the wake of which came a sharp depression which led to short-time working and unemployment. Recovery was greatly assisted by the outbreak of the Franco-Prussian War, shortly after which, in 1872, Dons achieved their biggest annual profit to date, of over £43,000. Rarely were anything like the same profits made in any one year (1880 and 1889 were the only comparable years for the rest of the century) and, indeed, in sharp contrast, in 1881 the firm made its biggest ever loss, of over £21,000. On the other hand, it is worth noting that although this was the period of the so-called 'Great Depression' (1873–96) for the British economy as a whole, Don Bros, Buist & Co did maintain reasonably high profit levels; this can be seen in Figure 5.2, which emphasises the fluctuating nature of the trade but also indicates that on a five-year basis, profit levels held up. If the brief period of extraordinarily high prosperity in the first half of the 1870s is removed, profitability in the following twenty years compares extremely well with that which was achieved in the period 1866–70.

Secondly, however, and in spite of this, in common with other firms which were heavily committed to flax-spinning, the company began to suffer severe competition as a result of penetration of home and overseas markets by foreign manufacturers, mainly from Continental Europe.[49] Dons, it must be assumed, were unable to hold on to their leading position in the Spanish market, and were squeezed elsewhere in Europe, where their yarn business had been concentrated. It was a challenge which many firms failed to meet and in the second half of the nineteenth century Scottish flax-spinning capacity was reduced by 50 per cent. It was not just the Scots who were feeling the pinch though, and in September 1885 J. C. Buist attended, as one of two Scottish representatives, a European Congress of Spinners, held in Antwerp, which was held to address the problem of the deterioration of the Russian flax crop.[50]

Dons did not succumb, however. One reason why the company succeeded during the later years of Victoria's reign, when business problems were mounting, was that they had a large weaving department in Forfar. As has been seen in Table 5.4, cloth production provided a steady income for the partners from the outset, and suffered much smaller losses than those which were sometimes incurred in Dundee. Furthermore, as Figure 5.1 revealed, by the end of the century the relative contributions of Ward Road Mills and the St James' Road weaving factory were changing. Over the five years from 1890–5, average profits from St James' Works were more than twice those of Ward Mills.

Yet the existence of weaving capacity alone was no guarantee that a company would survive in a situation in which over-production was leading to periodic gluts and where competition, notably from Calcutta, was cutting into Dundee's traditional markets for jute.[51] Even during the worst periods, however, some firms escaped relatively unscathed – Dons was one of them. Thus, for instance, while 1884 was a particularly bad year for Dundee generally, Dons' profits were only down by around a fifth compared to the previous year. What appears to account for this is that Dons – like Messrs J. & A. D. Grimond, another leading firm which did reasonably well during the depression – had managed, as in earlier times, to carve out a special niche in the market-place for their products, and demonstrated great flexibility in adapting their product range to the requirements of the market.[52]

They had, however, been forced down-market by the third quarter of the century. As early as October 1844 either W. G. or John Don (or both) had decided to disregard their father's distaste for jute and used some 32 pieces (around 2,304 yards) of 'jute weft tow sheeting' which were sent to Rylands & Son.[53] In February 1845 they made their first pieces of all-jute cloth, calendared jute osnaburgs, and in October the Dons dispatched a quantity of sheetings which were composed entirely of jute.[54]

By 1849 Robert Don's strictures against jute had been entirely forgotten, with 986 pieces and 50 cuts (some 72,792 yards) of jute sheetings being sold.[55] This was not far short of their sales of flaxen sheetings. In 1868, it was estimated that Ward Mills would prepare and spin 1,244 tons of flax, mostly from Riga, and 2,090 tons of jute, 300 bales of which they used each week.

The move into jute, however, was not complete, and as late as 1913 the company was still in a position to claim that 'at least' half of their total production was linen. From the mid-1840s until the 1880s they continued to depend heavily on sales of 'Brown Tow Sheeting Canvas' (tow sheetings), or 'Forfars'. However, although sales figures for the middle and later decades of the nineteenth century are not available, there are indications that the 1840s marked the beginning of a decline in their popularity, with sales falling from some 349,382 yards in 1844 to 257,720 in 1849, a drop of 26 per cent.[56] Over the same period, flax sheetings saw an even more marked decline, falling to just under 35,000 yards.[57] A sharp drop also occurred in sales of loom dowlas, which in its wider finer varieties was the best cloth the Dons produced.

Of more importance for the immediate future, it appears, was a recovery of interest in Forfar's staple cloth, osnaburg. Output of this rose from 219,676 yards in 1844 to 373,912 in 1849, an increase of some 41 per cent.[58] Osnaburgs, however, earned less for the company than sheetings and canvas unless the volume of sales was very great, owing to their lower selling price – between 2¼d and 4½d in the early 1840s, for example, compared to almost double that for tow sheetings and even more for flax sheetings.[59] By the end of the 1870s the company's range of osnaburgs had been much reduced and in 1881 they were removed from Dons' price lists.[60]

Nevertheless, sales of some varieties of canvas, including duck, also rose during the 1840s. It was just as well that the Dons did make this type of cloth, for war-induced demand for canvas for sails, tenting, sailcloth and the like, when it came, was usually intense. Again though, evidence drawn from the company's price lists reveals the existence of serious problems for this type of cloth by the late 1870s, and price falls of around 15 per cent for cream and white duck between 1876 and 1882 appear to have led the company to cease manufacturing these articles sometime between March 1882 and November 1884.[61]

During the course of the 1840s Dons began to move into bag and sack production. Demand for sacking was growing worldwide as trade in bulk commodities such as grain, flour, sugar and coffee expanded. By manufacturing bags and sacks themselves, the Dons were able to benefit from part of the price advantage which was obtained from selling these items direct. A bag which could be sold for 8d, or a three-bushel sack of 'best twilled hemp' at 1s 1½d, made a considerably greater profit than could be obtained from the sale of an equivalent quantity of unmade-up cloth.[62]

Although John and W. G. Don could not have known it in the 1840s, the company's future was to depend heavily on 'crash', towellings and bedding. Goods of this sort returned extremely low prices, unfortunately – roller towelling for instance, admittedly the cheapest variety of cloth they made, sold for 1½d a yard in 1876.

The pressure then to reduce production costs was enormous – and growing. This can be clearly seen from the company's price lists, which show both long and short-term falls, interspersed with brief periods of recovery. As might be expected, the decline was especially marked in linen goods. In August 1876, for instance, fine flax sheetings of between 30″ and 72″ wide, 24 to 32 porters, could fetch between $3^{10}/_{12}$d and 15d a yard. By March 1888 the narrower widths were selling at 3½d, wider pieces of the best quality at 13½d a yard, or between 8 and 10 per cent less, despite an improvement from 32 to 34 porters in the last case.[63] In the same period the selling price of padding canvas fell by between 12 and 14 per cent.

The company's size after the merger with A. J. Buist was an important factor in enabling the Dons to overcome such problems. With experience in manufacturing a wide range of cloth types they could concentrate production in those areas which brought the best returns. Being in both linen and jute also gave them a degree of flexibility which others lacked. How this factor could operate in their favour can be seen in an example drawn from June 1899, when sales of linen 'crash' were poor. ('Crash' was a type of linen which was generally used for domestic purposes, as in teatowels, aprons, etc.) The company responded to this by fitting up a number of looms to make jute hessians which, although their price had fallen, could at least be sold. As Don Bros, Buist & Co were strong enough to survive downturns in trade which broke the backs of some smaller companies, they were able to take up the slack which the others' departure had created. Thus the fall in the price of jute hessians just referred to was clearly advantageous to Dons, with one of their number reporting that:

> The price of low grade hessians . . . it may be said of all hessians, has been so unsatisfactory that a great many looms have been thrown out of work and broken up in Dundee. For ourselves, firstly no doubt owing to this, and from other causes, we have got filled up very largely, and in some widths cannot book any orders for months to come.[64]

Having greater access to capital than some of their rivals, Dons could take more radical steps when the need arose. Thus at the end of the nineteenth century it was clear that their trade in linen crash to the United States of America was declining rapidly. During the 1890s it had fallen in value from $167,063 to $88,750, or by 47 per cent.[65] This had been exacerbated by an increase in US tariffs. The company, however, able at the end of 1898 to dispose of '48 looms for making crashes', and replace them 'by others making goods we could sell'.[66]

Another way in which Dons dealt with falling prices was simply by producing more, if possible more cheaply. Such a policy was not always successful though, as in the case of Andrew Lowson, a flax-spinner and cloth manufacturer in Arbroath, whose efforts to counter decreasing profits by increasing production left his company tragically overextended at the time of his death in 1897.[67] Dons were more fortunate when they pursued this strategy. Furthermore, like Cox's of Lochee, Halley's of Wallace Craigie in Dundee, and other successful firms in the period, they raised productivity by periodically renewing numbers of their looms and fitting models which reduced labour costs. They also improved efficiency by purchasing the 'first saleable and workable dynamo and light in Dundee' and installing electric light in Ward Mills in 1878. Such was the benefit of this innovation that electric light was also introduced to both Forfar works in 1893 and 1894, at a total cost of £2,002.[68]

Despite being pushed down-market in the terms of types of

cloth they produced, Dons continued to maintain the tradition which went back into the eighteenth century, of ensuring that the company's goods were of the highest standard. In 1851, for example, their brown sheetings had won a commendation at the Great Exhibition at Crystal Palace. At the turn of the century Dons felt confident enough to claim that 'it has always occurred to us that we were at the top of the tree not only in Spinning and Manufacturing, but also in finishing'. That they felt they had been 'second to none' in the matter of finish for twenty years or more was ascribed to the quality of work put out from their own calendar, erected at St James' in the early 1870s. It was as well that they had taken such care for as crash linen was mainly used in the domestic environment, only well-finished goods from abroad had any chance of succeeding in the highly competitive US market, where Dons were the biggest exporters from the United Kingdom in the late nineteenth century.[69] Until 1893 they were represented by a New York firm of wholesalers, Adamson, Churchill & Co, and for a decade thereafter by their own agency, Wm & John Don & Co of New York.

The long-distance operation resulted in a major crisis in 1902, however, which forced both John and Robert B. Don to cross the Atlantic. In New York they were appalled to find 'matters here among our own people far worse than we could have expected'. The situation was such, they concluded, that 'it would be quite impossible to continue in any shape or form the existing arrangements'.[70]

In short, Mr Allan, one of the agency's representatives, had failed to carry out his duties conscientiously and was accused of failing to keep in touch with the New York office when on tour, drinking to excess and not pushing Dons' goods hard enough. He had, John Don wrote, 'lost all sense of whatever *dignity* of the position he occupied as representative of a firm of our standing and position'. As a result the two men decided to close the New York office forthwith and try to appoint the highly recommended George W. MacCutcheon (nephew of the proprietor of the long-established firm of George Riggs & Co) as a commission agent. 'Liked and trusted by buyers', and with numerous contacts in areas of the trade where Dons were currently excluded, MacCutcheon was also the US representative of the

Dunfermline fine linen firm, Hay & Robertson. Appointing the right agent was a critical matter for all linen and jute firms. There was little point in developing new lines if the agent did not then make the effort to sell them, preferring instead the easier option of selling standard goods for which demand was steady, but returns low.

Conscious that buyers of Hay & Robertson's tablecloths, napkins and damasks might also be interested in their complementary range of domestic goods, Dons determined to come to some sort of agreement with both MacCutcheon and the Fifers. They were completely frank about why they had made their approach – they were in the wrong location. It was not simply a rehearsal of the old argument though, for Dons' difficulty in 1903 was perceived not to be the burden of additional transport costs. Rather, they argued, being based in Forfar, they were 'out of the regular route' taken by buyers from the US. Even when Dons had offered to come to Dunfermline, they complained, they were 'not unfrequently [*sic*] told not to come'.[71] The outcome of their efforts was an arrangement whereby samples of Dons' cloth, along with their price lists, were put on view at Hay & Robertson's Dunfermline offices, while MacCutcheon became their commission agent in New York, in addition to the agency which he conducted for Hay & Robertson.

This was not the company's first experience of forming a closer association with other firms in order to secure orders, though links were not always entirely satisfactory. From around 1888 Dons had come to an agreement with the Manchester-based Packing Materials Association, and, in return for regular orders from the Manchester firm Dons undertook not to trade with anyone who was in competition with them. For more than a decade the arrangement appears to have worked – to the extent that in 1901 John B. Don, Gilbert W. Don and John W. Adamson bought 5,000 6 per cent cumulative preference shares in the Packing Materials Association. By the end of 1903, however, there were signs that things were not to the Scottish company's satisfaction, their Manchester agent being instructed to inform the Packing Materials Association that unless they mended their ways, they would 'exercise a free hand' and dispose of their goods to 'anyone who will offer the best price for them, a thing we have refused to do for more than the last *15* years.'[72] Relations between the two organisations were finally severed in 1905, when those directors of Don Bros, Buist & Co, who had shares in the Manchester firm, sold them.

The company was also disappointed with a trading agreement they had come to with the 'Tarring Combine', which was also based in Manchester. Although they were supposed to give Dons regular orders for PH hessians, it became apparent to the directors early in 1903 that the Manchester men had found another supplier. Obviously upset, they noted disapprovingly that, 'for a mere small vulgar fraction they passed us with the bulk of their business' and of late were 'only making a convenience of us'.[73]

The connection with MacCutcheon and Messrs Hay & Robertson then was a rare bright spot in a trading environment which was extremely gloomy in the years immediately prior to the company's incorporation.[74]

Yet even with George MacCutcheon working on their behalf in New York, Don Bros, Buist & Co could in fact do little to improve their fortunes in the US market. It was only in Belfast that he was able to make any impact.

As has been seen, crash sales had fallen sharply during the 1890s. By the early 1900s the threat to this aspect of the company's trade had become even more serious, as had been observed by one of their directors, J. W. Adamson, while on a trip to New York at the end of 1901, when he had seen some 'common' crashes in the market there which were very similar to Dons.[75] To make matters worse – rather incredibly, but perhaps hoping to win favour at a time of growing economic nationalism, and in the Scots' eyes to 'bulldoze' them out of the market – the US producers of the goods in question, the Stevens Linen Co of Webster, Massachusetts, raised a court action against Dons, alleging that they had made improper use of the stamps on their bales.[76] Dismissed by the judge and seen by Dons as a 'merely frivolous & vexatious action', it nevertheless presaged the company's eventual withdrawal from the New York crash market. In July 1902 the Massachusetts firm began to engage in the cut-throat practice of reducing all their prices by 1 per cent at a time of rising flax and yarn costs, in order to extend their market share.[77] Although Dons did consider buying a controlling stake in the Stevens Linen Co, this proved impracticable and eventually they simply had to admit defeat, although they continued to sell crash in the US until the 1920s.

In spite of the partial compensation which an increase in sales of burlaps provided, the strain of fighting what appeared to be a losing battle was clearly beginning to tell on the partners, with John B. Don, for example, responding to the writer of an over-long and apparently illegible letter from their own New York agency in 1902 by suggesting that 'if all the sheets' he had written on been order forms they would have been more welcome, and that in future the correspondent might use a typist to send not 'elongated opinion' but 'effectual business communications'.[78]

The strain which Don was clearly under was not helped by the critical situation which firms such as his faced over the supply and price of flax at the end of Queen Victoria's reign. Flax and tow, which were described as being in a 'very excited state' in January 1901, had risen by between 10 and 15 per cent over the previous twelve months. Furthermore, supplies of imported flax, long a weak link in the chain of production for the Scottish coarse textile industry, were becoming increasingly unstable. News of a bad flax harvest in Russia towards the end of 1903, and fears that the quantity available might be anything between 50 and 75 per cent below normal led to price increases of up to 25 per cent. Worse was to follow in 1904, when Russia went to war with Japan. Although war had traditionally brought prosperity to Dundee and Forfar, on this occasion its immediate effect was to create considerable uncertainty, with John B. Don having heard reports that 'in some parts of the Flax growing districts the Peasants have been summoned to the War', leading to worries about whether the flax crop, which already looked like being late, would be harvested.[79]

The period immediately prior to the company's incorporation then was an extremely difficult one, although conditions could change remarkably quickly. In July 1903, for instance, over 100 looms were stopped and short-time working, of 36 hours a week, was introduced; by October full-time shifts were being worked at both St James' and Station Works.[80] Nevertheless, markets for certain of their products were shrinking, notably, as has already been observed, for crash linen in the US, a problem which led the company in 1904 to consider stopping more looms or taking some further 'desperate step'. 'We must get business and new business, if we are to survive at all,' John B. Don wrote in an anguished letter to R. Crawley, their London agent of some 25 years' standing.[81] Later in the year, Don wrote to MacCutcheon in New York in similar vein, remarking that the company needed 'every penny' they could get and that their manufacturing accounts were in a 'deplorable' state.[82] It was little wonder that Don felt in October that 'There is a good deal to worry one in the state of business', concluding with the admission that 'I sometimes wish I were out of it'.[83] His response on this occasion, however, may have been overly pessimistic and influenced by the recent death of his mother, about which he was deeply upset. This was not the only time in his business life when John B. Don appears to have been less capable than some of his peers of distinguishing the short-lived upheavals which periodically afflicted the linen and jute trades and the fact that there was still considerable life left in them, at least for those who were willing to seize the opportunities for survival which presented themselves.

Chapter Five: Expansion

1 SRO, SC 47/40/24, Record of Inventory Books, Vol 24, Forfar, 5 May 1857.
2 SRO, Record of Inventories, Vol 36, 1886; SC 70/1/253, Record of Inventories, Edinburgh, 1886.
3 See relevant entries in A. Slaven and S. G. Checkland (eds), *Dictionary of Scottish Business Biography 1860–1960: Vol 1* (Aberdeen, 1986).
4 See Dundee Chamber of Commerce's *Centenary Souvenir, 1836–1936* (Dundee, 1936).
5 For a discussion of overseas investment from the Scottish linen region in general, see B. Lenman and K. Donaldson, 'Partners incomes, investments and diversification in the Scottish linen area, 1850–1921.' *Business History*, XIII (1971).
6 DUA, MS 100/1/3/6, Cash Book No 1, 1845–1852.
7 The style is used in legal agreements from 1845. See records held by Shiell & Small, solicitors, Dundee. Deed Box No. 2. This material is now held in Dundee University Archives.
8 DUA, MS 100/1/2/3, Letter Book, 1840–42, W. G. Don to George & John Lindsay, 12 October 1842.
9 DUA, MS 100/1/8/2, Despatch Book, 1846–49.
10 National Library of Scotland, Melville Papers, MS 642, f66, Petition of Alex and John Brown, 31 July 1804.
11 For background on east coast shipping see B. Lenman, *From Esk to Tweed* (Glasgow, 1975). The process largely by-passed Forfar.
12 DUA, MS 100/1/8/1 & 2, Despatch Books, 1843–46 and 1846–49. There was a maximum of only five customers per year between 1844 and 1847.
13 DUA, MS 100/1/2/2, Letter Book, 1814–17, William Don to Cowley Son & Sancton, 5 July 1815.
14 DUA, MS 100/1/2/1, Letter Book, 1809–1814, John Don to James Ogilvie, 18 December 1814.
15 Shiell & Small, Deed Box No 2.
16 Ibid.
17 Ibid.
18 Lenman *et al*, *Textile Industry*, p30.
19 *Forfar Dispatch*, 3 June 1954.
20 A. J. Warden, *The Linen Trade Ancient & Modern* (London, 1864), p654.
21 DUA, MS 100/1/3/1, Private Ledger No 1, 1865–97, p5.
22 Shiell & Small, Deed Box No 2.
23 DUA, MS 100/1/3/1, Private Ledger No 1, 1865–97, p7.
24 Lenman *et al*, *Textile Industry*, 32.
25 DUA, MS 100/1/3/1, Private Ledger No 1, 1865–97, p19.
26 See DUA, MS 100/1/3/6, Cash Book No 1, 1845–52.
27 DUA, MS 110/1/3/1, Private Ledger No 1, 1865–97.
28 Buist family papers, Letter Book of James Buist, 1831–7.
29 Obituary in *Dundee Year Book*, 1901, pp57–60; biographical details from typescript notes on members of the Buist family compiled by the late Frank D. Buist.
30 Warden, *Linen Trade*, pp656–7.
31 DUA, MS 100/1/3/1, Private Ledger No 1, 1865–97, p1.
32 Ibid, p27.
33 Ibid.
34 Quoted in an advertisement placed with the *Telegraph*, 6 June 1927. For the draft text of this advertisement see DUA, MS 100/1/2/7, Letter Book, 1927–34.
35 DUA, MS 100/1/3/1, Private Ledger No 1, 1865–97, p19.
36 See Shiell & Small, Deed Box No 2. See too M. Watson, *Jute and Flax Mills in Dundee* (Dundee, 1990), pp63–4, 118.
37 DUA, MS 100/1/3/1, Private Ledger No 1, 1865–97, p19.
38 Ibid, p124.
39 Ibid, p94.
40 Ibid, p95.
41 Slaven and Checkland, *Dictionary*, pp300–1, pp367–9.
42 DUA, MS 100/1/2/5, Letter Book, 1899–1926, 7 May 1904.

43 DUA, MS 100/1/3/1, Private Ledger No 1, 1865–97.
44 Slaven and Checkland, *Dictionary*, pp318–20.
45 DUA, MS 100/1/1/2/3 (1), Annual Return, 1908; *Angus Herald*, 10 July 1931.
46 Compiled from DUA, MS 100/1/3/1.
47 See Figure 5.1.
48 Lenman *et al*, *Textile Industry*, p30.
49 Durie, *Linen Industry*, p168.
50 Dundee Archive and Record Centre, DCC/GD/CC/6, Dundee Chamber of Commerce, Minute Book, 9 September 1885.
51 Lenman *et al*, *Textile Industry*, p31.
52 Ibid.
53 DUA, MS 100/1/8/1, Despatch Book, 1843–6, p28, October 1844.
54 Ibid.
55 DUA, MS 100/1/8/2, Despatch Book, 1846–49.
56 DUA, MS 100/1/8/1 and 2, Despatch Books, 1843–49.
57 Ibid.
58 Ibid.
59 See DUA, MS 100/1/2/3, Letter Book, 1840–42.
60 Price lists held at St James' Works, Forfar.
61 Ibid.
62 See DUA, MS 100/1/8/1, Despatch Book, 1843–46.
63 Price lists held at St James' Works, Forfar.
64 DUA, MS 100/1/2/5, Letter Book, 1899–1926, Don Brothers, Buist (hereafter DBB) to John Blackwell & Sons, 26 June 1899.
65 Ibid, DBB to Mr Churchill, 29 July 1899.
66 Ibid, DBB to Mr Churchill, 2 August 1899.
67 Slaven and Checkland, *Dictionary*, p301.
68 DUA, MS 100/1/3/1, Private Ledger No 1, 1865–97, pp109–10.
69 DUA, MS 100/1/2/5, Letter Book, 1899–1926, DBB to Mr Restallick, 11 December 1901;
70 This section is based on letters from Robert B. and John Don to the company in Scotland which are currently in the possession of Mrs Mary Drysdale, Dunblane.
71 DUA, MS 100/1/2/5, DBB to George W. MacCutcheon, 9 July 1903.
72 Ibid, DBB to D. E. Anderson, 19 December 1903.
73 Ibid, unaddressed, February 1903.
74 Ibid, DBB to Mr Restallick, February 1903.
75 Ibid, unaddressed, probably October 1901.
76 See DUA, MS 100/1/9/3, copy decision of US Circuit Court, Southern District of New York, 1906.
77 DUA, MS 100/1/2/5, Letter Book, 1899–1926, DBB to Mr Harkness, 15 July 1902.
78 Ibid, DBB to D. E. Anderson, 19 December 1903.
79 Ibid, John B. Don to Thomas Brown, 23 June 1904.
80 *Forfar Herald*, 16 October 1903.
81 DUA, MS 100/1/2/5, Letter Book, 1899–1926, John B. Don to R. Crawley, 7 September 1904.
82 Ibid, John B. Don to George W. MacCutcheon, 21 December 1904.
83 Ibid, John B. Don to George W. MacCutcheon, 5 October 1904.

CHAPTER SIX

From Incorporation to the First World War, *c.*1904–18

Conditions during the first year of the company's incorporation appeared to justify John B. Don's gloom. The Russo-Japanese war showed no signs of easing up, leading him at the end of March 1905 to express the fear that if the fighting continued, the seed time would be missed, and result in a flax famine.[1] A visit he made to the Continent in the spring in search of orders brought little in the way of tangible results. Not surprisingly, in May he reflected despondently that 'We have, unfortunately, all of us, fallen amidst bad times.'[2] Yet Dons did benefit in part from the demands of the war – as did most other Dundee textile firms – and, as will be seen below, well before the end of the year the US crash market had recovered. Indeed, gross profits for the year to May 1905 were respectable enough at £10,503 to allow the directors to carry forward a small sum, £1,564. Furthermore, the profit figure for 1904–5 was not much below that for 1905–6 – recovery, which had begun in the summer of 1905, was so strong that 1906 was described locally as 'an astonishing year' in which Dundee broke away from a long period of low prices.[3] For Dons, however, 1906 was less good, largely it seems because it was the jute firms which reaped the richest rewards from the war, owing to the inability of the Calcutta makers to meet the intense demand which this created.

Even so, at no time between 1904–5 and 1917–18 did the company lose money. There is little sign of what historians have called 'third-generation entrepreneurial failure'. With few other viable business outlets available in the region and his capital largely locked up in linen and jute, perhaps John B. Don had no choice but to carry on and make the best of things, but nevertheless, under his chairmanship (until 1916), vigorous efforts were made to maintain and expand Dons' market share while considerable attention was paid to ways of improving the various works' efficiency. Having survived the bad year of 1907, when there was a business depression in the USA, as well as the dull years of 1910 and 1911, Dons were in a position to benefit from an upturn in Dundee's trade from 1912, and after the outbreak of the First World War in 1914, to supply some of the vast quantities of yarn and cloth which were required during the ensuing conflict.

Profits, Sales and Markets, 1904–18

Only once, in 1907–8, did the company come close to making an operating loss. For the rest of the period under review, what is revealed in the table below is a pattern of fluctuating profit levels, which over time grew larger until they reached their wartime peak in the year ending May 1918, although it should be noted that owing to rampant wartime inflation this was rather less spectacular than appears at first sight.

Table 6.1 *Don Bros, Buist & Co Ltd, Profit (and Loss) Accounts (and amounts carried forward after AGM dividend distribution etc), 1904–5 – 1917–18*

Year	Balance at 31 May £	Carried Forward £
1904–05	10,503	1,564
1905–06	11,380	763
1906–07	10,584	1,999
1907–08	1,731	1,437
1908–09	9,557	1,964
1909–10	14,587	2,720
1910–11	20,367	3,720
1911–12	16,447	3,175
1912–13	27,119	9,097
1913–14	21,004	2,980
1914–15	39,138	16,338
1915–16	91,613	59,338
1916–17	151,053	173,528*
1917–18	229,666	80,063

* Includes £50,000 added after government reassessment of excess profits tax.

Source: Minute Book No 1, 1904–44

John B. Don of Maulesden (1858–1948), W.G. Don's son who played a leading role in the company's affairs until his retirement in the early 1930s

The main source of sales income in the early post-incorporation years was the USA where, despite the difficulties reported in the previous chapter, the company's linen crash trade experienced something of a recovery. This was not simply a fortuitous event, but a temporary upturn in Dons' fortunes in this market which owed a good deal to the directors' decision, taken in 1905, to open a linen agency in Belfast. This was done in conjunction with George MacCutcheon, their New York agent, and Hay & Robertson from Dunfermline, along with John A. Lowry of Belfast. This strengthening of the ties between Dons, MacCutcheon and Hay & Robertson took the form of a business which traded from a Belfast office under the name of George MacCutcheon, Lowry & Co but was financed by the two textile firms, who provided £10,000 starting-up costs, and guaranteed bank overdraft facilities of £2,000 in the first instance, and £10,000 by 1907.[4]

High hopes were entertained for the new company, which was to conduct a 'merchant business . . . [in] addition to the ordinary commission business done in Forfar and Dunfermline goods.'[5] The agency was conducted on a large scale, with several staff being employed in the company's office. This was for good reason: firms such as Dons and Hay & Robertson had much to gain from having an effective presence in Belfast. The city was the main destination for American buyers of the finer linens when they came to Europe, and with MacCutcheon's New York connections they were clearly in a much more favourable situation than they would have been had they simply stayed put on Scotland's east coast. What was more, MacCutcheon was an exceptionally able agent, who was congratulated by Don Bros, Buist & Co Ltd in November 1905 for sending 'a record season's orders' in crashes. It had been several years since one of the company's correspondents could confess that he lived 'in fear and trembling lest we get into trouble for not delivering in time . . . All round, in every width of loom, we are busier than we have been for many years'.[6]

Although it is impossible to say precisely how far MacCutcheon and Lowry influenced events in their favour, Dons certainly believed that they had made a difference. From 1905 until 1907 the American market was a lucrative one for the company, with much business being channelled through their Belfast office. The extent of this can be seen in a letter written by the company to MacCutcheon in New York in August 1907:

> The monthly payments for September, October and November amount to about £7000 . . . the actual Capital available, including £10,000 of Bank overdraft, is about £32,000; the sales are estimated at £60,000 and there is a stock or option, or purchases yet to sell amounting to £15,000 . . . the whole history, short though it is, of the Belfast business shows that under favourable conditions a big business can quickly be done; but it shows also how fast one can outrun one's capital.[7]

In fact, the rather high stock levels reveal the precariousness of the Belfast operation, and within two months the situation had been transformed for the worst, when the buoyancy of the US market was punctured and a 'serious all round fall in values' triggered a general slump in the linen trade which lasted throughout 1908 and into the early months of 1909. Shortly afterwards the Belfast agency was converted into a limited liability company, two years after MacCutcheon had suggested such a move.[8]

As was indicated in the previous chapter, the long-term outlook for linen was poor, and in 1912 the Belfast subsidiary was wound up. The fact was that the US crash market was to an increasing degree governed by the Stevens Linen Co. Dons' prices were effectively set by Stevens, which left the Scots at the mercy of their US rivals. Dons had hoped that they would be able to raise their prices, but could only do so if the Stevens Linen Co raised their rates. This the US company was not prepared to do, much to the discomfort of John B. Don, whose frustration is to be seen in a letter to MacCutcheon in which he wrote of his anxiety to maintain his company's reputation as 'cheap sellers', but also insisted that he was not 'in the business as a philanthropist'.[9] The US crash market then was becoming an increasingly difficult one for Dons to survive in, even though they made an attempt to find somebody in Belfast to 'look after our interests there, and buttonhole American buyers'.[10] Apart from a brief involvement with the Flax Society Ltd in 1918, in a scheme designed to grow flax in Ireland with Canadian seed, it was not until 1923 that the company again became directly linked with Belfast.[11]

Nevertheless, because of their manufacturing capability in both jute and linen, the problems associated with declining crash sales were not as serious for Dons as might have been the case otherwise. Those textile firms which had not diversified were driven to accept whatever price the market for their more limited range of products offered. Thus, for example, Dons had stopped making flax sheetings several years prior to 1908 due to the 'ruinous prices which have prevailed for so long'. Yet in spite of this and the 'unpleasant fact' that flax sheetings 'were not wanted', 'certain manufacturers', one Manchester correspondent was informed, 'go on making, *because they must*'.[12]

There was little that Dons could do during 1907 and 1908, however, when demand for both their jute and linen products was weak. It was unusual for both commodities to be in the doldrums concurrently. The company was very much aware of the advantage this gave them, as in January 1909 when there was an upturn in the prospects for linen. 'The improvements in Linens will enable us to curtail our production of Jute goods, should demand be slow,' John B. Don wrote, 'and thus make us independent, more or less, of any adverse conditions which may arise.'[13]

It was as well that they could turn to jute, for such periods of prosperity in linen were becoming less common. By October 1911 more crash looms had been stopped and others were to follow, with their operators being transferred to other work. Jute had 'taken a turn for the better', prices were 'on the upgrade' and demand was 'vigorous'.[14] Indeed, for the next two years it was their jute trade which was Dons' principal support.

In order to strengthen their position, the directors embarked on a major electrification scheme of all their plants in Forfar in January 1910. A 500 hp steam engine which had been built at St James' Works in 1900 by the Dundee engineers Messrs J. & C. Carmichael was used to provide power transmitted by cables to drive motors at Station Works, the Bleach Works, South Street Works and the finishing machinery at St James'. By rationalising their power supply Dons were able to effect considerable reductions in their energy costs by making it possible for them to get rid of the Corliss engine at St James', a steam engine and gas engine at South Street, and also the dynamos for lighting at all their works.[15] A turbine was added to the Carmichael engine at St James', which utilised waste steam to produce electricity; two generators were also added, together rated at 600 kilowatts.[16] The installation gave Dons their own private grid some eighteen years before electricity was introduced to Forfar by the Grampian Electricity Co. The engine which lay at the heart of the system, which became known as 'Auld Maggie', remained in operation until 1955, when it became necessary to link up with the Hydro-Electric Board's supply.[17]

It was as well that the company did pay such attention to this aspect of their production costs. Competition was forcing them to extend the length of their bales and pay even closer attention to the quality of their weaving and finishing. In this regard at least John B. Don was content, reflecting in 1909 that as far as the company's hessians were concerned, 'the finish was never better, and never was more care given to it'.

The outbreak of the First World War in August 1914 confirmed the importance of jute to Dons, with sales rising almost immediately.[18] Linen, on the other hand, was in a bad way. A request in March 1915 from the Forfar Factory Workers Union for the payment of a war bonus was turned down on the grounds that the linen trade was 'bad'. Adam Farquharson, the union secretary, was informed that:

> Our American trade is dead, and the ordinary Home trade outlets for Linens are shut down. We have over 100 looms standing for want of orders, and consequently we cannot keep our winders and others on full time.[19]

Linen sales remained sluggish until the summer of 1917. Demand for jute products on the other hand was buoyant, and the company's decision on wages in March notwithstanding, they were persuaded in May to pay a war bonus of 1s, followed by a further 1s in July, on condition that workers did a full week's work.[20] Production targets had not been met, partly due to absenteeism. The bonuses then, which had been paid first in Dundee, and then Forfar, were introduced as an inducement to workers who were 'irregular in their attendances' to put in a full day's work.[21] A suggestion from the FFWU, made around the same time, that work should cease on a Saturday at 10 a.m., was rejected on the grounds that this was 'not the time to reduce production, when for the most part our output is needed directly for the use of the army'.[22]

Although production figures are not available, net profit figures for the company's manufacturing operations have survived. These reflect not only the profit increases referred to earlier, but also point to a reversal of the pre-war trend where the weaving factories in Forfar had been playing an increasingly important part in the company's financial success. Table 6.2 reveals that from the outset, the company's wartime profits came mainly from Ward Mills.

Table 6.2 *Don Bros, Buist & Co Ltd. Net Manufacturing Profits (£), 1914–15 – 1917–18*

Year	Dundee (Ward Mills)	Forfar (St James/ Station Wks)
1914–15	27,708	22,000
1915–16	66,051	35,412
1916–17	109,602	42,846
1917–18	107,451	74,275

Source: Minute Book No 1, 1904–44

At first sight this appears to have been a return to the traditional situation in the textile trade, where the greatest profits were made in spinning and yarn sales, usually as a result of successful speculation in the purchase of flax and jute.

During the war though, the normal trading mechanisms were interrupted. For example, before 1914 flax had been bought cif (cost, insurance and freight) and paid for by bills of lading when it arrived in Dundee. In 1915 and 1916, however, Dons had found it necessary to buy on 'interior' terms, whereby firms based in Russia acted as buying agents, bought flax and stored it until it could be shipped from Archangel. In order for this to work properly Dons had to provide the funds for flax when it was purchased, and pay for insurance and transport.[23] Understandably, the directors were extremely uneasy about this system, which involved major risks should the buying agents be unable to 'safeguard' them in the event of any flax not being 'forthcoming'.

This was also a worry for the British government, which in March 1916 decided that it would become the sole buying agent for the Russian flax crop. In August the government similarly intervened in that year's jute crop.[24] These were moves which were generally welcomed by Dons; at a meeting of Dundee Chamber of Commerce in January 1916 John B. Don had urged that the government should intervene much more directly in the jute trade, by taxing all raw jute which was exported from India, with rebates to be given to purchasers in the British Empire along with the allies. The policy of free trade should be abandoned, he argued in a speech which echoed some of the prevailing Germanophobia, for, in effect, firms such as his had been engaged in 40 years of 'commercial warfare and strife' with Germany. 'Commercial aggression' from this direction, he was convinced, would continue after the military conflict was over, and would require the sort of assistance he was talking about if it was to be overcome.[25] In fact, Don's fears about the German commercial threat were largely unfounded.

During the war, the government's role was not restricted to the purchase and supply of raw materials. By March 1916 it was reported that Dons was 'largely engaged in work both for the War Office and Admiralty', a situation which was to continue well into the following year.[26] This had its advantages, but there were drawbacks, although these could be – and were – over-emphasised. Thus in February 1917 the company turned down a demand for a wage increase from the FFWU on the grounds that they were 'obliged to make whatever the War Office demands', with yarn supplied by the government, which also set the prices of both the yarn and the cloth. In such circumstances, it was claimed, 'there is no margin for profit', although, their workers were assured, 'we are content so long as it helps to bring the war to a speedy end'.[27] Evidently this was part of the posturing which often accompanies the collective bargaining process, for in May 1917, wage rises of 10 per cent for males, 7.5 per cent for females, were granted, and back-dated to 16 March.[28]

The fact is that state involvement in the textile industry was providing much greater stability – and higher profits (even allowing for inflation) – than had been seen in the pre-war years. On top of this, Dons benefited in the second half of 1917 from a sharp upturn in free market demand for linen from North America. Indeed, so intense was this that the company had to turn away some business, with their Manchester agent being informed early in July that:

> Our whole output in Crashes is engaged quite up to the end of September for America, Canada and the home trade, and we have additional orders from the United States at much higher prices, which, if they go through, will keep us busy for another two months . . . in Crepes and such like we are engaged far beyond the end of September.[29]

Good times, it seemed, were back again – but not for long. Indeed, even before the end of the war, in the winter of 1917–18, most Dundee works were put on short-time, as the government cut the supply of raw jute to 10 per cent below the 1916 level. The misery of the considerable numbers of workers who were thrown out of work altogether was only partly eased by the industry's establishment of a benefit scheme for those who were unable to find other employment.[30]

Chapter Six: From Incorporation to the First World War

1 DUA, MS 100/1/2/5, Letter Book, 1899–1926, J. B. Don to Thomas Brown, 29 March 1905.
2 Ibid, J. B. Don to Thomas Brown, 18 May 1905.
3 Lenman, *et al Textile Industry*, p36.
4 See Minute Book No 1, 1904–44, p23, p31 and p35.
5 DUA, MS 100/1/9/4, Agreement regarding Belfast office, July 1905.
6 DUA, MS 100/1/2/5, Letter Book, 1899–1926, DBB to G. W. MacCutcheon, 22 November 1905.
7 Ibid, DBB to George W. MacCutcheon, 28 August 1907.
8 MacCutcheon suggested the move in September 1907, see DUA, MS 100/1/2/5, Letter Book, 1899–1926. The establishment of a limited company was agreed in July 1909, see Minute Book No 1, 1904–44, p51.
9 DUA, MS 100/1/2/5, Letter Book, 1899–1926, J. B. Don to G. W. MacCutcheon, 1 July 1907.
10 Ibid, J. B. Don to G. W. MacCutcheon, 27 May 1912.
11 See Minute Book No 1, 1904–44, 23 August 1918 and 25 October 1918.
12 DUA, MS 100/1/2/5, Letter Book, 1899–1926, DBB to D. E. Anderson, 15 October 1908.
13 Ibid, DBB to D. E. Anderson, 11 January 1909.
14 Ibid, DBB to George W. MacCutcheon, 5 October 1911.
15 Minute Book No 1, 1904–44, 21 January 1910.
16 See *Forfar Dispatch*, 29 December 1955.
17 Ibid.
18 Minute Book No 1, DBB to D. E. Anderson, 6 January 1915.
19 Ibid, DBB to Adam Farquharson, 9 July 1915.
20 St James' Works, Wages Book, 1914–48.
21 DUA, MS 100/1/2/5, Letter Book, 1899–1926, DBB to Adam Farquharson, 31 March 1915.
22 Ibid, DBB to Adam Farquharson, 9 July 1915.
23 Ibid, DBB to Seyd & Co Ltd, 17 January 1916.
24 S. Pollard, *The Development of the British Economy, 1914–1980* (London, 1983), p20.
25 *Forfar Herald*, 28 January 1916.
26 DUA, MS 100/1/2/5, Letter Book, 1866–1926, DBB to H. J. Wilson, 20 March 1916.
27 Ibid, DBB to James Taylor, 7 February 1917.
28 St James' Rd, Wages Book, 1914–48.
29 DUA, MS 100/1/2/5, Letter Book, 1899–1926, DBB to D. E. Anderson, 4 July 1917.
30 DUA, MS 84/3/1(3), Association of Jute Spinners and Manufacturers, Transfer Book No 1, General Committee Minutes, 15 March 1918.

CHAPTER SEVEN

Labour Relations and Industrial Conflict, *c.*1880–1918

Notwithstanding John B. Don's inherent tendency to look on the dark side, some justification for his gloomy view of the company's late Victorian and early Edwardian circumstances can be seen in the industrial relations arena, which was becoming increasingly troublesome.

Unfortunately, little can be ascertained about the labour management strategies of Don Bros, Buist & Co prior to the 1880s. What evidence there is, both before and after *c.*1880, suggests that industrial relations were strongly tinged with paternalism. As far back as William Don's time, efforts had been made to generate a sense of respect for and loyalty to the firm in Forfar amongst those who worked for them. With centralised production, firmer methods of control were necessary in order to achieve the full benefits which large-scale manufacturing under one roof could bring. The inclination of hand-loom weavers where it was possible to determine their own work rhythms, for instance, had to be replaced by a regular work routine at hours fixed by their employers – which were announced by the works' bell at St James'. Habits had to be reformed, especially as regards alcohol: to this end, in 1885, the company purchased a public house in North Street, Forfar, which was next to Station Works, with the express purpose of closing it down.[1] Occasional acts of charity served to enhance the sense of obligation which the inhabitants of Forfar felt towards the company, the fortunes of which (as it grew) were having an increasing impact on the town.

The firm's contributions were often small but nevertheless

significant, as in 1907, when Dons erected children's swings at a park beside their Station Works. In 1908 John B. Don arranged for the transfer to the burgh of Forfar of a site 'presently tenanted as dwelling houses and workshops', and an adjoining piece of land, upon which, with a financial donation from Andrew Carnegie of Skibo, public baths were built.[2] A grateful town council rewarded Don and Carnegie by making them freemen of the burgh in 1910, the first people to be honoured in this way since 1869. In 1913 Don donated a further £1,000 in order to fit up and provide materials for a small clinic at the baths where minor accidents to factory workers and others could be treated.[3]

In Dundee, the company's works' school at Ward Mills was one of the better examples of its kind, and employed a staff of five or six (headed by a separate teacher for the boys' and girls' departments) at the turn of the century. Indeed Don Bros, Buist & Co were congratulated by the Factory Inspectorate in 1884 for the excellence of their school provision, not least because the company was at the forefront in Dundee in raising the educational standards of its younger workers.[4] There is evidence too of small payments being made to sick, injured and aged workers, although no trace of the rules which governed the disbursements of such sums of money seems to have survived, though good performance was almost certainly a condition of assistance. Thus the gestures which the company made at times of national mourning or celebration, as on the day of King Edward VII's funeral in May 1910, when the mills were shut down at 12 noon, were almost certainly welcome. The mills had closed even earlier – 9 a.m. – on Queen Victoria's Jubilee in June 1897. Yet on both occasions it was only those workers who had no absent time against them who were paid in full.[5]

In their turn, both the Dons and the Buists could find themselves in receipt of acts of gratitude on the part of their workers. Thus Gilbert Don, who managed the Forfar works until his premature death in 1913, was given what were described as 'handsome gifts' by the workers at St James' and Station Road on the occasion of his silver wedding anniversary.[6] Such expressions of respect were not confined to Forfar. The retiral of A. J. Buist from active involvement in the firm inspired a demonstration by the workers at Ward Mills at which they presented him with an illuminated address.[7] No hard-faced

1840 1893

Presented to

Alexander Jefferson Buist, Esq.

Dear Sir,

We the present Employees of Messrs Don Brothers, Buist & Co. herein seek to convey to you the high appreciation in which we hold you as an employer of labour, and to express our deep gratitude for the manifold kindnesses and voluntary acts of courtesy and consideration extended by you to your employees during the 53 years of your business career.

You have manifested throughout the whole of these years an eminent degree of business capacity, your outstanding ability as a spinner and manufacturer is recognised on all sides, and your sound judgment and strict integrity in all your dealings have always been gratifying to customer and worker alike.

We would join in hearty congratulations, now that you have retired to enjoy a period of well-earned rest, that in your son we have every confidence as one who will in all respects follow his father's worthy example and share in the high esteem in which you are held.

It is also a great pleasure to us to hand to you with this address, a token of our regard for Mrs Buist, the worthy partner of your joys, in the form of A Silver Cake Basket, and we ask that she may accept it with the hearty good wishes of all the workers who have an interest in her, both for her own and for your sake.

You will, we trust, pardon the privilege we take in expressing here to you, our high admiration of the unassuming acts of charity and generosity bestowed by you upon the public institutions of the city and neighbourhood.

In asking you to accept this address and accompanying gift, we pray that you may both be long spared to your family circle and friends, and to the city in which you have so long been an honoured and honourable citizen: and that the remaining years of your life may be peaceful and happy; till it please God to call you to that higher sphere, for which your noble life here has so admirably fitted you.

Signed on behalf of the Employees

Gilbert Fraser
William Miller
John R. Walker
Robert Ross
Robert Anderson
Peter Craighead
John C. Downie
John B. Millar
John Forrester
Donald Noble
David Fisher
Robert Sime
John Marten
James Lees
David Marshall
Alexander J. Robertson
William Stewart
Peter Summers

3rd April 1893

John Leng & Co. Illuminators & Designers, Dundee

Illuminated scroll presented to A. J. Buist by the employees of Ward Mills on his retirement in 1893, after 53 years in business. Reproduced by kind permission of J. B. Watson

Victorian of the Gradgrind school of business, he had been an advocate of shorter hours and an active philanthropist who was involved in several of Dundee's charitable societies, such as the Poor Nursing Society and the Curr Night Refuge, as well as being a prominent temperance reformer, a cause which attracted remarkable support from all social classes in Dundee.[8]

Yet paternalism is a reciprocal relationship which is conditional upon mutual respect and satisfaction with the other's conduct, and there were circumstances when it could break down.

THE GREAT STRIKE AND LOCKOUT OF 1889

One such occasion was in 1889. This was a year of considerable labour unrest throughout the country, with the London Dock Strike being one of the best known industrial disturbances of the period. In Dundee, strikes, which had spluttered on and off since 1885 when a series of wage reductions had occurred throughout the jute trade, had allegedly brought the industry there to a state of 'anarchy'. Partly as a result, a series of wage rises of between 10 and 20 per cent were awarded.[9]

In 1885 the Revd. Henry Williamson's Mill and Factory Operatives Union had been formed in Dundee. Although the union did have branches in the smaller textile towns such as Arbroath, Brechin and Montrose, none was apparently formed in Forfar. Why this was so is not clear, but it is conceivable that this was due to hostility directed towards Williamson's union outside Dundee, on the grounds that his organisation was seen to represent only the interests of Dundee workers.[10]

Whatever the reason, by 1889 an independent union, the Forfar Factory Workers Union, had been formed. Led by its president, a Mr Farquharson, and the secretary, a Mr Roy, its objective in the final months of 1889, following the wage rise which had been achieved by Dundee's textile workers in September, was to obtain an increase in the wage rates then paid in Forfar, which it was claimed with much justification, were the lowest in the whole of the textile district.

This can be seen clearly in the case of male wages, which are listed in the following table. It is possible, however, that the wages given for Dundee and elsewhere were exaggerated by the union. Unfortunately though, relatively few long runs of reliable wage data for the linen and jute trades have survived. Certainly the figures listed below are somewhat higher than those given in other sources, although as wages could fluctuate sharply from year to year, it may well be that these are an accurate record of wages paid in the year they represent.

Table 7.1 *Average male wages (weekly), Tayside, 1889*

Category	District	Weekly Wage
Tenters	Forfar	19s – 26s
	Dundee	27s – 30s
	Kirriemuir	20s – 24s (plus bounty)
	Brechin	21s – 27s
Laffers	Forfar	10s – 18s
	Dundee	18s – 22s
	Kirriemuir	17s – 20s
	Brechin	12s – 17s
Dressers	Forfar	15s 9d – 22s 9d
	Dundee	25s 3d – 27s 6d
	Kirriemuir	16s 6d – 22s
	Brechin	*c*.19s – 22s

Source: Forfar Herald, 16 September 1889

Forfar's male factory workers got no comfort when they looked further afield for comparisons: wages for the same work in other textile towns such as Aberdeen, Kirkcaldy and Markinch were always higher than those obtainable in Forfar.

The differential between women's work in Forfar (which was mostly in weaving) and the other textile towns was believed to be marginally less substantial, allegedly ranging from 10 to 35 per cent less than the wages which were paid elsewhere, compared to the 20 and 35 per cent less paid to males.[11]

A distinction, however, has to be made between linen and jute, although, in both, the wage rates paid to Forfar females were substantially lower than those paid to their Dundee counterparts – who also were required to make less cloth. Thus it was argued by the FFWU that linen-weavers in Forfar had to turn out 50 yards more cloth per week than a Dundee weaver, for a wage of 12s 6d, whereas a Dundonian would receive 14s 7d.[12] This was a differential of some 24 per cent; in jute this was even greater – 35 per cent – with Forfar jute-weavers being paid around 12s 3d, compared to 15s 9d in Dundee. The main reason for this was the basic wage rate, with a 'cut' of cloth (of which a weaver might produce 14 in a week) in Forfar bringing a reward of 10½d compared to 13½d in Dundee.[13]

Incensed by the fact that the wage increases obtained in Dundee had widened the gap between 'Juteopolis' and Forfar, the union directed its attentions to Dons, firstly because they employed more textile workers than anyone else, and secondly because they were (with good reason) accused of paying, overall, lower wages than the other local firms.

After initial unsuccessful approaches had been made to Forfar's employers, the dispute rapidly escalated, beginning with a strike at Messrs Craik's Manor Works. Neither side, however, managed to achieve the solidarity which each had anticipated. The union had hoped to mount an organised campaign, first bringing out the workers at Dons, and then, if necessary, those at smaller works.

Dons at this stage were firmly opposed to the principle of trade unionism and preferred instead to carry on with their established method of 'bargaining', which was to pass on information to foremen and others of similar status, who in turn were expected to communicate this and discuss it with those beneath them at shop-floor level, and in this Dons were not atypical. The workers' demand for a modest 5 per cent increase, however, became confused with a struggle over trade union recognition. Within days of the first approach by the FFWU to Dons, who had refused to meet with union representatives, short-time working had been introduced, leading to strikes throughout the town over which the union had no control. On Wednesday 2 October a series of lock-outs was commenced.

One firm, however, Lairds, broke ranks and offered to pay their workers an additional 5 per cent.[14] Dons held firm though, and argued through public notices and the columns of the local press that despite union suggestions to the contrary, they were unable to pay more as they had large stocks on hand.

Tenters, Forfar, late nineteenth century. These were always men and were the best-paid production workers. Back row *(from left to right): James Prophet, James Keas, John Esphin;* Middle row: *Alex Paterson, Charles Samson, William Duff, W. Gibb, G. Petrie;* Front: *William Young, D. Duncan, D. Ramsay, Alex Smart, David Hill*

Wages in Forfar had to be lower than in Dundee, they claimed, owing to the excess costs they incurred in transporting raw materials into Forfar and getting cloth to Dundee. Although no figures relevant to this issue have survived from this period, data presented by the firm to a Jute Board questionnaire in 1933 suggests that its inland location did at that time create an additional burden of 9s 8d per ton of jute, mainly in the form of transportation costs.[15] There is no reason to suppose that this was any less serious a problem in the 1880s. Harder to counter in 1889 though was a union assertion that Dons' property charges were significantly lower than those incurred by Dundee's textile companies. The highest feu duty paid by any Forfar manufacturer, the FFWU alleged, was 3s 4½d per pole, whereas in Dundee it could be anything from 16s to 21s a pole.[16]

Weavers, Station Works, late nineteenth century. The two men are tenters. Back row *(from left to right): Christian Hutcheon, unidentified, Maggie Cook, Isabel Herald;* Middle row: *Mary Craik, Mary McClaren, Jean Gracie, Jessie Tarbet;* Front: *G. Prophet, Mary Laird, M. Laird, J. Fenton, John Esphin*

The workers received moral support for their cause from the radical *Forfar Herald*, which tended to see the dispute in terms of class warfare, accusing the masters in general and Dons in particular, of being 'bent on crushing the Factory Workers' Union'.[17] With passions running high, within a week of the lock-out beginning, clear signs of tension began to appear. G. W. Don opened the door of his house in Glamis Road on the morning of Saturday 5 October to discover 'a large crowd at the gate, who shouted and booed and made various noises' as soon as he emerged. Undaunted, he made his way past them, to be followed all the way to the works in St James' Road, and at one point was pelted with 'stones, mud, divots, potatoes, etc'.[18] Who was actually guilty of the assault was difficult to ascertain, as most damage was done when Don's back was turned. The bulk of the accused – charged with assault and breach of the peace – were boys aged between eight and 16, who were dismissed after a warning from the magistrates. Only one identifiable factory worker, Betsy Smith of Glamis Road, was charged – with assault and forming part of a disorderly crowd – but witnesses to support the prosecution could not be found.

Soon the town was teetering on the edge of more violent confrontation, with G. W. Don again being subject to threats from hostile crowds, this time in the company of his fellow director, J. W. Adamson, along with two of Forfar's other textile employers, James Moffat and James Craik. The four men were in the habit of travelling by train to Dundee on Mondays and Fridays, but by the end of October they were being regularly trailed on their walk to the station by large crowds, whose attitude and behaviour made it expedient for them to have a police escort.[19] It was a cat and mouse game, of which the *Forfar Herald* strongly disapproved, the editor writing that 'their [the employers concerned] parading of the principal streets surrounded by constables is an exhibition of ignorant bravado that does not deserve police protection'.[20] The arrest on one occasion of several people on the charge of 'mobbing and rioting' suggests that whatever the wisdom of the actions of Don and his colleagues, they certainly needed protection.

Potentially much more serious was a rumoured drift away from the town of some of the 'best weavers', who during the lock-out sought work in Dundee, Lochee, Alyth and Coupar Angus, and even the south of England.[21] Consequently, on 22 November, almost two months after it had begun, the dispute was brought to an end when the employers agreed that the question of a wage rate increase should go to arbitration. The arbitrators were the respected Dundee lawyer Thomas Thornton and Provost William Hunter of Forfar. They awarded a 7.5 per cent rise to all men whose wages were below 14s a week, whilst those earning between 14s and 17s obtained 5 per cent. Women were to get 5 per cent, 'should trade continue to improve'.[22] Of importance for the future was an agreement, in principle at least, that wage rates in Forfar should rise at the same time as those in Dundee, and not later, as had been the case hitherto. For Dons' employees, this was undoubtedly a step forward. Furthermore, for better or worse, a union had been established, a development which would require Dons to re-think their approach to the management of labour.

Hours and Wages to 1918

In the short-term, however, little changed. The end of the 1889 dispute had been hailed by the *Forfar Herald* as a victory in the struggle of labour to free itself from 'the slavery of capital'. The FFWU, the paper asserted, had been 'made' by the struggle: where, the editor asked rhetorically, 'was this ever more needed than in the county town of Forfar?'[23]

The sentiments were noble; the outcome somewhat more prosaic. Dons continued to communicate to the workforce through senior workers of their choice. And despite the union officials' dislike of this practice, it was only with difficulty that they were able to persuade the workers to make representations to the company on the union's behalf. In May 1894, however, Farquharson did manage to persuade four women to volunteer to represent St James' and Station Works following proposals from the company that unless they accepted a 10 per cent cut in their wages, which would make it possible to operate both St James' and Station Works full time, the latter would be closed down, with the best weavers being transferred to St James' and those 'less capable' turned out.[24] The union's argument, not unreasonably, was that workers who had been selected by the Dons or J. W. Adamson to negotiate on behalf of their colleagues would be less likely to challenge their employers, 'for if they did they would be discharged'.[25] On the other hand there was in Forfar and in Dundee considerable faith, born of the paternalist spirit which prevailed in many works, that the masters (but less so the managers they employed) would be sympathetic to their grievances.[26]

Accordingly, in general, the union's attitude to the firm was accommodating. Anyway it was difficult for the FFWU to present a determined and united front in a situation where, faced by the wage cuts just referred to, it was decided that they should attempt to negotiate with the company on the basis that they would accept a reduction of 5 per cent for women workers as long as male rates remained unchanged. The decision was taken partly on the justifiable grounds that 'male workers were paid too little already'. Clearly, though, the Victorian belief that a woman's place was in the home – where she should be content to be provided for by a man – was prevalent amongst Forfar's early FFWU members, one of whose number agreed that 'there were a lot of young women in Forfar who were looking out for husbands, and if they went against this question they would be hurting themselves.'[27]

In the face of Dons' resolution to act in the manner they deemed best, the FFWU could do little but engage in futile protests. The company wanted nothing to do with the FFWU's suggested compromise and announced the temporary closure of Station Works. Despite union claims that 2,000 of Forfar's 2,500 textile workers were 'connected' with them, in fact in June only 79 people (67 of whom were women), about half the number thrown out of Station Works, were receiving unemployment benefit (for which they had had to pay subscriptions to the union for six months) from the FFWU, suggesting that material support for the union was rather weaker than its leaders wanted to believe. Hopes that those workers retained in employment would donate 10 per cent of their wages to help support those who had been laid off appear not to have materialised.[28]

Even so, in the longer run, the FFWU did manage to obtain a semblance of recognition by the company. This can be seen in July 1897 when Dons made an offer to the union directly, that if they accepted a sliding wage scale, the company would keep the workforce fully occupied. It was only after the union had rejected this suggestion that Dons appealed to their workers over the heads of the FFWU leadership. This was done by issuing a leaflet which, after outlining the difficult market circumstances in which the firm was operating (without a 'single order on our Books from America'), urged them to accept a wage cut and keep the looms going.[29] Such frankness about the company's situation (although there was no question of them revealing anything about their operating costs and profit levels) was far from universal amongst Tayside's textile employers and the strategy may have served to maintain something of the belief that Dons and their employees shared mutual interests. Around 1912, however, there was a shift in the attitude towards trade unions amongst Dundee's textile manufacturers, when they began to see the wisdom of cultivating trade union leaders as a means of preventing strikes at a time of growing industrial militancy elsewhere.[30]

In reality, though, there was little the FFWU could do to affect wage levels. These, and the extent of short-time working and even plant closures, were determined first and foremost by the company's trading situation, which was extremely volatile in the decades preceding the First World War. Secondly, as far as Forfar was concerned, wages were influenced by Dundee rates, of which, owing to their inland location, the company always had to be acutely conscious. Accordingly, and regardless of the agreement which had been reached in 1889, Forfar wages tended to follow those of Dundee, although when a cut appeared to be on the way, as in May 1894 when Dons were losing money, the company was accused, perhaps unfairly, of wishing to 'have the honour of leading the van' in what the FFWU's president declared to be 'this very questionable reduction of wages'.[31] In fact, Craiks appear to have been the least popular employers in Forfar, their workers allegedly being the first to come out on strike in the event of a dispute.[32]

Not surprisingly then, trends in wages both at Ward Mills and in the company's Forfar works appear to have been very similar to those of the rest of the coarse textile district, with a run of reductions from the mid-1870s until the mid-1880s which reduced wages (in Dundee) by some 25 per cent. Thereafter a series of rises was obtained, which, in money terms at least, meant that by 1912 most workers were as well off or perhaps even marginally better-off than they had been in the early 1870s. In real terms however their living standards were considerably lower.[33]

The years immediately prior to the outbreak of the First World War saw further improvements in money wages, especially for Dons' male workers.[34] The war brought further gains, partly at the prompting of the FFWU, but largely it seems, because of the growing success in Dundee of the Jute and Flax Workers' Union, which had benefited greatly from government intervention in the jute industry. It was hoped that by deliberately strengthening the union's position greater harmony in the trade would result.[35] Invariably then, Dons' workers in Forfar had to wait until their Dundee counterparts had obtained an increase before they could have any hope of an advance. This occurred in May and July 1915 for instance, when a war bonus of two shillings was paid – after it had been introduced in Dundee.[36] In September 1916 there was a 'general advance of wages in Dundee', which led to parallel increases in Forfar – two shillings a week to dressers, tenters and joiners, three shillings for mechanics and blacksmiths and five per cent for all other workers, male and female.[37]

Over the period of the war, most of Dons' workers more than doubled their money wages. Thus the weekly wage of the head tenter at Station Works rose from 23s 10d in 1913 to 62 shillings at the end of 1918; lower down the works' hierarchy, female darners saw their weekly wage rising from 12s 6d in 1913 to 29s 2d; the wages of female apprentice winders rose from 7s to 16s over the same period.[38] Production workers though could still feel the pinch of short-time, although by the end of the war this was not such a trial as it had been beforehand. Thus in July 1918 St James' was put on a 40-hour week, while both Station Works and South Street Works were closed down. In spite of the loss of fifteen hours' work at St James' however, those affected were to receive 25 per cent of their actual wages (for 40 hours' work) in addition, up to a maximum of 7s.[39]

The biggest rises were secured by the mechanics, who in August 1917 joined the Dundee branch of the Amalgamated Society of Engineers. It was a move which brought almost immediate benefits, their craft status and separate organisation allowing them to negotiate with the company in their own sectional interest, and shielding them from the fluctuations in wages which affected the firm's production workers. Slowly but surely, collective bargaining was becoming part and parcel of the everyday business of managing the company.

Chapter Seven: Labour Relations and Industrial Conflict

1 DUA, MS 100/1/3/1, Private Ledger No 1, 1865 – 1897, p95.
2 *Forfar Herald*, 14 June 1907, 10 April 1908 and 2 September 1910.
3 Ibid, 11 April and 18 July 1913.
4 British Parliamentary Papers, *Reports of the Chief Inspectors of Factories and Workshops, 1884 – 86*, Vol XV, C4369, p34.
5 The information for this paragraph is largely drawn from the pocket book of R. R. Taylor, a former clerk of the company. I am indebted to Mr Tom Scotland for lending it to me.
6 *Forfar Herald and Kirriemuir Advertiser*, 11 July 1913.
7 *Dundee Year Book, 1901*, p59.
8 *Dundee Year Book, 1888*; W. M. Walker, *Juteopolis: Dundee and its textile workers, 1885 – 1923* (Edinburgh, 1979), Chapter VIII.
9 Ibid, 149; Letter, A. Forbes to *Forfar Herald*, 11 October 1889.
10 Walker, *Juteopolis*, pp162 – 3.
11 Stated by FFWU officials at a public meeting, see *Forfar Herald*, 16 September 1889.
12 Ibid.
13 Ibid.
14 *Forfar Herald*, 11 October 1889.
15 DUA, MS 100/1/2/7, Letter Book, 1927–1934, DBB response to Jute Trade Board questionnaire, October 1933, p387.
16 *Forfar Herald*, 11 October 1889.
17 Ibid.
18 Ibid.
19 *Forfar Herald*, 1 November 1889.
20 Ibid.
21 *Forfar Herald*, 18 October 1889.
22 Ibid, 29 November 1889.
23 Ibid.
24 *Forfar Herald*, 25 May 1894.
25 Ibid.
26 Walker, *Juteopolis*, pp292 – 3.
27 *Forfar Herald*, 25 May 1894.
28 *Forfar Review*, 27 November 1914.
29 *Forfar Herald*, 25 May and 8 June 1894.
30 Walker, *Juteopolis*, p313.
31 *Forfar Herald*, 25 May 1894.
32 See, for example, *Forfar Herald*, 11 October 1889. According to the FFWU representatives, 'the reason that the employees there are generally the first to strike in Forfar is perhaps best known to the Messrs Craik.'
33 See also, DUA MS 100/1/2/5, Letter Book, 1899 – 1926, J. B. Don to W. A. P. Hewins MP, secretary to the Tariff Commission, 4 April 1912, pp590–1.
34 Ibid, DBB to Adam Farquharson, 27 August 1912, 613.
35 Walker, *Juteopolis*, p397.
36 See DUA, MS 100/1/2/5, Letter Book, 1899 – 1926, DBB to Adam Farquharson, 14 May and 9 July 1915, p655 and 661.
37 Ibid, DBB to Provost Meffan, 27 September 1916, p676.
38 St James' Road, Wage Book, 1914 – 48.
39 *Forfar Dispatch*, 21 March 1918.

Chapter Eight

Gloom and Reconstruction: The Inter-war Years

The years between the First and Second World Wars were the most difficult in the company's history. In this Dons were not alone, for the linen and jute industry of Dundee and Angus as a whole, this was a 'testing time'. No company came through the period unscathed. Amalgamations were commonplace and indeed by the end of the period, two firms, Jute Industries Ltd and Low & Bonar, accounted for over half of Dundee's jute trade. Rationalisation, however, meant the closure of some works, while some firms had to give up the fight altogether.

Yet, in some respects, in the first two years of peace it all looked so different, as the following table demonstrates.

Table 8.1 *Don Bros, Buist & Co Ltd, Profit (and Loss) Accounts, 1918–19 to 1938–39*

Year	Profit or (Loss) £	Carried Forward £
1918–19	171,908	82,307
1919–20	321,786	143,742
1920–21	4,259	459
1921–22	49,797	18,997
1922–23	24,975	16,425
1923–24	33,537	15,136
1924–25	40,770	19,720
1925–26	7,471	3,671
1926–27	8,278	4,478
1927–28	36,404	3,104
1928–29	11,162	4,987
1929–30	4,594	794

1930–31	(19,952)	(20,002)
1931–32	(24,233)	(24,283)
1932–33	(30,998)	(31,048)
1933–34	(14,135)	(14,185)
1934–35	4,559	4,509
1935–36	9,001	8,951
1936–37	(1,452)	(1,502)
1937–38	(8,148)	(8,198)
1938–39	17,811	10,261

Source: Minute Book No 1, 1904–44

As can be seen, the high profit levels of the First World War continued after peace had been restored. Indeed in 1919–20 the company's profits were better than they had ever been, although war-induced inflation meant that in real terms they were somewhat lower than the figures alone suggest. The transition from wartime production, however, was not achieved overnight; in March 1919, at the first annual meeting of the newly-established Association of Jute Spinners and Manufacturers (with J. C. Buist as vice-chairman), it was reported that private business was small. The outlook, it was concluded, 'is not bright'. The rest of 1919 though, was better, especially for jute-spinners. Weavers on the other hand were 'not in such a happy condition'.[1] Neither sector enjoyed the spectacular post-war boom conditions which many other industries experienced. And almost immediately after the picture had brightened – this time along with much of the rest of British industry – Dons fortunes crashed (from an annual profit figure of £321,786 to £4,259), as the post-war bubble – such as it was in linen and jute – burst.

Nevertheless, for the rest of the 1920s the company did reasonably enough, despite declining linen sales in the USA, where Dons were being driven out of the crash market. The Great Slump and the Depression which followed brought four consecutive years of losses, and on top of the virtual disappearance of their US linen trade, making a period of crisis for the company. Although Dons weathered the storm, and a modest recovery in the company's fortunes occurred in 1934–35 and

1935–36, two further loss-making years followed. Respite came in large part because of the threat of war with Germany, which encouraged the government to build up stocks of sandbags.

Although to a large extent the directors of Don Bros, Buist & Co Ltd were simply the victims of world events and market forces over which they had no control, they did not simply lie down and accept their fate. As this chapter will demonstrate, during the inter-war decades Dons engaged in a major restructuring of their organisation and production methods. Understandably, there were times of despair, and others when the company was inclined to seek the easy way out, campaigning, for example, for the erection of a protective tariff wall for their industry; but at no time did the directors surrender. Generally their record during a period of prolonged commercial adversity is impressive.

Personnel Changes and the Legacy of War

The fatalities which occurred during the Great War had a profound impact as far as the company's leading personnel were concerned. Even before the outbreak of hostilities, Gilbert Don, who had been extremely active at St James' and Station Works in Forfar, died in July 1913 at the age of 53. Perhaps because Gilbert's death was not entirely unexpected, having been preceded by a long period of ill-health, one of his sons, Frederick W. R. Don had begun to train with the firm prior to his father's death. Unfortunately though, Frederick, apparently a popular manager, died prematurely in 1916, before making his mark on the company. Ironically, he never saw action in the war, having met his death after falling ill at Leamington Spa, *en route* to join the army. He had been predeceased by his brother Reginald, who lost his life at the battle of the Marne in 1914.[2] Before this Frederick had been joined in the business by one of his cousins, one of John B. Don's sons, William Gilbert Don, whose career with the Royal Navy was cut short in 1912, almost certainly owing to pressures on him to help fill the gap which Gilbert Don's growing incapacity was creating within the firm.

Gilbert's brother and fellow-director Robert B. Don died in 1917. In addition, two of his sons lost their lives during the course of the war, Archie at Salonika in 1916, and his brother

Robert in Greece in 1917.[3] Two of Robert's other sons did later become shareholders in the firm, although they played no part in its management. And while the fifth son, John A. Don, was on the board between 1943 and 1951, he does not appear to have made a significant contribution to the company's development prior to that.

Gilbert and Robert Don were the sons of one of the company's two great Victorian leaders, John Don. The son of his brother and partner W. G. Don, John B. Don, also lost one of his sons, Valentine Grantham Don, at the battle of Loos in 1915.[4]

A consequence of this catalogue of family tragedies was that during the war, instead of being taken over by the younger men, the company continued to be run by an older generation of directors, John B. Don, J. C. Buist and the company secretary, Charles Hill. Indeed in 1917, as partial compensation for what the first two at least may have considered to have been an unexpected burden, the three men awarded themselves £1,000 each, in recognition of the 'extra duties' they had had to perform.[5] Their business lives were drawing to a close, however: Charles Hill was the first to go, in 1929, two years before his death; John B. Don retired from active involvement from the firm in the early 1930s, although he lived in retirement until 1946; and J. C. Buist retired in 1933, although unlike Hill, he did enjoy several years in retirement until his death in 1944 at the age of 92.

With the deaths of so many natural heirs, some of whom were being groomed for senior positions within the company, new men with comparatively little or no experience in the industry had to be brought in. John Don's side of the family came to be represented by the Hills, descendants through the distaff side. One of his daughters, Mary Anne Don, had married Michael Hill, a merchant from Hull. Although Hill himself appears to have had no connections with the company, one of his sons, Lionel E. Hill (b.1884), who through his distinguished army service ultimately reached the rank of colonel, first became involved with Don Bros, Buist & Co Ltd after the end of the war and was appointed a director in 1922. The 'Colonel', as Lionel Hill came to be known, was joined on the board by William Gilbert Don, who after the outbreak of war had been sent to Gallipoli, and later Egypt. Badly wounded, Captain Don, as he

Captain W.G. Don (1888–1961), was involved with Don Bros, Buist & Co Ltd from 1912 until 1961, except during the First World War. He played an important role (with Lionel E. Hill) during the 1930s and throughout his career was credited with maintaining peaceful industrial relations in the company's Forfar works. This photograph was kindly supplied by J. Gavin Don; the original hangs in Gardyne Castle, Forfar

had become, once more commenced work with the family firm.[6]

Although he had been a director since 1904, Robert Hay Adamson, the son of James W. Adamson, was to play a much more prominent role after the war, notably in Forfar. Amongst the pre-war directors, Adamson (b.1869) was unusual in that he had a technical background, having studied engineering at university as well as receiving further practical training with James F. Low in Monifieth, after a period in Leeds before joining Dons at Ward Mills in 1893. In spite of this, he concentrated on the commercial side of the business. He too saw war service and rose to the rank of colonel.

J. C. Buist's son, Frank D. J. Buist, also joined the company, although it was not until 1933 that he became a director, along with James Strickland Oliver.[7] Like W. G. Don, Buist (b.1900) had embarked on a career in the Royal Navy. With the death of his brother on wartime service, however, it was clear that his future would be with the family firm, and after studying engineering at Cambridge, he was sent to Mackie's in Belfast to learn more about textile machinery. Similarly, Oliver (b.1898) had hopes of following his father Col William James Oliver into the army. Nevertheless, after serving in France during the war, largely as a bombing instructor, and with plans laid thereafter for a spell in India with the 30th Lancers, he was persuaded to join Don Bros, Buist & Co – 'a nice kind of job', he reflected.[8] Almost certainly his decision to opt for a career in business was due to family pressure: his mother was Margaret Christie Don.

Just how far the introduction of so many new and relatively inexperienced faces influenced the company's fortunes in the following decades is impossible to say. Indeed the fact that for most a career in textiles had not been envisaged might at first be assumed to have been a drawback. There are indications though, and they can be no more than that, that after they had familiarised themselves with the industry, the new recruits appeared more ready than might otherwise have been the case to break with the past and carry through the changes in company organisation and working methods which became necessary in the bleak economic circumstances which marred the inter-war years. In so doing, they created a solid basis from which the company was able to develop after the Second World War, although it goes without saying that this was not their intention at the time. For a long time their aim was simply to survive. Significantly, three of the younger men, Buist, Hill and Oliver (who in the early 1920s lived together in The Vennel, Forfar), were technically competent too. Oliver had a passionate, even obsessive interest in textile machinery. In co-operation with the company's technical staff both he and in a rather more tangible way Hill were over the next three or four decades able to make a series of important modifications to their weaving machines. As will be seen, Dons' in-house conversion of their narrow linen looms to jute weaving, and productivity gains made on older machinery, were important factors in accounting for their improved fortunes in the later 1930s, as well as the best part of the two decades after 1945.

THE END OF AN ERA: THE DEMISE OF LINEN

The return of peace and the ending of government controls on the supply and price of flax, which had risen nearly ten-fold during the war, from £36 to £350 per ton, brought into sharp focus the problems the company had first faced in this area prior to 1914.[9] The Russian Revolution made the supply of flax even more uncertain, and owing to their inability to obtain any flax, some firms even gave up making linen altogether. As in former times, however, Dons' involvement in both jute and linen was a considerable advantage. With their income from jute sales, they were able to ride the storm which followed the brief period of post-war prosperity and by September 1921 could benefit from the departure from the flax market of some of their rivals. Their favourable position in this respect is revealed in a letter sent to their London agent, who was informed that 'We shall have no abundance of flax for years . . . if there were not so many Mills standing idle, we should long ago have exhausted supplies, and there would have been an absolute famine.'[10]

Despite these obstacles the directors were convinced that there was still some life left in the linen trade and a market for their products. To this end, late in 1921, after an absence of some nine years, it was decided once again to try to trade through Belfast, which for John B. Don had become 'in a business way . . . a closed book'.[11] This connection had proved beneficial before the war and, it was hoped, might do so again. Belfast was still the most important British centre for the sale of linen goods in the US. An advantage of trading there was that exporters were able to obtain the endorsement of invoices for goods sent across the Atlantic from the US consul, which secured for firms a fixed rate of exchange, agreed on the date of dispatch. Such a system was not then in use in Dundee, which had been noted by Dons in 1919; because of this, a disgruntled but anonymous correspondent on their behalf had written that 'As usual, Belfast seems to get ahead of the world in true Irish fashion'.[12] Accordingly, in order to benefit from the more secure trading arrangements which Belfast could provide, Col Hill was dispatched to Ulster to re-establish the firm's presence there and in May 1923 they came to an agreement that M. Wallace MacDowell & Co should be their agents.[13]

The renewed efforts made by the company in Belfast were unfortunately not a success. They managed to transact only £70,000 worth of business in the US in 1926, £40,000 in 1927, and £41,000 in 1928. By March 1930 it was noted that sales of crash were only one-tenth of what they had been formerly and that the chances of revival were 'remote'. The spirited fight which Dons had conducted in the US crash market had simply become a losing war of attrition, with looms being converted for jute-weaving ever since the end of the First World War. Instead of 400 looms allocated to the weaving of crash, there were only 84 by 1928. Although the company had resisted going out of linen altogether, by 1931 not even the suggestion from W. B. Erwin of Belfast that there might be an opening for them in the 'Heavy Suiting and knicker Linen trade with the USA' could tempt Dons back to large-scale production. They were by then 'too much occupied in other directions' to be able to give the matter their attention.[14]

Why this momentous departure in terms of the company's product range should have occurred requires explanation. In one sense there was little that Dons could do. By 1925 the US duty on imported linens of the sort produced by the Scots had risen to 55 per cent, and it was relatively easy for their old rivals, the Stevens Linen Co, to take total command of the market. They were also subject to intense competition in the manufacture of crash from Ireland, Belgium and Czechoslovakia: 'For every competitor we had before the war we have a dozen now', was the way their New York agent saw things.

Yet the company has to take some part of the blame for the loss of the linen trade. Conservatism, tinged with complacency, was the culprit. One reason why the Czechs had had some success in the crash trade, for instance, was that they had introduced colours to their cloth. Dons followed suit, and began to finish theirs with fancy borders and to hem the tea towels they exported in packages of a dozen.[15] A fashion change had occurred in kitchen goods, where colour and better quality finishes were being sought: Dons had recognised this later than some of their rivals (they only had one cross-border loom working satisfactorily in December 1926), and suffered as a consequence.

Ironically, another weakness, which Dons shared with many other British firms in a variety of trades, was that they had, by trying too hard to satisfy their customers' requirements, developed too wide a range of crashes. In 1907 they had been making something like 59 varieties of this cloth: 'There is no house who can show a range of Crashes as you,' Dons were informed by MacDowells in Belfast, 'most run only a very few Nos, but they try to concentrate on them.'[16] For this reason Dons were unable to benefit to the same extent as some of their competitors from the savings which could be obtained from long production runs. Thus Dons were advised, rather late in the day, to concentrate their production in eight or twelve of their best-selling lines and price them 'on the basis of big production'.[17]

The company's main failing though, again born of conservatism, lay in their marketing arrangements. As has been seen, they had long depended on agents to sell their goods for them, and indeed, their dependence on these increased during the 1920s. Again in partnership with Hay & Robertson they employed W. R. Begg in Toronto, Canada, from 1924, and Fred Higgenbotham in Montreal from 1928. Although their Paris agency (which had commenced around 1885) had diminished in importance as their dealings in linen in Europe declined, they maintained a French connection along with one in Holland, where Dons were represented from 1925 by Van Meenen & Stratum. They also had a German agency and others in New Zealand (from 1904) and South Africa and Rhodesia (from around 1923 to 1940). Nearer home were their agencies in London, Birmingham, Leeds, Kidderminster, Manchester and Glasgow.

It was not the agencies as such which were the cause of the problem, although Dons' traditional dependence upon them seems the likely reason for the company's failure to act on advice of MacDowell & Co in Belfast in 1928 that they should send a representative direct to New York in January, before the main buying season (which was spring), and the US buyers left for Europe.[18] More significant – and damaging – than this was the company's attitude to their agents.

In the nineteenth century, both the company and its agents dealt largely with wholesalers. By the 1920s, however, a major change in retailing had got under way, first in the US and later in Britain, with the emergence of chain stores which preferred to deal direct with the manufacturers and purchase either individually or in concert with others. With the formation of companies in Britain such as the Drapery & General Investment Trust Ltd and Selfridge Provincial Stores Ltd, with their own central buying offices, the wholesalers were squeezed out of business.[19] Yet it was the wholesalers with whom Dons had conducted their business from the very beginning. Sensibly enough, for without much haggling over price, wholesalers of long standing were usually prepared to take large quantities of cloth.

In this way, and even when they were selling through agents, Dons were able to maintain control over the selling price of their goods. Indeed they insisted on this, and continued to do so. This is to be seen in their agreement with D. E. Anderson of Manchester, which included two articles which specifically restricted the agent's freedom of action. The first gave Dons the sole right to set the selling prices of any of their products sold by Anderson, while the second made it clear that all orders were subject to Dons' approval and control.[20] In other words, the price lists which the company published, usually once a year, were to remain unchanged until such time as a new one was compiled.

This system, which had obviously served Dons well, imposed considerable restrictions on their agents and was not suited to the more competitive conditions of the 1920s. Customers wanted to negotiate prices, yet as late as May 1928 Dons were still being urged to give MacDowell's in Belfast their asking price and their 'minimum' and to 'let them work between these'.[21] Furthermore, in spite of the recognition by their allies Hay & Robertson that it was probably best to deal direct with retailers, the directors were unwilling to countenance change, preferring instead to sell 'only through recognised channels'. Observing what had happened in the US and fearing that the same would be likely to follow in Britain, in 1926 the company urged the London-based Wholesale Textile Association to take a 'strong line of action' or 'Wholesale Houses will be driven out of business'.[22]

Their loyalty to the wholesalers was misplaced. That conditions had changed was recognised in December 1926 when the directors concluded that the time had arrived when 'we should risk losing what small business we still do with Wholesalers, and try to establish a new clientele with these large combines'. Wholesalers, it was pointed out, had 'practically ceased doing business with us', preferring instead goods from mainland Europe. In addition, it was felt that they had treated Dons 'with gross unfairness as to carrying stocks etc' and therefore it was concluded that it was 'no longer possible for us to do business exclusively with Wholesalers as in the past'. The company's decision to change their ways came too late though, and that a mistake had been made was acknowledged in April 1928 when it was admitted that the 'old time jobbers' had been succeeded by department store buyers, 'who do not know the name of Don as the old jobber buyers did in pre-war days'. Having recognised and responded to this change somewhat belatedly, the directors realised with some apprehension that the task they faced in recapturing a place in the linen market would be extremely difficult, as the departmental store buyers had 'got well in' with other manufacturers.[23] They were right; in fact, it was well-nigh impossible.

Depression – and building for the future

The demise of the linen trade and lower profits after 1925 (except for a brief upturn in 1927–28, largely owing to a temporary surge in demand for hessians), forced the directors to conduct a major review of the company's operations. The onset of the worldwide 'Great Slump' in the latter months of 1929 might reasonably have been expected to have deepened their gloom. Indeed, earlier in the same year the industry as a whole had been subjected to a renewed attack from India, where Associated Mills had reportedly increased their employees' hours of work from 54 to 60 a week, apparently in the hope of flooding the world market with jute and driving out their competitors.[24] The Slump itself led to severe cutbacks in Dundee and Forfar, where Dons' factory output in July 1930 was only 35 per cent of capacity.[25] Neither the directors nor the shareholders can have derived much comfort from the report and prognosis of the chairman, John B. Don, at the cheerless annual general meeting held on 14 July 1931. First of all he had to inform shareholders that the company had made a loss of £54,952 during the previous twelve months, before £35,000 was transferred from the General Reserve Account, to reduce the figure to £19,952. This was the biggest deficit ever, and the first since 1895. With a sharp fall the previous year in the value of both raw jute and cloth, the company had had to write down the value of their stocks by 'at least the equivalent of £10 per ton'. All cloth production was being carried on at a loss. 'Looking to the future,' Don reflected despondently, 'one cannot see a single ray of hope anywhere in the business outlook.'[26] It was a situation which only the week beforehand had persuaded the directors to resolve to write down the value of the company's shares 'to such an extent as will wipe out this year's loss'. This they proposed doing by writing down the value of their 9,500 Ordinary £10 shares to £1, which would reduce the company's capital by £85,500.[27] They also proposed to reduce the value of the company's property and plant 'as nearly as possible, to £50,000' (at a time when this was valued at £95,000). This was a drastic step which was vehemently opposed by one of their bankers, J. M. Kellas of the British Linen Bank. Both he and the company's legal advisers urged the directors to take a longer term view and adopt a more patient approach to their problems. If such a scheme became publicly known, Kellas argued, the company's credit and prestige would suffer 'a severe blow'.[28] Such a step, he went on:

> would in fact be proclaiming to the business world that the company had sustained serious losses and it would be inferred by a good many people that the directors were writing down capital partly with a view to assuring payment of dividends on an earlier date than would otherwise be possible. You can readily understand that such a policy would not readily commend itself to Bankers, as it would appear that the directors had made no firm resolve to retrieve the position.

Anxious to persuade the directors to change their mind, Kellas appealed to their pride, warning them that, 'the affairs of the company would be discussed in the jute market and elsewhere to the[ir] chagrin and humiliation', a sorry situation for a body of men who had 'always prided themselves on the outstanding position the company had earned itself'.

Kellas's pleading was as unsuccessful as his advice was sound. The main instigator of the devaluation had been John B. Don, who, as has been seen already, was at the sight of any major downturn in the company's fortunes inclined to adopt a rather less optimistic view of the future for coarse textiles than those around him. In 1931 too he was close to retirement. Although the directors eventually decided to overturn their earlier decision, Don remained unrepentant, and wrote from his retirement home in Bournemouth in June 1933 that 'in spite of bankers & everyone else' he still believed that the company should write down some of its assets.[29]

Whilst in the continued depression of the early 1930s John Don's dismal prognostications are understandable enough, the fact is that by 1930 the company was in a much stronger position than he reported. Paradoxically, publicly – indeed at the very meeting at which he had pronounced so gloomily about the future – he was prepared to say that when trade revived, the company would be 'in a position to take advantage . . . thanks to much reorganisation both in Dundee and Forfar'.[30]

John B. Don himself may not have been entirely convinced by the positive stance he had been obliged to adopt in order to reassure the company's shareholders and others interested in Dons' future, but even so, there was much truth in the words he spoke, for the period of introspection referred to above had not been one of self-pitying inaction. It was true that linen was in rapid decline. Accordingly, the company was becoming increasingly dependent upon jute, the outlook for which was felt by most of the directors to be considerably better, Calcutta notwithstanding – although only if the company could sharpen its competitive edge. Thus the first step in the review process referred to above was taken in July 1927, with the appointment of a sub-committee comprising Charles Hill, Col R. H. Adamson, Col L. E. Hill and Capt W. G. Don, the aim of which was to produce an 'exhaustive' report on the company's current situation and make recommendations 'for the improvement and benefit' of the business. Specifically, the sub-committee, which had been set up on the suggestion of Col Hill, was to consider the ways in which their jute operation could be improved. Hitherto jute yarn had been obtained from the company's Ward Mills in Dundee, where flax-spinning was also carried on. In 1927 though, with demand for common hessians, the firm's leading line, at a high level, the question of opening a jute-spinning facility in Forfar, where the company's weaving operations were located, was raised. Another consideration was the company's requirement for yarns which were 'more regular in spin and superior in quality to the average which can at present be obtained'.[31]

The sub-committee reported in November, following which it was decided to establish a 'half-system' at Forfar's South Street Works, which had lain idle since 1915. Subsequently (in 1929) renamed Strang Street Mill, possibly in order to disassociate it from the old power-loom factory at South Street, the conversion was begun almost immediately, with the machinery being supplied at a cost of £14,650 from James Mackie & Co of Belfast, a company which was to become a major supplier of textile machinery in Dundee. The total cost, including winding frames, electric motors, building work and fitting out the factory, was put at between £20,000 and £25,000.[32]

The aim was to be 'fully competitive with Calcutta, or any other low wage country'.[33] The directors were confident that their answer to Indian competition, which was centred on the installation of the best machinery available, was unanswerable, as their rivals' dependence on low wages gave them little incentive to re-equip their mills and factories. Working on a small scale at first, spinning only 30 to 40 tons of common hessian cops weekly, the Strang Street development appears to have been an immediate success. Short-time working, for instance, which was introduced at St James' and Station Works in November 1929, did not affect Strang Street. The directors were pleased and noted that, 'Much benefit to our own trade had accrued already, and seems likely to increase rapidly', as a result of their ability to produce 'clean, high coloured goods, regular in weight and appearance'.[34] This they felt, was in large part due to the control they were now able to exercise over the spinning process, which had not been possible at Ward Mills, which had enjoyed a semi-independent status within the company.

Spinning their own yarns had another advantage. Although the use of whale and fish oil in the jute batching stage was less common from the end of the nineteenth century, the practice was still carried on in the 1920s. Accordingly, a sizeable proportion of Dundee's jute yarns and cloth was alleged by customers to have been distinguished by a distinct 'fishy odour'. While buyers had simply had to accept this when Dundee and Angus had had a virtual monopoly of the world's supply of jute products, the rise of competition enabled them to adopt a more critical attitude to the yarn and cloth which came out of Dundee. By the later 1920s, though, little use was apparently made of whale and fish oil in jute processing anywhere – except in Dundee. Calcutta mills, for instance, used mainly mineral oil, which gave their products a 'sweet and pleasant smell compared with the smell of Dundee goods', an objection which was particularly strong when these were being used for food packaging.[35]

Dons were made conscious of the problem by some of their customers, and accordingly the company made representations to the AJSM in Dundee in 1927 in the hope that concerted action would be taken to abandon the use of whale and fish oil in the industry. While sympathising with Dons, the AJSM felt that it could do no more than urge members to refrain from the use of such softening agents. Anyway, not all members of the AJSM (from which Dons had withdrawn in 1928) accepted that their rivals were using only mineral oil. The only way of improving matters, Dons were informed, was for manufacturers to specify that yarns they purchased from spinners 'must be free from any fishy smell'.[36] Although it is not clear whether such considerations played any part in the decision to transfer some of their jute-spinning to Forfar, that the company did so can only have been beneficial in this respect. By moving part of their spinning operation to Forfar, Dons could – as in the early days – disassociate themselves from Dundee and the 'prejudice' which existed (and they believed this was increasing) against jute made there.

The move proved a good one for more tangible reasons too. By 1930 Strang Street Mill was demonstrably lowering the firm's production costs and producing yarn which was much in demand from other manufacturers.[37] Strang Street was thereby kept fully occupied, and provided, in the directors' view, 'an excellent advertisement for our spinning mills generally'. They were at the forefront of modernisation schemes in the Angus textile region, and although Baxter Bros in Dundee built a mill which was four times the size of Strang Street, and the recently established Jute Industries Ltd had begun to build another, Dons were confident that their more modest venture, which turned out high-quality specialised yarns, at least half of which they could use themselves, was the better long-term proposition.

The directors' efforts in re-equipping and reorganising their works did not end with Strang Street however. In the belief that 'the best and cheapest time to undertake such work is when times are most depressed', a course of action which had benefited many of the region's most successful textile firms in the past, they began early in the spring of 1929 to bring up-to-date automatic looms into Station Works.[38] Their introduction was not entirely straightforward, owing to fears on the part of the workforce about the impact the new machinery might have on their earnings and employment prospects. In May 1929 the suppliers of their looms, Whittaker Automatic Looms Ltd of Blackburn, were informed that 'Our old employees here are inclined to be conservative . . . we have not been very successful with automatic looms so far.'[39]

Yet ultimately they were, and in fact by the end of the year a number of automatic looms had been installed, under the guidance of Alex Grossett, who was appointed as a foreman specifically to oversee the introduction and operation of the new looms. He was paid £4 per week (about twice the wage of the best weavers) and had rent-free accommodation.[40]

Although described as a 'young mechanic', by the time he arrived in Forfar, Grossett had had experience in the textile industry in both Dundee and India. He had received formal training about automatic looms at Dundee Technical College and was sent by Dons to discover more at Whittaker's Blackburn factory.

FFWU representations on behalf of weavers who were concerned about reductions in their piece rates were met with the response that the new looms had larger shuttles and beams and 'other advantages' which would enable them to earn higher wages than beforehand, and more too than most other weavers in the trade.[41]

The decision to create a spinning mill in Forfar obviously called into question the future of Ward Mills in Dundee. These, which had served the company so well for so long, had ceased to do so by the end of the 1920s. Ward Mill's original function had been to spin flax, yet in the 1920s only 'small and varied orders for Flax and Tow Yarns' could be obtained. Furthermore, most of the machinery was old, and the mill had been organised for the production of short runs of a wide range of specialised yarns. Accordingly, in July 1929 the sub-committee which had proposed the development at Strang Street was called upon again, although without the services of Charles Hill, who retired at this time after being connected with the company for 62 years. The three men who remained, Adamson, Col Hill and Capt Don, were to investigate ways in which Ward Mills could be made more efficient and either make profits for the company or at least 'reduce the loss to the house'. In order to achieve this they were given considerable powers, and were free to cut salaries and overheads, stop or renew machinery and reorganise as they saw fit. In short they were to do 'whatever may be necessary to bring the Mills up to date in methods & in the production of yarns which can be readily sold & produced at a minimum cost'.[42]

With the 'old trade' in linen dying, the board took the inevitable but momentous decision in March 1930 that 'the flax-spinning end of the business at Ward Mills should be abandoned'.[43] Less easy to decide was what role Ward Mills should play in the future. Closure was a step which the directors would take only with 'extreme reluctance', and instead they debated two alternative strategies. One possibility was that a more efficiently run Ward Mills could carry on as before, as 'an independent unit with its own sales operation'; in this case the Forfar factories would be 'a casual customer on the same terms as any other'.[44] The other was to tie Ward Mills firmly to the Forfar operation and spin yarns exclusively for the company's own use. This would have the advantage of making it possible to eliminate the independent sales organisation and introduce other economies, both in the mills and the offices.

In the end the board decided on a compromise. The main yarns to be spun at Ward Mills were jute yarns for the carpet trade. The company had been involved at least since 1927 in spinning carpet yarns, for which jute was particularly appropriate as it did not stretch as much as other fibres. Although the British carpet industry was in the doldrums for most of the 1920s, demand for carpets was expanding. Ward Mills had been producing in the region of 12 tons a week of these yarns, but after reorganisation it was hoped to almost double this, to 23 tons. The company aimed to capture something more than 19 per cent of the British market for carpet yarns, which in 1930 stood at around 9,000 tons per annum. The house-building boom of the 1930s, however, created a significant additional demand for carpets and, by 1938, Ward Mills was in fact able to turn out 55 tons of carpet yarns each week.[45]

As well as spinning carpet yarns, capacity at Ward Mills was retained for producing fine yarns, to be made from 'the best jute picked out of the raw material bought for Strang St & Ward Mills'.[46] As this suggests, Ward Mills was now much more tightly integrated with Forfar, a necessary departure it was felt by the board, if their decision to utilise automatic looms proved to be successful commercially. Henceforward, Strang Street was to be run as a department of Ward Mills. Between them it was anticipated that their spinning capacity could be expanded considerably, from 2,000 tons of jute and 1,500 tons of flax per annum, to 5,550 tons of jute.[47] There was a human cost to all of this; to permit the requisite building to take place, the plant at Ward Mills had to be closed down between May and August 1930. When production recommenced, there was work for only 400 people as opposed to 700 previously.[48]

Despite the board's rationalisation measures, it was some time before they could benefit from them. Although, as has been noted already, yarn output rose – even during the trough of the Slump, jute cloth production dipped steeply in 1930–1 and did not surpass that level until 1933–4, as the following table shows.

Table 8.2 *Jute Consumption and Production Figures, 1929–30 to 1933–4.*

Year	Jute consumed (tons)	Yarn spun (tons)	Spindles woven	Cloth produced (yards)
1929–30	3,972	3,022	1,280,099	17,802,210
1930–31	3,367	3,171	712,040	9,893,180
1931–32	5,298	5,127	985,919	13,542,581
1932–33	6,587	6,147	1,265,807	17,217,450
1933–34	7,760	7,493	1,692,838	22,884,587

Source: Trading Accounts, St James' Works, Forfar

Losses continued to be made until May 1934. Indeed, as Figure 8.1 reveals, the company made an average annual trading loss of £16,944 between 1929–30 and 1933–34. Dons' financial situation would have been much worse had the directors not been able to benefit from the sale of 5 per cent War Loan Stock, £25,000 worth of which had been purchased in January 1917.[49]

This proved to be an invaluable if fortuitous step, for not only did its value rise substantially, but the company was also able to sell portions of their holdings in order to raise much-needed finance. The first sale occurred in August 1929, when £60,000 was raised to reduce the company's overdraft at a time of what for contemporaries were relatively high interest rates (5.5 per cent with the Bank of England, 6 per cent with the US Federal Reserve).[50] In September 1931 another tranche was sold, which raised £30,000, while in November more units were disposed of in order to raise the company's bank overdraft facilities in Dundee from £50,000 to £70,000.

This was necessary, it appears, 'to provide for the purchase of the Company's increased requirements of jute'.[51] Prior to this, in December 1930, following a marked drop in the value of both their stocks of raw jute and cloth, the company had had to adopt a much more cautious policy where jute purchases were concerned, with chief buyer Col R. H. Adamson being instructed by the board not to purchase more than a month's supply.[52] The last recorded sale took place the following summer, when a total of £69,150 was taken out of the War Loan account.[53] In all, the company's initial investment of £25,000 provided a return of £179,150, a rate of return of over 700 per cent.

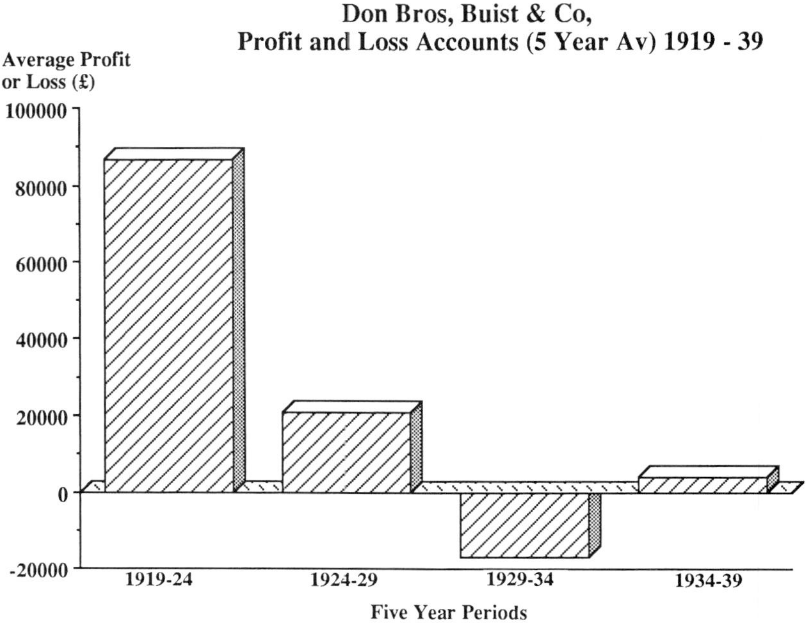

Don Bros, Buist & Co, Profit and Loss Accounts (5 Year Av) 1919–39

Even this fillip, however, and the restructuring which has been referred to, were insufficient to make the 1930s anything other than a bleak period for Don Bros, Buist & Co Ltd. The profit and loss accounts which bear this out have already been examined. That no ordinary dividends were paid between 1929 and 1943, nor dividends on preference shares between 1931 and 1939, and the fact that no sums for depreciation were written off in the same period, further confirms that this was the bleakest decade in the company's recent history.

The fact is that whatever a textile firm such as Dons did, it was extremely difficult to overcome competition from Calcutta. Some attempt was made to dampen the Indians' impact within the British market, principally through the AJSM, which conducted a campaign to persuade the government to impose tariff duties on Indian imports. Their efforts were partly rewarded in the spring of 1932 with the Import Duties Act which levied duties of 20 per cent on imported cloth, bags and carpets and 10 per cent on yarns.[54]

At this level, however, the tariffs provided only a partial defence for the jute manufacturers. The difference between the purchase price of raw jute and the sale of the finished product (which in the worst years of the early 1930s was between £17 and £18 a ton) was considered to be 'totally inadequate to meet the costs of spinning and weaving even in modern mills & factories with all the latest machinery'.[55] Only when the margin rose towards £25, which it did in 1933, could a profit be made. As always, the price which the company had to pay for raw jute was a crucial factor, and while the board itself provided general guidelines as to price for Col Adamson when he was purchasing jute – instructing him in June 1931, for example, to pay no more than £16 per ton – considerable responsibility lay upon his shoulders to obtain the requisite quantities at an acceptable price. Adamson continued to exercise his considerable skills in this area until his death in June 1936.

Dons continued to press for further state assistance. In a letter to a member of the great Cox dynasty of jute masters, in Lochee, now leading lights in Jute Industries Ltd, Capt Don advocated an agreement with India which would guarantee to Britain the markets of north-west Europe and West Africa, and allow free rein to Calcutta in the rest of the world. Such a step, he urged, was imperative, 'now that we also have Japan hammering on the door'.[56] And indeed concerted action on the part of Dundee's jute manufacturers, both on their own part and in the form of continued pressure on the government, did bring some favourable results. Exports of cloth to Denmark and Argentina increased, for instance, following government assisted agreements with those countries. Dundee Chamber of Commerce was able to secure outlets with the Baltic republics of Estonia (1934) and Lithuania (1935) for bacon and ham wrappers.[57]

Nevertheless, for Dons, as for the rest of Dundee's textile firms, simply keeping going was a hard, sometimes bitter and always exhausting struggle. Some failed. Capt Don probably encapsulated the feelings of his fellow directors when, in the aforementioned letter, he justified his support of further protection for the industry largely on the grounds that it would obviate the need for more mill and factory closures, as well as further 'amalgamations or changes in our present organisation'. Competition between the various firms, he argued, would keep cloth prices reasonable, but 'the adequacy of the market would render cut-throat competition between them unnecessary'.[58] Don had good reason to look for stability: almost certainly one of the factors which had contributed to the breakdown of his marriage, which ended in divorce in 1932, was the long periods he had had to spend away from home on company business during the critical years at the end of the 1920s.

Despite continued representations from the industry to government, relief on the scale which Don envisaged did not come until the era of Jute Control, and from 1935 until the outbreak of the Second World War, the Indians were able to flood the British market with cheap jute goods, which drove the price of unfinished cloth down to rock-bottom levels: in February 1936, for example, Calcutta cloth was selling for £30 a ton. Dons simply could not compete, and the directors determined 'not to follow this market down indefinitely, unless a corresponding fall occurred in jute'.[59] Dons could go no lower than around £37 a ton, which was the current price for their 8oz 40-inch hessians, of which there was a 6.5-fold increase in imports between 1928 and 1938.[60] A major factor in the Indians' favour was their wage costs: Indian workers, on average, were believed to be paid between 32s and 34s a week less than their Scottish counterparts, a differential which was calculated to be giving Indian manufacturers a cost advantage of some £8 to £10 per ton.[61] As a result, Dons felt they had no alternative but to close their Forfar works between July and December 1936.[62] When they reopened early in 1937, it was on a restricted scale of output.

Only with rearmament, as the political climate in Europe turned chillier, did the situation improve. In 1938, Dons, like most of the jute manufacturers in Dundee and Angus, were working on a government sandbag contract, which had been negotiated in such a way, the company chairman James S. Oliver explained to anxious shareholders in July 1938, 'as to exclude the possibility of Indian hessians being used'.[63] The quantity required, however, was less than the industry would have liked, and the work was spread thinly over two years. Nevertheless, the importance of the sandbag contract for Dons should not be underestimated: in 1938, 240 (or one-third) of the company's 750 looms were standing idle, and 210 (28 per cent) were employed on uneconomic work in more or less direct competition with India. 140 looms (19 per cent of the total) were being used for 'special' goods not made by the Indians. 160 (21 per cent), that is more than half of those which were working profitably, were employed in the manufacture of sandbags.[64]

Stemming the Tide: Further Change and Innovation in the 1930s

Although government orders for sandbags were clearly crucial for Dons in the year which preceded the outbreak of the Second World War, they did take steps during the 1930s to seek out and supply alternative markets.

Indian competition in 'standard goods', such as cloth for bag manufacture, both abroad and within the home market, simply could not be matched by jute manufacturers in Dundee or anywhere else in the textile region of east central Scotland. It was therefore essential for Scottish firms to seek out lines in which the Indians showed either little or no interest. It was true in the former case of linoleum, hessians, brattice cloth and clothing paddings for instance, and in the latter with carpet yarns, cables, ropes and twines. Tayside firms also made cloths in weights and widths for specialist markets. Again, the Indians paid little attention to these.[65]

Dons were very much in the forefront of the search for markets for non-standard goods. Their commitment to carpet yarns at Ward Mills has already been noted, but the search for new possibilities did not end there. In August 1932 Capt Don wrote to Alexander Low that unless some 'new outlet' for bulk goods appeared, he thought that the 'highest endeavour' should be directed towards the discovery and promotion of 'as many minor or subsidiary uses [for jute] in our own country as we can'.[66]

He recognised that the quantities required of each of these would be relatively small, but was convinced that their aggregate significance could be considerable. Amongst the uses to which jute cloth could be put, apart from its traditional function as bagging and sacking material, were coverings for herring barrels, motor tyre wrappings, book bindings, wall coverings (instead of lathe and plaster), and oven cloths. Those which most attracted the attention of Dons were 'cleavage surface' for concrete roads and binding material for tarred roads. Don took a personal interest in the first of these and in July 1934 published an article on the subject in a transport journal, in which he pointed to experiments which were taking place with the process in the USA, Germany and India, evidently in the hope of attracting the attention of the road construction industry.[67] In December the company launched its own product under the trademark 'Cleavecrete'.[68]

Unfortunately, from the surviving records it is not possible to ascertain how successful this particular product was for Dons. They did, however, continue to endeavour to develop new lines 'which would not be subject to competition', and in 1937 the directors felt confident enough to report that they had made progress in this direction.[69] That in 1938 140 of the company's looms which were in production were making 'special goods' is an indication that their confidence was justified. There was a limit, however, to how far it was advantageous for them to increase their output of such specialist goods, as over-production where the size of the market was limited had the effect of driving down their price.

Although competition and the failure of the industry's leaders to persuade the government to provide a higher level of protection weakened some spirits in the boardroom, Dons' corporate resolve remained unbroken, except for a few weeks in 1931 when John B. Don's proposal for writing down the value of the company looked as though it would be implemented. Instead, as had been seen, the directors strove to find means by which the company could carry on and grow. Furthermore, and equally importantly, the rationalisation of the company's organisation which had commenced in 1927, the introduction of new machinery, and other means of improving productivity, continued through the 1930s.

The success of Strang Street Mill persuaded the directors to extend there from July 1932.[70] New machinery worth £9,000 was to be installed in what was a move to further integrate production in Forfar. By July 1933 the work had been completed, when it was reported that the mill, which could now spin an additional 30 tons of yarn each week, was 'running very efficiently'.[71] Output at Strang Street rose to 80 tons a week.

What appears to have been a remarkable stroke of good fortune enabled the company to make even further progress at Station Works, and subsequently in their Forfar operation as a whole. Although a number of automatic looms had been introduced, there were still large numbers of older looms both at Station Works and St James'. Some 346 of the company's looms were of either 42 or 46-inch reed space, and over 100 were of 54 inches. These widths were too narrow for the contemporary market, and clearly the company was faced with a major financial outlay if they were to be replaced.

On 29 August 1932, however, what the *Forfar Dispatch* described as 'the outstanding local event of the week' in Forfar occurred, with the outbreak of a major fire at Station Works. The fire, which broke out at between six and seven in the morning, and 'cast a vivid glare in the sky and attracted hundreds of spectators', destroyed three sections of the roof covering the loom shed, a warehouse which was largely filled with cloth, and also caused substantial damage to 100 of the 54-inch looms. The cost of the conflagration, which was not as great as was feared at first, was put at £12,500.[72]

Such was the extent of the damage which was done to 'Little Donnie's', as Station Works was known locally, that the company was compelled to carry out a wholesale reorganisation of the Forfar factories. In essence, this involved transferring some of the older, narrower looms from St James' to Station Works, and replacing those which were moved with new wider models. In consequence, the number of 42 and 46-inch looms in Forfar was reduced from 346 to 268, while three dozen 50-inch looms, forty 80-inch looms and four 62.5-inch looms were brought in to replace them. The warehouse at Station Works was abandoned and replaced by a new one at St James', a more convenient location. Further warehousing space was acquired by the company in 1935, when the trustees of W. Laird were persuaded by Capt Don and Col Hill to dispose of their empty factory, Canmore Works.[73]

By 1938 a fully integrated manufacturing and finishing operation had been established in Forfar, and at the AGM in July 1938 the directors were able to report to those present that the two plants (for spinning and weaving) working in conjunction

Station Works, Forfar. The fire on 29 August 1932 caused extensive damage both to the roof and the looms below

had produced a profit during the first six months of the year, 'and during the last six months operated without a loss'. Forfar, it was believed, 'could hold its own with the trade under present conditions'.

No such sanguine expectations emanated from Dundee. Although output of carpet yarns had more than doubled during the 1930s, the costs of production using what the company admitted was 'old fashioned' machinery, were high. As long as demand for carpet yarn remained buoyant, this situation was tolerable, and no losses were sustained. However, during the first half of 1938 there was a slump in carpet sales – the first for several years – and Ward Mills, which depended heavily on demand for carpet yarns, suffered accordingly.[74]

The downturn provided another impetus for the directors to reconsider their already far from strong commitment to Ward Mills. July 1935 appears to mark the beginnings of what for Dons was a long retreat from Dundee, a process which was only reversed, and then none too successfully, in the 1970s. On this occasion part of their office accommodation was let for £650 per annum, a move which was followed in December with the sale, to the Postmaster General for £16,000, of a tract of land lying to the south of Willison Street.[75] In November 1939 trade was sufficiently bad to cause the directors to order that the works be closed down, with only tentative plans being made for re-opening 'about the New Year, if Jute is available'.[76]

One final aspect of the company's efforts to improve its competitive position in the 1930s remains to be examined: labour management.

LABOUR

The efforts of the company from 1927 at least, to achieve significant productivity gains, clearly had profound consequences for the labour force. This had been anticipated by the first sub-committee of directors which had looked into the possibility of spinning at the disused South Street Works. Before making their final proposals the members of the sub-committee had endeavoured to satisfy themselves that a two-shift system could be operated, with male workers, and that this would not be opposed by the FFWU.[77]

In fact, the new arrangements appear to have been introduced relatively smoothly, with the exception of the cop-winding department. As women were debarred by law from working at night, the only way in which the company could operate a two-shift system was to employ males. Their efforts to train men as cop-winders were not successful though, and after a year of trying, the FFWU was informed that, 'They [the men] cannot, or will not, attain anything approaching the efficiency of the girls doing the same work in our Dundee mill.'[78] As a consequence, the men who were employed at this work on the day-shift were replaced, but not by local females, as the company felt it had already spent enough on training, but by 'skilled female winders from Dundee'. Even so, 87 per cent of employees in Strang Street Mill were male in March 1934 – a remarkably high figure and a clear break with tradition. In Dundee at the end of Victoria's reign the ratio of females to males in the mills had been 2:1, and on the spinning flats, 8:1.[79]

Lionel E. Hill (1884–1969). Related by marriage to John Don (1823–86), he played a crucial role in the rationalisation of the company during the 1930s. After the war he was not only a leading figure in Don Bros, Buist & Co but also contributed much to the jute industry generally through his work with the Association of Jute Spinners and Manufacturers

Interestingly, given that linen and jute were industries which as a whole had traditionally been dominated by female labour, the proportion of all Dons' Forfar workers who were male rose from 45 per cent in 1930, to 63 per cent in 1935.

Dons, of course, were not alone in having to face the challenge posed by low Indian wages, though the company's inland location meant that the directors were if anything even more acutely conscious than their counterparts in Dundee of the importance of reducing marginal costs. In October 1933 it was estimated that the extra cost of manufacturing a ton of cloth in Forfar, compared to Dundee, was 9s 8d, most of which was incurred in the transportation of coal, raw materials and stores to Forfar.[80] The company's position was made even more difficult by the imposition by the Board of Trade of uniform minimum wages in the jute industry. The firm's protests were generally made through the Forfar and Kirriemuir Manufacturers' Association. Their complaint was not without foundation, with Dons and Craiks Ltd, another Forfar textile firm, being convinced that they were suffering from unfair competition from Northern Ireland – a 'self governing Dominion' which it was alleged was benefiting from the fact that Board of Trade legislation was not applicable there, thereby making it possible for Irish manufacturers to pay lower wages.[81] The constraints on female workers, which had necessitated the arrangements referred to above, were also felt to be an unwarranted and unhelpful piece of interference on the part of the state: parliament, Dons' directors felt in August 1932, had been 'unduly restrictive in respect of textile factories'. It was not obvious to them 'why it should be worse for a woman to work at a loom after 6 p.m., than to work as a night housemaid, or as a programme seller in a theatre'.[82]

Two main methods of reducing labour costs were adopted by the company. First, where possible, numbers were cut. The reduction from around 700 to 400 at Ward Mills has already been noted. Even with the development of Strang Street, the numbers employed in Forfar fell too during the worst years of the Depression, from 600 in 1930 to 561 in 1933. By 1935, however, the number had begun to rise again, to 693, with the biggest increase coming from the ranks of males under the age of 21 who were employed at Strang Street Mill.[83]

More important for the medium-term as far as costs were concerned was the introduction of the 'Bedaux System of Labour Measurement', a method of work analysis which had been devised by a Belgian, Charles E. Bedaux. The system was based on a series of productivity assessments which then formed the basis of a fixed minimum wage rate. Earnings beyond that figure were dependent upon workers achieving certain output targets, for which bonuses were paid. From the outset – Dons first contact with Bedaux Ltd was in May 1930 – high hopes for the scheme were entertained, with Frank D. J. Buist being co-opted from the board of directors to work with Bedaux Ltd's H. M. Melville-Smith on a full-time basis.[84]

The system was not introduced in Forfar without considerable difficulties. This was not unusual, as worker resistance to it generally was substantial, and frequently resulted in strikes. Dons were faced with one which lasted more than a fortnight.[85]

Another dispute had resulted from an attempt by the company to use an overseer to measure loom output, which was seen by the weavers as an uncalled-for intrusion into their working lives. As a result, the directors decided in September 1931 to fit pick meters on all the looms at St James' to obtain in a more precise manner 'daily records of output . . . to secure the highest efficiency'.[86]

Two further related reasons account for the hostility of workers in Forfar to the Bedaux system. First, workers disliked the young graduates who were employed by Bedaux Ltd to measure their work. Indeed, despite (and also because of) the interest that they had in introducing the system, Dons did share some sympathy with the resentment and mistrust felt by their older experienced hands towards some of the Bedaux employees. If the system was to work, it had to be seen to be fair. This was not the case in November 1930, when mistakes made on behalf of Bedaux Ltd by one of their representatives caused Dons to conclude (and complain) that they could not 'force through any unpopular or revolutionary proposals of his in the way we should certainly otherwise do'.[87] Later, in November 1931, Dons wrote to Bedaux Ltd to demand an explanation of how a Mr Muehleck had arrived at his 'final averaged values', as these appeared to have been fixed 'in an approximate and arbitrary manner'.[88]

The second objection which the workers had was that they perceived the system to be one which was designed to cut their wages. It was an understandable fear, which the directors had to work hard to dispel. They had no choice but to admit that basic rates would be cut. On the other hand, they argued, with the mill and factory reorganisation which had taken place (better yarns, bigger cops, new machinery and semi-automatic attachments on the looms), their weavers could earn more than they had in the past. In order to drive home their point, in March 1932 they compared the earnings of three weavers on four 56–inch looms. The basic pay for this work was 31s, on top of which the weavers had earned bonus payments of 4s 3d, 4s 9d and 5s 9½d respectively. These sums, they claimed, represented weekly increases of approximately 3s over the old method of wage calculation.[89]

Yet despite the initial opposition, the principles of the Bedaux system were adopted by the company, and indeed Dons were on occasion called upon to provide testimonials on its behalf. Where possible, however, Dons preferred to cajole their workers into an acceptance of change rather than enforce it. During a dispute over the measurement of loom output in September 1931, for example, Capt Don had addressed a meeting of 300 female weavers from St James' and argued that it would be in their interests to allow an investigation into their working methods to take place as some of the machines being used had been designed in 1867. Only by this means could the best type to replace them be determined.[90] Throughout his period with the firm (which lasted from 1912 until 1961), Capt Don was at pains to maintain good relations with those on the mill and factory floors.[91] During the 1930s he was assisted in this by the majority of his fellow directors who, for instance, rejected the Dundee custom of working two shifts (of four and a quarter and four and a half hours per day, with four and a quarter hours on a Saturday) in favour of the traditional Forfar system of three three-hourly shifts during the week, on the grounds that they considered a 'yoking' of the length of time in Dundee as 'far too long'.

Indeed Dons, along with some other Forfar firms, arranged for a free issue of tea around 3.30 or 4 p.m., prior to the last hour's work of the day.[92] They took care too to record their appreciation of the efforts of their employees on the company's behalf, with company chairman J. S. Oliver, allegedly the most hard-headed of the directors in labour matters, paying tribute at the AGM in July 1938 to their 'unflagging zeal' and the quality of their work. This was in spite of the fact that the level of wages paid in jute was 'as low as any in the country'.[93] It was not a fact of which anyone was particularly proud, but neither was there a practical alternative.

Chapter Eight: Gloom and Reconstruction

1 DUA, MS 8412 (1), Annual Report of Association of Jute Spinners and Manufacturers, 28 March 1919.
2 *Forfar Dispatch*, 30 November 1916.
3 See *Archibald Don: a memoir* (Privately printed, 1917).
4 Recorded on the family memorial, Newmonthill cemetery, Forfar.
5 Minute Book No 1, 1904 – 44, 8 June 1917, p112.
6 *Forfar Dispatch*, 30 March 1961.
7 Minute Book No 1, 1904 – 44, 1 August 1933, p245.
8 For providing me with selected extracts from some of the letters of J. S. Oliver I am grateful to his son – in – law John Hurst.
9 P. K. Livingstone, *Flax and Linen in Fife Through the Centuries* (Kirkcaldy, 1951), p20.
10 DUA, MS 100/1/2/5, Letter Book, 1899 – 1926, DBB to R. Parker, 19 September 1921.
11 Ibid, John B. Don to R. J. McKeown, 28 December 1921.
12 Ibid, DBB to W. B. Fenton, 9 October 1919.
13 See Minute Book No 1, 1904 – 44, p163.
14 DUA, MS 100/1/2/7, Letter Book, 1927 – 34, DBB to W. B. Erwin, 22 May 1931.
15 DUA, MS 100/1/2/5, Letter Book, 1899 – 1926, DBB to Crawley and Parker, 9 December 1926.
16 DUA, MS 100/1/2/6, Letter Book, 1926 – 29, M. Wallace McDowell & Co to DBB, 13 April 1928, p110.
17 Ibid, 10 May 1928.
18 Ibid.
19 DUA, MS 100/1/2/5, Letter Book, 1899 – 1926, DBB to Crawley & Parker, 9 December 1926.
20 Ibid, DBB to D. E. Anderson, 5 April 1922.
21 DUA, MS 100/1/2/6, Letter Book, 1926 – 1929, W. B. Fenton & Co, 12 April 1928.
22 DUA, MS 100/1/2/5, Letter Book, 1899 – 1926, DBB to Wholesale Textile Association, 30 October 1926.
23 DUA, MS 100/1/2/7, Letter Book, 1927 – 1934, DBB to W. B. Fenton & Co, 12 April 1928.
24 DUA, MS 100/1/2/5, DBB report for AGM, 14 July 1931, pp305 – 6.
25 Ibid, p22.
26 Minute Book No 1, 1904 – 44, J. B. Don to AGM, 14 July 1931, pp305 – 6.
27 Ibid, 234.
28 St James' Works, (copy) letter, J. M. Kellas to DBB, 22 December 1931; see also DUA MS 100/1/9/10.
29 St James' Works, letter, J. B. Don to unknown recipient, 17 June 1933.
30 Minute Book No 1, 1904 – 44, J. B. Don to AGM, 14 July 1931, pp305 – 6.
31 Ibid, 1 July 1927, p198.
32 See DUA, MS 100/1/9/8, DBB internal document, 1930, p2.
33 Ibid, p1.
34 Ibid, pp1 – 2.
35 DUA, MS 100/1/2/7, Letter Book, DBB to AJSM, 9 September 1927.
36 Ibid; See too DUA, MS 84/3/1(3), Minutes of AJSM General Committee, 22 September, 21 October 1927.
37 DUA, MS 100/1/1/2/5, DBB report for AGM, 1930, p2.
38 Watson, *Jute and Flax Mills*, p22.
39 DUA, MS 100/1/2/7, Letter Book, 1927 – 34, DBB to Whittaker Automatic Looms Ltd, 8 May 1929.
40 Ibid, pp138 – 9.
41 DUA, MS 100/1/2/6, Letter Book, 1926 – 29, DBB to FFWU, 29 August 1929.
42 Minute Book No 1, 1904 – 44, 5 July 1929, p211.
43 Ibid, 18 March 1930, p220.
44 Ibid, pp219 – 23.
45 Ibid, J. S. Oliver to AGM, 8 July 1938.
46 Ibid, pp220 – 1.

47 DUA, MS 100/1/1/2/5, DBB report for AGM, 1930, p5.
48 Ibid.
49 Minute Book No 1, 1904 – 44, 30 January 1917, p110.
50 Ibid, 13 August 1929, p214.
51 Ibid, 10 November 1931, p241.
52 Ibid, 23 December 1930, p231.
53 Ibid, 12 July 1932, p248.
54 DUA, MS 100/1/2/7, Letter Book, 1927 – 34, p285.
55 Minute Book No 1, 1904 – 44, L. E. Hill to AGM, 18 July 1933, p309.
56 DUA, MS 100/1/2/7, Letter Book, 1927 – 34, W. G. Don to Mr Cox, 28 March 1934.
57 DUA, MS 100/1/2/8, Letter Book, 1934 – 39, Dundee Chamber of Commerce to DBB, 11 September 1934; 18 May 1935.
58 DUA, MS 100/1/2/7, Letter Book, 1927 – 34, W. G. Don to Mr Cox, 28 March 1934.
59 Minute Book No 1, 1904 – 44, 18 February 1936, p267.
60 Ibid, J. S. Oliver to AGM, 8 July 1938, p318.
61 Ibid, W. G. Don to AGM, 14 July 1936, p315.
62 Ibid, p336.
63 Ibid, J. S. Oliver to AGM, 8 July 1938, p317.
64 Ibid, p318.
65 'Survey of United Kingdom Jute Industry', *The Times Weekly Review* (1952), p8.
66 DUA, MS 100/1/2/7, Letter Book, 1927 – 34, W. G. Don to Alexander Low, 12 August 1932.
67 *Highways and Bridges*, July 1934.
68 DUA, MS 100/1/2/8, Letter Book, 1934 – 39, p42.
69 Minute Book No 1, 1904 – 44, L. E. Hill to AGM, 16 July 1937, p316.
70 Ibid, 4 July 1932, p246.
71 Ibid, 11 July 1933, p253.
72 Ibid, 23 December 1932, pp250 – 1.
73 Ibid, 3 September 1935, p264.
74 Ibid, J. S. Oliver to AGM, 15 July 1938, pp317 – 9.
75 Ibid, see pp341 – 2.
76 DUA, MS 100/1/2/8, Letter Book, 1934 – 39, DBB to unknown recipient, 15 November 1939.
77 Minute Book No 1, 1904 – 44, 15 November 1927, p199.
78 DUA, MS 100/1/2/7, Letter Book, 1927 – 34, DBB to FFWU, 1 September 1933.
79 For the composition for the labour force in Dundee's mills and factories, see E. Gordon, 'Women and the Labour Movement in Scotland 1850 – 1914' (unpublished PhD thesis, University of Glasgow, 1985).
80 DUA, MS 100/1/2/7, Letter Book, 1927 – 34, DBB response to Jute Trade Board questionnaire, October 1933.
81 DUA, MS 100/1/2/8, Letter Book, 1934 – 39, Craiks to DBB (copy), 12 April 1934.
82 DUA, MS 100/1/2/7, Letter Book, 1927 – 34, DBB to Alexander Low, 19 August 1932.
83 St James' Works, Wage Book, 1914 – 48.
84 Minute Book No 1, 1904 – 44, 12 August 1930, p229.
85 DUA, MS 100/1/2/7, Letter Book, 1927 – 34, DBB to W. Wood & Son Ltd, 11 November 1932.
86 Minute Book No 1, 1904 – 44, 10 September 1931, p239.
87 DUA, MS 100/1/2/7, Letter Book, 1927 – 34, DBB to Charles E. Bedaux Ltd, 27 November 1930.
88 Ibid, 27 November 1931.
89 Ibid, DBB to FFWU, March 1932.
90 *Angus Herald*, 24 April 1931.
91 *Forfar Dispatch*, 30 March 1961.
92 DUA, MS 100/1/2/8, Letter Book, 1934 – 39, DBB to Charles Kerr MP, 25 July 1934.
93 Minute Book No 1, 1904 – 44, J. S. Oliver to AGM, 15 July 1938, p319.

'Benholm', Glamis Rd, Forfar. A former mansion-house, the property was purchased by Dons in 1948 and converted into a hostel for women from outside Forfar, at a time of labour shortages

Dining-room of 'Benholm', Glamis Rd, Forfar, in the early 1950s. There was room for 38 women, most of whom slept in dormitories

Chapter Nine

War and Peace, 1939–*c*.1960

As the outbreak of hostilities became imminent, orders burgeoned for jute products, chiefly sandbags, and at the AGM in July 1939 F. D. J. Buist was able to report a 'substantial improvement' in the affairs of the company. The brighter situation is reflected in Dons' profit and loss accounts, which show that in 1938–39 profit levels were higher than they had been since 1927–28. Table 9.1 reveals that steady if unspectacular profits continued to be made throughout the period of the Second World War.

Table 9.1 *Profit (and Loss) Accounts (£), Don Bros, Buist & Co Ltd, 1938–39 – 1944–45*

Year	Balance (31 May)	Carried Forward
1938–39	17,811	10,261
1939–40	24,312	16,262
1940–41	40,663	25,613
1941–42	39,860	24,810
1942–43	46,628	19,223
1943–44	35,713	23,308
1944–45	37,842	25,437

Source: Minute Book No 1, 1904–44; Minute Book No 2, 1945–55.

In fact, these figures somewhat understate the company's real financial condition, which was good enough to enable the directors to build up substantial cash reserves. Even with higher wartime taxes, sums of between £40,000 and £60,000 a year were being deposited into reserve accounts during the war.[1]

This was in spite of the fact that in the final years of the conflict the company was working at only half capacity; in common with the rest of the jute industry on Tayside, Dons found their activities constrained by severe labour shortages from 1943, mainly owing to the manpower requirements of the armed services. As in the First World War, the directorate was depleted too, and with F. D. J. Buist and J. S. Oliver on war service, only Capt Don and Col Hill were left of the pre-war board. In order to boost the numbers, and to utilise their experience, both the ageing J. C. Buist and John B. Don were brought back on to the board in 1939, although Buist died in August 1944. Don died shortly after the war, in April 1946.

In 1946 prognostications on the jute industry were overwhelmingly gloomy,[2] though Dons appear to have been notably less concerned for the future than most of their counterparts. In August 1944 for instance, looking forward to the return of peace, Capt Don remarked that in spite of all the 'war troubles etc' the financial position of the company was sound, and they were 'well set to take advantage of any post-war demands that may arise'.[3]

Ideally, this chapter should be concerned with the company's wartime operations and the first 15 post-war years. With the acquisition in 1960 of the Dundee firm of merchants, Low Brothers & Co (Dundee) Ltd, a new era in the company's history began. Few records from the period 1939 to 1945 have survived, however, and minute-book entries are brief. Accordingly, the bulk of what follows deals with the immediate post-war years, during which, in one form or another, Jute Control was in existence. There seems little doubt that without this and the import protection it provided, the jute industry in Scotland would have been virtually eliminated.[4] As will be seen, Dons benefited enormously from its functions, especially in the 1940s and early 1950s. Yet it can reasonably be argued that partly owing to the reorganisation which they had undertaken in the 1930s, especially with regard to the establishment of an integrated works in Forfar, Dons were in a better condition than most to take advantage of Jute Control. Their product range was such that they depended somewhat less than other firms upon the protection it provided for 'standard' goods, in which Indian competition was more intense. What is clear, however, is that like much of the rest of the textile industry on Tayside, Dons acted positively behind the protective barrier and ensured that when the functions of Jute Control were finally ended in 1969, they were well prepared to face the colder winds which freer market conditions brought in their wake.

Dons and Jute Control

Jute Control was set up by the government at the outbreak of the war in September 1939, and continued for three decades. Essentially, it was a means of protecting the UK industry from Indian competition, and although originally concerned only with raw jute, by 1942 it had also become the sole importer and seller of jute goods, with profits from sales being used to subsidise raw jute purchases. A licensing system for spinners and weavers was introduced, as too were controls over the end-uses of jute and the prices which could be charged at each stage in the manufacturing process. Production quotas were set with remarkable precision. In September 1950, for example, Jute Control sought to increase the quantity of British hand-made hessians available to the domestic market, only half of which was then being supplied by British manufacturers. Their proposal for the achievement of this was that hessian manufacturers should work an extra 36 minutes overtime.[5]

Unlike most wartime regulations, however, Jute Control remained in being long after hostilities had ceased, although by the time it finished considerable relaxation and amendment of its functions had taken place. In September 1952, for instance, the jute cover scheme was wound up. This had been designed to protect manufacturers against stock losses caused by customers who had failed to take up their orders. More importantly, in 1954, trading in raw jute was returned to private hands.

Nevertheless, a Board of Trade report on jute in 1946 had argued that such was the severity of competition from Calcutta that some form of protection was necessary if the industry was to survive. There was considerable concern, especially in Labour Party circles, about the level of unemployment in Dundee and district which would result from a resumption of unregulated trade. In return for continued protection, the industry was required to undergo a programme of re-equipment and reorganisation, with small firms amalgamating to ensure a minimum size of 15,000 new-type spindles. Protection was in the hands of

Jute Control, which operated a scale of duties the rate of which depended on the type of yarn and cloth in question. In this, as will be seen, Dons played an important role. There was some flexibility in the system, with Jute Control adjusting the prices of imported jute goods on the basis of 'equated prices', or 'mark-up prices', which was the preferred standard after 1957. 'Mark-up prices' were determined by the landed prices of imported goods, with the mark-up price reducing over time: thus in the mid-1950s it stood at around 47 per cent; in July 1957 it was set at 30 per cent; and in January 1960 it was cut to 20 per cent.[6] In May 1969 all imported jute goods which had been subject to Jute Control were freed from restrictions.

One consequence of protection had been the establishment by Dundee producers of price agreements, which were facilitated by the necessity of Jute Control to publish the prices of imported goods. These arrangements, however, which had taken the form of seven registered trade agreements, were declared to be against the public interest by the Restrictive Practices Court in March 1963, and thereby provided the industry with another competitive spur, although not immediately.[7] Reluctant to give up its privileges without a fight, the industry's leaders set up the Jute Information Bureau, the function of which was to provide participating firms with lists of each others' prices, which, it was claimed somewhat unconvincingly, left them 'free to charge their own price'.[8] The Bureau was given up in February 1966.

One of the most important functions of Jute Control was its intervention in the raw jute market, which provided an element of price stability which had not existed beforehand. Nevertheless, even with Jute Control, jute supplies were uncertain and subject to sharp price fluctuations in the troubled political conditions which followed the Second World War.

Indian independence and partition in 1947 caused considerable concern in Dundee and Forfar as most raw jute was grown in East Pakistan, while the mills and baling stations where the jute was processed were situated in and around Calcutta. Jute prices rose dramatically. Prior to the war the price of a ton of jute was in the region of £20. Although this had doubled to £43 in the immediate post-war years, by 1948 it had risen to £100 a ton.[9] The outbreak of the Korean War made matters worse by driving the price up to the unprecedented level of £275 a ton (in April 1951). In the financial year 1951–52 Dons' raw materials bill rose from £635,657 to £939,159, the equivalent of almost 70 per cent of their sales income.[10] Previously raw materials had accounted for under 50 per cent of sales income. This was partly the result of stockpiling on the part of the USA, in response to global conflict or their expectation of it. Thus the Suez crisis brought 'violent' price rises, while news in 1961 that the USSR was testing atomic weapons led the USA to buy up vast quantities of hessian for sandbags.

After 1954, when responsibility for jute purchases was back in the company's hands, a combination of foresight, business acumen and good fortune on the part of their buyer, D. L. Urquhart (see below), was required if adequate supplies were to be maintained at reasonable prices. Indeed in both 1961 and 1965, considerable stock profits were made by Dons through the purchase of 'spot' and 'afloat' jute just before major price rises took place, in the latter instance owing to the renewal of hostilities between India and Pakistan.[11]

Although Jute Control could make little impression where the sharpest price rises were concerned, they could do something when circumstances were less volatile. In 1949, for example, owing to the situation in the jute-growing and shipment region, Calcutta prices fluctuated between £70 and £120 a ton; Jute Control, however, was able to provide British users with raw jute at £90 per ton.[12]

The most important contribution of Jute Control was that it freed spinners and manufacturers from the necessity of holding large stocks of raw materials, and thereby reduced significantly the costs this incurred. The fact that Jute Control carried the bulk of the jute trade's stocks was worth considerable sums of money to Dons, as the directors recognised in 1948:

> Raw Jute is now more than five times the pre-war price, and had the company to carry and finance its existing pre-war working stock at today's prices, this would not only require all the present surplus of liquid resources, but an additional £200,000.[13]

In these circumstances the company was able to double its cash reserves, which had risen to £200,000 by 1951–52. This was almost wholly due to the operation of Jute Control, which enabled them to purchase only what jute they required to meet current orders, plus a bit more. Instead of six months' or even a year's supply, which it was not unusual for Dons to be carrying, in 1950 the maximum they were required to stock was eight weeks' supply, the minimum four. With the withdrawal of Jute Control from the raw jute market, however, companies once more had to arrange their own supplies and on 8 October 1954 Dons' first private post-war shipment of raw jute arrived in Dundee aboard the SS *City of Stafford*.[14] With the continuation of protection, however, and the likelihood that manufacturers would be assured 'of a fair share of the home market', Dons were not unduly worried about the future.

A time for 'study and experiment', c.1945–54

With Jute Control carrying what Capt Don called 'our former burdens', along with the rest of the jute trade, Dons found themselves relieved somewhat from the cut and thrust of normal business conditions. This lull provided an opportunity for them to engage in 'study and experiment'.[15] Dons were in a rather more fortunate position in this regard than many of their rivals, for the reorganisation of their operations and the introduction of much new machinery in the late 1920s and the 1930s spared them the 'crippling expense' of such activity 'at inflated post-war prices'.[16] Between 1945 and 1951 an estimated £4 million was spent by the industry on re-equipping.[17] Little of this came from Dons, who concentrated their attentions on ways of utilising raw jute more efficiently, adapting and improving existing machinery and developing new product lines.

There was investment in new machinery, though, but this came towards the end of the period. Dons were one of the first companies in the region to order and install Ecco looms with automatic shuttle loaders. Also introduced during the autumn of 1952 were some Schweiter automatic cop machines, which were said to have caused a 'substantial' drop in the quantity of cop waste produced by shuttle loading.[18] An additional eight Ecco looms were in use by 1953, and more followed thereafter.

These machines had three main advantages over their predecessors: they were more efficient; they were wider, up to 126 inches; and as many as four could be operated by a single weaver.

Before 1953 little additional capital was laid out on Strang Street. Instead, efforts were made to ensure that the company's reputation for spinning high-grade yarns was maintained. Jute Control paid little attention to the quality of jute they sent out and on occasion there were difficulties for Dons in achieving their preferred mix of batches which, in the case of dark jute, comprised 40 per cent 'Crack Daisee' (or Dundee Tossa) and 60 per cent 'Grade Daisee' (otherwise known as Continental Tossa). The white jute varieties were 'Mill Firsts' and 'Mill Lightnings', of which similar proportions were desirable.

Costs were also examined, and ways sought to reduce them. A partial answer in the short-term was to make greater use of salvaged jute, and experiments with this were conducted in 1953 following the purchase in April of jute salvaged after a fire on the SS *City of Colchester*. The advantage of buying such jute, of course, was that although it was damp, it could be obtained at a hefty discount. The 165 tons which were bought by Dons cost them only £11,900, compared to the current market price of £14,850.[19] As this quantity of jute was sufficient to make up 924 bales, and the company was using some 605 bales a week at that time, purchases of imperfect jute were judged to be worth making, when possible.

A much more pressing problem which faced Dons immediately after the war was an acute labour shortage – in stark contrast to the situation which had prevailed a few years earlier. The principal factor governing the volume of production, according to Capt Don in 1947, was 'not limitation of demand, but scarcity of labour'. He would have had the sympathy of earlier generations of the firm's leaders when he added that this was 'particularly during summer months when outside work was most attractive'.[20]

Nor was the shortage easily or quickly overcome, either in Forfar or Dundee, as former jute workers turned their back on the industry. As late as September 1953 the percentage of the insured population unemployed in Forfar (and Kirriemuir) stood at 0.7, compared to 3 per cent in Dundee and 3.4 per cent in Scotland as a whole. It was a serious situation; Dons' inability to recruit tenters in June 1953, for instance, meant that the company could not increase the number of looms.[21]

Various steps were taken by a number of firms in and around Dundee both to hold what labour they had and to attract new recruits. Within Dons' works, in 1947, under the supervision of J. S. Oliver, Works Councils were set up, partly to give workers more direct access to the managers and directors. Working conditions were also improved in an attempt to make mill and factory workers more comfortable. In September 1953, following the examples of Low & Bonar at their Eagle Mills, and Jute Industries at Manhattan Works, both in Dundee, Dons began to look into means of installing 'artificial humidification' into their works. For precisely the same reason in October 1954 the company began laying 'sound deadening' tiles at their weaving factories.[22] Priority was given to the maintenance of good labour relations. The loyalty of those who were already employed by the company was rewarded on the occasion of the 50th anniversary of its limited liability status with the payment of an extra week's wages, while later, in January 1960, a similar payment was made by way of apology by the company to its workers for the disruption which had been caused by the reorganisation.[23]

In order to attract new recruits to the area, especially younger women who had traditionally formed the backbone of the jute industry's workforce, in 1948 Dons purchased 'Benholm', a mansion-house in Glamis Road, Forfar, for use as a hostel. Initially designed to house 20 workers, by 1951 it had been adapted for 38 women, who paid a weekly rent of between 30 and 33 shillings.[24] The other side of the coin was that Dons (who had had to create a pool of reserve weavers to replace absentees) could afford to extend little sympathy towards the efforts of those outside the jute trade who were attempting to generate alternative forms of employment in the vicinity of their works, either in Forfar or Dundee. In 1951 representations to Forfar Town Council were made by 'certain Forfar manufacturers' concerning permission which had recently been given for the erection of a fruit-canning factory on the south-west end of Forfar loch.[25]

Perhaps the most important departure for the company in the immediate post-war period was the manufacture on a large scale of lightweight jute scrim. 'Narrow scrims' had been produced in Forfar in the eighteenth century, prior to the introduction of osnaburgs, and by the late Victorian era they had become identified with the town. When Dons first made this type of cloth is not certain. During the late 1930s, however, they had begun to establish themselves as makers of lighter weights of jute cloth for industrial end-uses and there are indications that it was at this time that the company began to make narrow scrims. Twentieth-century scrim was used primarily by the building trade, where it served as a backing for insulating material, and also found uses in roofing felts and damp courses and as plasterer's scrim. For Dons this was a sensible production strategy, for lightweight jute scrims could be made on their older light linen looms, modified for the purpose by their own engineering staff.

Scrim is an open weave fabric, and in appearance takes the form of a grid of varying dimensions. Dons made three main sorts. The most popular was described as 4oz/40, meaning that a yard of this cloth, 40 inches wide, weighed four ounces. From the mid-1950s demand grew for a 3oz/40, while in addition, and virtually alone of all the textile firms in the region (although both W. G. Grant and R. G. Kennedy also made scrim), Dons made a scrim cloth composed of only two warp and two weft threads per square inch, which weighed only one and a half ounces, called No. 15 scrim.[26] Generally speaking, the lighter the scrim, the more profitable it was.

This cloth was Dons' speciality during the 1940s, 1950s and early 1960s, and indeed it remained a profitable product even when the company moved into the field of synthetic fabrics. Its attractiveness meant that not only did it account for a major part of Dons' total production (the average annual output of cloth in the 1950s was 4,745 tons), but also that the company could keep their looms working when downturns in demand were forcing temporary layoffs elsewhere. Over 100 looms at Station Works were employed in weaving scrim, each of which produced between 2,000 to 3,000 yards each week, depending on weight. Thus in February 1952, a time of general economic depression, and when Jute Control had instructed companies not to make goods unless they had received orders for them, Dons were able to maintain full production on those looms which were turning out scrim for the building industry.[27] Cloth sales as a whole were of increasing importance to Dons; whereas in 1945–46, 62.6 per cent of the company's sales revenue had come from cloth (the rest from yarn), by 1951–52 the proportion had risen to 93.9 per cent.

Yet their success in this regard, and especially light narrow scrims, was not wholly due to the company's achievements on the factory floor. In the post-war years, Col Hill played a leading part on the Association of Jute Spinners and Manufacturers' Price Committee, which negotiated with Jute Control – and jute merchants – to determine yarn and cloth prices. It is entirely conceivable that Hill's involvement with the AJSM (he was the chairman of the Price Committee from 1947) and the detailed information he was able to gather about the jute trade reinforced his belief in Dons' strategy of concentrating on 'specialties'. The industry's state-regulated profits arrangements meant that it was the firms which depended heavily on the 10oz/40-inch common hessians which struggled to keep their heads above water. As has been seen, even before the war Dons specialised in rather lighter weights, such as 8oz/40. What is beyond doubt is that Dons as well as much of the rest of the jute industry on Tayside owed much to Hill's knowledgeable and energetic chairmanship of the Price Committee – in which role, amongst other things, he co-ordinated the views of member firms, put their case forcefully to the Board of Trade, and vigorously upheld local price agreements and chastised those who broke them.[28]

Such was the value of scrim to Dons that they were encouraged to make every effort to maximise the efficiency of its production. Indeed, one element in the success of the product was the fact that Dons were not only able to deliver it in very long rolls, but also that these were tightly packed and fluff-free. These features were the result of a modification made to the conventional rolling gear, which involved adding a driven pressing roller to the head of the machine.[29] A further innovation in scrim production was introduced in the autumn of 1954. The beams on the looms weaving No. 15 scrim were removed and the machines adapted to weave from spool strippings on small banks attached to the back of the looms. Previously the spools had been put on the spindles manually by women who drew their supplies from barrows. This in-house modification, which made possible long uninterrupted production runs, led to remarkable efficiencies from the best weavers calculated at 95 to 96 per cent.[30]

Managers and directors

These major but easily overlooked innovations were in large part the result of careful observation and practical experimentation on the part of the company's senior employees. The pressing roller modification for example was one of many technical contributions made by Frank M. Thomson, works manager at St James' up to 1949, but who had been employed by Dons since he began his apprenticeship with them in 1898. The improvements to the No. 15 scrim looms were masterminded by E. W. 'Ed' Lee (along with Col Hill), when he was head of the weaving department. Lee had begun his working life as a soaper in a barber's shop, before entering the jute trade an apprentice mechanic. Similarly, Addison G. 'Ed' Stewart, for a time Lee's under-manager and who also served under Thomson, had entered the trade at the bottom in 1936 as an apprentice fitter with Moffat & Sons, jute manufacturers in Forfar, where his mother had been a weaver. He was identified by J. S. Oliver and Col Hill as a young man of considerable technical ability, and was invited to join Dons as a draughtsman after the Second World War (during which he served as an instructor in the Royal Engineers). Ultimately Stewart was to become the company's chief engineer, responsible for all of its plants during the 1970s, prior to his retirement in 1982.

Indeed, the role which was played by the company's employees in achieving improvements in production methods had become increasingly important from the time that W. G. and John Don had erected their first weaving sheds at St James' and extended Ward Mills. The contribution, for example, of Gilbert Fraser, Ward Mills' manager for many years until he retired in 1924 (after 38 years of employment with Dons), was recognised in the size of his annual pension, £400. Relatively little, unfortunately, can be discovered about such individuals from the company's records. One of the rare occasions when their role was publicly acknowledged was at the AGM in 1950 when it was argued that there was no need for concern over the fact that Capt W. G. Don and Col L. E. Hill would remain as the sole managing directors as Don Bros, Buist & Co Ltd possessed 'a highly trained staff fully capable of carrying on the daily routine management'.[31]

Yet at the level of the directorate there was continued involvement in the practical operations of the company's works. The abrasive J. S. Oliver, for example, who became company chairman in 1961, sought constantly for ways to obtain machine and other efficiencies, while Col Hill oversaw much of the technical development needed to keep the company at the forefront of the industry, and was closely involved with Frank Thomson in the development of the pressing roller.

New faces were needed though, both on the board and in management. David L. Urquhart (1912–1975) became a director in 1952 following six years' service with the company which had begun in 1946, after having qualified as a chartered accountant, and spending ten years with a firm of accountants in London. Initially company secretary, he took over sole responsibility for purchasing the firm's raw jute around 1953, and throughout his career kept a scrupulous watch over the company's income and expenditure. Unusually amongst the ranks of the directors of Tayside's jute firms, Urquhart was also a Labour Party member, and deeply involved in local politics. He was not averse though to treading on the national stage, especially where the jute industry was concerned, and on two occasions he became chairman of the AJSM.[32] Not a man to mince his words, he condemned what he called the 'Suez escapade' on the grounds that it had 'cost us dear in prestige and in business to the Arab world', and early in 1958 castigated the influence of the south of England MPs whom he believed had been behind the Board of Trade's decision to relax tariffs on Indian sacks. Dundee and district employed 20,000 people, Urquhart argued, whose future had been 'jeopardised in favour of possible help to small sack-sewing English firms', who employed only 1,500.[33]

He was elected as Provost of Forfar in 1956, becoming the third member of Dons to do so; J. W. Adamson had held the office between 1901 and 1906, while Col Hill followed for a similar length of time, between 1937 and 1942. Although an outsider, Urquhart, who was ennobled on the recommendation of Prime Minister Harold Wilson in 1967 to become Lord Tayside, was appointed as company chairman in August 1966 and continued in the post until his death in March 1975. In his rise to prominence within the company, Urquhart was accompanied by Francis Gerald Anderson. Anderson was the son of David E. Anderson, who had been the company's Manchester agent earlier in the century. He joined his father in business in 1920 and succeeded to it after the latter's death in 1931. He had first become directly linked with Dons in 1934, when he joined the company's sales staff, coming north to Forfar in 1937. During the war he served with the Black Watch, but in 1947 he was appointed sales manager, and joined the board in 1952, at the same time as Urquhart. The two men were leading directors in 1960 when Low Brothers were amalgamated with Dons.

Col Hill, a dominant force in the company from the 1930s, had retired in 1955. While the ageing Capt Don carried on as company chairman until 1961, he had by that time withdrawn from day-to-day involvement in the firm's affairs.

The management team, however, had been further strengthened in 1952 with the appointment as assistant company secretary of Ernest S. Gourlay, a Glasgow-trained chartered accountant who was promoted to the rank of company secretary in 1954. He later held directorships of some of the company's subsidiaries until becoming a director of the holding company (see below) in 1979.

The family presence within the firm remained strong. The Don interest on the board was strengthened by the presence of J. G. S. Gammell, Gilbert Don's grandson (through his father's marriage to John B. Don's sister Gertrude), an accountant who became a director in 1957, although his involvement with Dons was relatively short-lived and somewhat controversial. He was joined (though not without a struggle) by his near contemporary John Gavin Don (b.1927), Capt Don's son, who sat on the board until 1973. Col Hill's son Michael Henry James (b.1929), a Cambridge-educated chemist who had worked for a time with Boots, also joined the company (in 1954) and became a director in 1958. The Buists were represented by Frank Buist's nephew, John B. Watson, who joined the board as a non-executive director.

Concentration in Forfar: departure from Ward Mills, c.1954–60

With the ending of Jute Control's involvement in the purchase of jute in 1954 and the return of the responsibility for this to individual firms, there was a greater onus on them to improve their spinning efficiency, even though the home market continued to be protected. This, D. L. Urquhart urged, should be a matter of great rejoicing in Forfar, where jute was still the main industry and the largest employer of labour.[34] Even though the industry established a series of pricing agreements, it was clearly in the company's interest to reduce its production costs as far as possible. During the later 1950s a new competitive threat emerged in the shape of the proposed Common Market, which would have put the Scottish jute industry on an even footing with the advancing jute industries of France, Belgium and Germany. Ultimately, of course, and to the relief of the jute trade, Britain remained outside the 'Six', and instead joined the European Free Trade Association.

Urquhart's stress on Forfar was significant – and entirely appropriate – for in December 1947 the firm's head office was transferred from Ward Mills to St James' Road. With something like three-quarters of Dons' jute yarn being spun in the county town, and all of its weaving operations located there, this was a logical step. Accordingly, most of the new investment and innovation which occurred from around 1954 was based in Forfar. In 1954 itself, for example, the company's works were connected to the national electricity grid, replacing the private electrical generating system which had been used to supply St James' (and parts of Strang Street Mill and Station Works) since 1910. This change was expensive, and required in the region of £50,000 to achieve.[35] It was, however, a step which to a large extent was forced on the company, as spare parts for the ageing brush turbine could no longer be obtained. Dons took full advantage of the situation by fitting each loom with an individual motor, instead of running them off a belt drive from a main shaft, which brought important efficiency gains.

Some re-equipment at Strang Street had taken place prior to 1954, notably with the introduction of Fraser Roll Formers, made by Douglas Fraser & Sons of Arbroath. During 1956 and 1957 Strang Street Mill was almost entirely re-equipped and a 'sliver

Jute bales in raw jute store prior to preparation, Strang Street Works, Forfar, early 1950s

spinning' system introduced. Essentially this meant that whereas beforehand there were three stages between carding and winding – drawing, roving and spinning – there were now only two, with the roving process being eliminated. Reforms were introduced at St James' too, from the middle of 1955. The major problem with the factory was its 'multiplicity of rooms and departments', which made it unsuitable for housing such new looms as they bought, which were also capable of producing the more profitable long rolls of cloth. Accordingly, a 'spate' of building work took place at St James'. By 1960 the company had spent in the region of quarter of a million pounds on rebuilding and re-equipping its Forfar plants.

The rewards from the modernisation programme were substantial, and in 1959, when many Dundee firms were on short time, Dons were able to maintain production. As Table 9.2 shows, 1959–60 was the company's most profitable post-war year to date.

Table 9.2 *Don Bros, Buist & Co, Profit (and Loss) Accounts (£), 1946–47 – 1959–60.*

Year	Balance (at 31 May)	Carried Forward
1946–47	25,106	20,431
1947–48	46,813	37,463
1948–49	113,004	21,104
1949–50	57,792	22,943
1950–51	58,590	24,452
1951–52	49,845	17,548
1952–53	37,268	21,277
1953–54	99,957	24,914
1954–55	90,937	27,252
1955–56	108,385	28,571
1956–57	118,277	27,929
1957–58	81,040	21,285
1958–59	83,842	23,335
1959–60	126,785	28,555

Source: Minute Book No 2, 1945–55, and Annual Accounts, St James' Works, Forfar.

However, the best evidence for the success of the programme comes from the table below, which distinguishes Strang Street from Ward Mills.

Table 9.3 *Don Bros, Buist & Co Ltd, Spinning Output (Tons), Strang Street and Ward Mills, showing Profit (and Loss) (£) per Ton, 1951–52 to 1960–61.*

Year	Total Yarn	Ward Mills	Pft (Loss)	Strang Street	Pft (Loss)
1951–52	4,259	789	6.82	3,470	0.991
1952–53	3,917	877	(14.44)	3,040	(7.55)
1953–54	4,998	960	(9.39)	4,038	4.74
1954–55	5,078	1,179	(5.11)	3,899	11.91
1955–56	5,462	1,314	4.17	4,148	11.41
1956–57	5,657	1,323	5.03	4,334	13.94
1957–58	4,683	1,279	2.07	3,404	(8.41)
1958–59	4,902	242	–	4,660	5.17
1959–60	6,234	–	–	6,234	17.28
1960–61	5,938	–	–	5,938	30.12

Source: Annual Accounts, St James' Works, Forfar

Jute preparation department at Strang Street Works in the early 1950s. Earlier, it was at this stage that water and whale oil were sprinkled on to the raw jute to soften it. In the 1920s Dons were ardent opponents of whale oil as it gave the finished product an unpleasant smell

Drawing department of Strang Street Works, early 1950s. The machines on the right were built by James Mackie & Sons Ltd, Belfast, major suppliers of machinery to the Dundee and Angus textile industry

While profits per ton were greater at Strang Street throughout, these leapt substantially after 1958–59, when most of the planned modernisation had taken place, and by 1959–60 had surpassed £30.

The company's improved performance at the end of the 1950s can be seen too in Table 9.4, which shows sales revenue from both cloth and yarn from 1945–46 to 1960–61.

Table 9.4 *Don Bros, Buist & Co Ltd, Sales Revenue (£), Cloth and Yarn, 1945–46 – 1959–60.*

Year	Total Income	Cloth Sales	Yarn Sales
1945–46	656,925	411,660	245,265
1946–47	837,811	478,933	358,878
1947–48	805,298	685,205	120,093
1948–49	802,659	666,217	136,442
1949–50	na	na	na
1950–51	1,018,567	920,806	97,761
1951–52	1,342,513	1,260,909	81,604
1952–53	807,827	797,998	9,829
1953–54	1,042,100	1,018,647	23,453
1954–55	1,095,447	1,087,269	8,208
1955–56	1,076,796	1,067,763	9,034
1956–57	1,165,181	1,156,871	8,310
1957–58	1,092,997	1,085,821	7,176
1958–59	1,157,570	1,134,707	22,863
1959–60	1,459,777	1,305,984	153,793

Source: Annual Accounts, St James' Works, Forfar

After running at just over £1 million per annum for most of the 1950s, total income rose sharply after 1957–58, to just below 1.5 million. Significantly, a respectable proportion of the increased income came from sales of yarn made in Forfar.

What is clear from Table 9.3 is that by comparison, the performance of Ward Mills was poor, even though yarn output had almost doubled between 1951–52 and 1956–57, and some cost efficiencies had been obtained by scrapping the mill's steam engines and replacing them with motorised engines fitted to drive the line shafting for each flat individually. In fact, the company's commitment to Ward Mills had waned substantially

Coping department, Strang Street Works, early 1950s

by this time. Attention has already been drawn to the first visible sign, in the early 1930s, that Dons were inclined to favour Forfar rather than Dundee as the company's main production base. In 1950 there was further consideration by the board of whether to let more of their Ward Mills property, and eventually it was decided that the Old Mill building was surplus to requirements.[36] During 1951 and into 1952 though, Ward Mills did better, spinning not only the firm's own waste jute, but from November 1951, also that of other companies. At a time of high jute prices this was an extremely profitable operation, for jute waste could be obtained for around £40–£50 per ton, compared to the £200 plus which was the going rate for a ton of raw jute.

With the subsequent fall in raw jute prices, however, Ward Mills' future again became uncertain and understandably, worker morale was low. The sale of machinery in 1952 and 1953 did nothing to allay fears for the future, although for Dons, machinery sales were a profitable sideline. In February 1933, for example, Dons sold two Ayrton Cone Winding Machines from Ward Mills to J. & L. F. Goodbody in Eire for £3,000. Their original cost, in 1933, had been £840.

These Schweiter automatic cop winding machines were first introduced in 1951, and reduced considerably the amount of cop waste produced by shuttle loading. Strang Street Works, 1960s

By the mid-1950s Ward Mills had become a loss-making operation. Improvements in performance were obtained for the most part not by new investment – in 1951 the possibility by putting in more second-hand machinery was considered – but rather by modifying existing equipment, cutting down on waste and instigating work studies, although in this last regard Dons were by no means alone. Throughout the industry close attention was being paid to ways in which shop-floor efficiency could be improved. Further gains in productivity were in fact achieved by this means, with the workforce being cut in 1953 from 109 to 80, half of its immediate post-war level, following recommendations by Associated Industrial Consultants Ltd, a company which had been contracted by the AJSM in 1950 to undertake a 'base rate analysis' of the jute industry in Dundee. That this should be done was of vital importance in persuading the government to provide support for the industry.

As far as hours, wages and conditions in Forfar were concerned, Dons were their own masters, inasmuch as these were agreed by the Forfar and Kirriemuir Manufacturers'

Finishing (calendaring) department. The calendar was completed in 1872. St James' Works, Forfar, early 1950s

Weaving shed, narrow looms. Note how cramped conditions were and contrast with St James' after the Sulzer looms were introduced. St James' Works, early 1950s

Pressing rollers, St James' Works. Dons' tight and neat rolls of cloth gave them a considerable advantage in the marketplace

Association. Jute trade matters in general and Dundee wage rates, which were to be standardised throughout the district, were the province of the Dundee-based AJSM, of which, as has been seen, Dons were also prominent members. In a sense, membership of both gave them the best of the two worlds, as they were privy to AJSM decisions concerning the industry as a whole, yet they were able through the FKMA to enjoy 'autonomy in all local matters', including wage rates.[37] This, however, did not apply to any manufacturing Dons carried on in Dundee.

Consequently, and reluctantly, on 29 August 1958, the directors decided to close Ward Mills and concentrate all production in Forfar. The crucial short-term consideration was the decision by Jute Control in July 1957 to reduce the mark-up price on imported hessians from 47 to 30 per cent. At the end of 1961, by which time Dons had been associated with Ward Mills for almost a century, the mills and the land upon which they stood had been sold off. F. R. Evans (Leeds) Ltd acquired the

Switchgear for the works' electrical generating system, which Dons had introduced in 1910. It was not until 1954 that Dons' Forfar works were connected to the national grid. St James' Works, early 1950s

mill area for £39,000, while Robertsons Ltd, house furnishers, bought the site of the old pond for £10,000. The directors decided that the total profit of £85,959 should be distributed amongst the company's shareholders.[38]

Chapter Nine: War and Peace

1 Minute Book No 1, 1904–44, p354, p356, p358, p361.
2 Howe, *Dundee Textiles*, pp17–22.
3 Minute Book No 1, 1904–44, W. G. Don to AGM, 11 August 1944, p326.
4 See Howe, *Dundee Textiles*, pp163–4.
5 Minute Book No 2, 1945–55, 13 September 1950, p66.
6 J. M. Jackson, 'Leading Industries', in J. M. Jackson (ed), *The Third Statistical Account of Scotland; The City of Dundee* (Arbroath, 1979), p110.
7 Ibid, p111.
8 Minute Book No 4, 1961–66, 19 April 1962, p282.
9 Minute Book No 2, 1945–55, W. G. Don to AGM, 8 September 1948, p346.
10 Figures prepared for 1952 AGM.
11 Minute Book No 4, 1961–5, 16 June 1961, p226; 10 September 1965, p390.
12 Minute Book No 2, 1945–55, W. G. Don to AGM, 7 September 1947, p349.
13 Ibid, 16 August 1948, p26.
14 Ibid, 14 October 1954, p210.
15 *Forfar Dispatch*, 13 January 1949.
16 Minute Book No 2, W. G. Don to AGM, 17 September 1952, p363.
17 Howe, *Dundee Textiles*, p18.
18 Minute Book No 2, 1945–55, 12 October 1951, p106.
19 Ibid, 16 September 1954, p206.
20 Ibid, W. G. Don to AGM, 19 August 1947, p343.
21 Ibid, 18 June 1953, p167.
22 Ibid, 14 October 1954, p210.
23 Ibid, 15 October 1954, p193; *Forfar Dispatch*, 21 January 1960.
24 Minute Book No 2, 1945–55, 14 January 1948, pp22–3; W. G. Don to AGM, 8 September 1948, p346.
25 Ibid, 18 January 1951, p80.
26 I am grateful to Mr Michael Hill for his attempts to familiarise me with the complexities of the scrim market.
27 Minute Book No 2, 1945–55, 20 February 1952, p118.
28 DUA, MS 84/5/4, Association of Jute Spinners and Manufacturers, Transfer Book, Miscellaneous Section, 1936–52, includes minutes of Price Committee, and see for example entry for 1 May 1952.
29 Information provided by Mr M. Hill.
30 Minute Book No 2, 1945–55, 18 November 1952, p218; I have also benefited greatly from discussions I have had with Ed Stewart on this subject.
31 Minute Book No 2, Report of AGM, 13 September 1950, p353.
32 *Dundee Courier*, 13 March 1975.
33 *Forfar Dispatch*, 9 January 1958.
34 Ibid, 6 January 1955.
35 Minute Book No 2, 1945–55, 10 September 1954, p203.
36 Ibid, 15 November 1950, p71.
37 Ibid, 16 August 1948, p29.
38 Minute Book No 4, 1961–65, p221; 19 May 1961, p224; 12 January 1962, p242.

Chapter Ten

Low Brothers and Diversification, 1960–65

The 1950s had been a decade of not inconsiderable reorganisation and modernisation for Dons. In lighter jute cloth and scrims they had a saleable specialist product range (the best of its sort, according to a one-time employee of a rival company), which was geared towards industrial users. They had made respectable profits, which on average had doubled between the three years 1950–53, and 1957–60. Furthermore, between 1953–54 and 1960–61 the company had been in a position to build up substantial reserves, with an average of £55,363 per annum being set aside for this purpose.[1] The sums ranged from the equivalent of 8.7 per cent of sales, in 1953–54, to 3 per cent in 1957–58 and 1958–59. Cloth output too had risen over the course of the decade, as is shown in Table 10.1. Margins, though, were tightening.

Table 10.1 *Don Bros, Buist & Co Ltd, Cloth Output (tons) with Profit (and Loss) per ton, 1950–51 to 1959–60.*

Year	Output (tons)	Profit (Loss) per ton (£)
1950–51	4,048	16.41
1951–52	4,098	14.09
1952–53	3,848	19.85
1953–54	4,751	27.86
1954–55	4,943	21.30
1955–56	5,168	22.02

1956–57	5,279	20.90
1957–58	4,801	21.35
1958–59	5,108	16.27
1959–60	5,336	16.81

Source: Annual Accounts, St James' Works, Forfar

The jute trade was at a low ebb, and the outlook insecure, especially for weavers. The level of protection enjoyed by the UK industry was being reduced. Since the end of the war India had been making inroads in the market for better-quality jute products. In the packaging market, a traditional outlet for jute goods, new products such as paper for multiwall paper bags, and polythene, and new methods, principally containerisation, were making their presence felt. Demand for jute for linoleum backing, which was Dundee's second-most important customer, had peaked in 1955.[2] It was during the mid-1950s too, that the output of the UK jute industry reached its post-war peak. Locally, a process of contraction in the numbers of firms began after 1958, when the membership of the AJSM began to fall, from 40 to 33 by 1960, reaching 14 by 1977.[3]

This then was a period of considerable uncertainty about the future, which to some extent is reflected in the accumulation of reserves. With the market for jute being squeezed, the company's survival depended upon the directors' ability to find and develop new business interests. Yet there were signs of entrepreneurial fatigue amongst some of the older family directors, the understandable long-term result perhaps of their enforced entry to second-choice careers and lifetimes spent in the business, which they had already steered through one major and prolonged crisis. Capt W. G. Don, in one view 'a quietly-spoken, unassuming man' and paternalist employer whose conversation was said to have been coloured by 'Victorian anecdotes and illustrations', was 73 when he died in 1961, still holding the office of company chairman. The mild-mannered Frank D. J. Buist, who in his earlier years had, like Don, made a major contribution to the firm (to which he had remained fully committed during the dark days of the Depression), was finding it increasingly hard to generate enthusiasm for the jute industry, and indeed by the 1960s he had no executive responsibility within the firm. Instead he found time to devote to his other major business interest, the Dundee, Perth and London Shipping Co, and his leisure interests such as golf and painting. Some of his considerable intellectual ability was directed towards part-time historical research. Attributes and characteristics which were perfectly adequate for the kinder conditions of the 1940s and 1950s (compared to the 1930s), may no longer have been sufficient as the covers of Jute Control were removed.

This chapter is concerned with the company's response to these challenges. Changes in personnel occurred and avenues which ultimately went nowhere were explored. Mistakes were made. Yet the search for alternative products went on relentlessly. Although the chapter deals with comparatively few years, it was to prove to be a period of the utmost importance for Dons.

The merger with Low Brothers (Dundee) Ltd

Merchanting firms had developed a reputation for squeezing prices down hard during periods of depression in the jute industry, and partly to avoid this a number of producers engaged in 'forward vertical integration' in the mid-1960s and acquired their own merchanting arms.[4] There was also a more positive aspect of this strategy for producers, namely the opportunities it provided for capturing additional and more secure outlets for their yarn and cloth.

Dons were one of the first jute producing companies to integrate themselves with a local firm of merchants. Although they had performed admirably in the 1950s in reorganising and redeveloping their production capacity, and maintained an excellent reputation for the quality of their products, there was room for improvement on the marketing front, especially overseas. Virtually all of Dons' sales were in the UK. Nevertheless, their lightweight scrims had done well and indeed the immediate outlook for this product looked bright in February 1961 when it was noted by the board that 'our mainstay is continuing to be in our lighter weights and scrims, in long rolls, in both wide and narrow widths'.[5] Indeed, when Dons first considered the possibility of buying a merchanting company it was to Alexander Laurie & Co Ltd, who sold most of their scrim, that they first looked. A further indication that Dons were

Frank D. J. Buist (centre), the last member of the Buist family to play an active role within the company. Buist (1900–80) was most powerful during the inter-war years, although he continued in his post after the Second World War and was company chairman for a time during the 1960s. He finally stood down in 1966

performing reasonably was that early in 1961 an informal approach was made to the company on behalf of Sir Hugh Fraser's Scottish & Universal Investment Trust Ltd about the possibility of a takeover. Fraser's group, which was in the process of extending their interests in textiles, was evidently impressed by the fact that Dons were not subject to 'as violent fluctuations' as other jute companies but, rather, 'were in good steady lines' with customers who liked what they made.[6]

From around 1954, however, a new outlet for jute had begun to appear: as backing for tufted carpets faced with man-made fibres rather than wool. Sales of tufted carpets burgeoned during the later 1950s and early 1960s, with UK production rising from 3 million square yards in 1957 to 13.3 million in 1961 and 33.3 million in 1964.[7]

Unlike the majority of the other jute producers in the region, Dons had previously shown relatively little interest in tufted carpets. They had had an early opportunity to share in the manufacture of this product, which had originated in the USA, when in November 1954 Dons were approached by representatives of four prospective tufted carpet manufacturers in Britain, including James Templeton & Co Ltd of Glasgow, with a view to supplying jute hessians for 'needletuft carpeting' – at a time when only one British company, Homfray & Co Ltd of Sowerby Bridge, was making it.[8] However, the jute cloth required had to be woven on broadlooms of either 168 or 210 inches in breadth, much wider than those which Dons normally used. Partly because entry to the new field would have involved a substantial capital outlay on new machinery, and perhaps due to a certain element of timidity – the directors had tried unsuccessfully to secure a five-year contract to supply wide carpet backing – Dons had apparently decided not to become involved. They were, after all, leading the market in their long rolls of narrow speciality scrims.

In the longer run, that Dons, almost uniquely, and unlike companies such as Low & Bonar and Jute Industries Ltd, had not invested heavily in carpet backing looms was to prove to be a fortuitous advantage when polypropylene emerged as a potential alternative to jute. (Dons did purchase some 30 or so looms for making wide carpet backing though, and located them at St James'.) In 1960, however, as demand for tufted carpet backing boomed, it appeared as though Dons might have missed a golden opportunity. What was quite clear was that the company needed to widen its markets and strengthen its sales effort. And such were the cash reserves which had been amassed during the 1950s that their search for a suitable candidate to perform this function was not constrained by a lack of financial resources.

While the pros and cons of purchasing Alexander Laurie & Co Ltd were still being considered, the opportunity appeared of forging a relationship with Low Brothers (Dundee) Ltd, a long-established, highly respected and successful family firm of jute merchants run by William Low, Peter S. Low and D. Murray Low since the death of their father William, in 1957. William, who had begun his business life in the Dundee office of the Samnuggur and Titaghur jute company, and his brother Peter (d.1955), had formed their own company, Low Brothers, jute bag sewers in 1913.[9]

What happened in 1960, however, was not simply a takeover on the part of Dons. Lows had already demonstrated a serious interest in integrating backwards by purchasing Alexander Henderson & Sons of South Dudhope, Dundee, a small manufacturing company. They had also developed business links with Dons, partly by selling their cloth but also through a friendship which had developed between Michael Hill and Peter S. Low. Significantly, they had become well acquainted during discussions over Dons' failure to dye properly 'striped backing', a wine and gold jute fabric used to back hearth rugs. After learning that Lows were anxious to become further involved in manufacturing, and recognising the value of the Low brothers' experience in the jute trade, Hill suggested that they might try to come to an arrangement with Dons.

The outcome was that the board of Don Bros, Buist & Co Ltd accepted the proposal, which Hill had made to his board with some trepidation, that the two companies should merge, and authorised the payment of what some members felt was a generous £153,002 for Lows.[10] William Low joined Dons' board, while D. L. Urquhart and Michael Hill sat on that of Lows'. Dons was also put on a firmer financial footing with a second share restructuring. The first of these had taken place in 1952, when each old share of £10 had been divided into ten new shares of £1 each, with the aim of making it easier to buy and sell the company's shares. At the same time the Articles of Association were amended by reducing the shareholding required by a director from £1,000 to £250 in an attempt to bridge the growing gulf between the ownership of the company and those effectively responsible for its management. Whereas in 1904 the great bulk of the shares had been owned by the active directors, by the 1950s leading lights in the company, notably D. L. Urquhart and F. G. Anderson (recruited largely to improve the company's rather inadequate sales arrangements) had only small shareholdings, of 130 and 150 shares respectively. Indeed both men had had to be loaned shares to qualify as directors in April 1952.

In 1961 each of the Low brothers was given 250 ordinary shares. In August, £287,250 was capitalised from the company's

William Low (b.1921). Initially of Low Brothers (Dundee) Ltd. Joined Dons' board in 1960 when Lows were acquired by Dons and thereafter played a leading role in establishing Dons as one of Europe's leading polypropylene companies. Finally left the company in 1989, when he retired from his post as non-executive chairman

large reserves and distributed in the form of a bonus issue of three for one. This raised Dons' issued ordinary share capital up to £383,000, and together with the £150,000 in preference shares, the total issued capital stood at £523,000.[11]

The benefits to Dons of their merger with Lows quickly became apparent and indeed, within a year, in April 1961, the directors noted that 'were it not for the support . . . given us by Low Brothers, we should probably have had to introduce short-time working long before now'.[12] Sales revenue, of £1,594,398 in 1960–61, continued the upwards trajectory which had been set in motion after 1957–58. In large part this early success was due to Lows' links with carpet manufacturers, so that by 1964 it was reported that 'very large quantities' of Dons' lightweight hessian cloth was being used to back needlefelt carpets.

Dons' continued to strengthen their merchanting connections and, in May 1961, acquired the small merchant company of

Stiven, MacPherson & Thomson, while three years later William Smith (Dundee) 1939 Ltd was also taken over. By May 1963 Dons had come to depend heavily upon the work provided by Lows' sales efforts, although 30 to 40 per cent of Low Brothers' sales were of cloth made by companies other than Dons. The significance of Lows' contribution was recognised in May 1965 when William Low (b. 1921) joined D. L. Urquhart as Dons' joint managing director. Although Dons had a long-standing reputation for the quality of their products, greater stress began to be placed upon this factor by the Low brothers, who were also more conscious than had been the case beforehand of customer requirements and the need to deal expeditiously with complaints, and insisted on closer collaboration between the marketing and production ends of the company, in order to meet agreed delivery dates.[13]

Partly as a consequence of this, there was a distinct move upwards in the quality of jute purchased by Dons, and during the autumn of 1962 a complete revision of the composition of their warp and weft batches for common hessian backings was undertaken. Although the cost of the jute batch was higher, the quality of yarns which resulted from a series of tests were found to give much better machine efficiency, which more than compensated for the increased cost.[14]

JUTE: KEEPING GOING AND CUTTING COSTS

The decision of the Restrictive Practices Court in 1963 that the registered price agreements between the jute producers were against public interest and should be abandoned, made it essential for companies who wanted to survive the return of price competition to examine ways of further reducing their production costs. Yet with the unpromising outlook for jute, Dons were reluctant to invest large sums in new looms – sensibly enough as those then available could not operate at higher speeds, while the sand content in jute made it unsuitable for weaving in fine machinery. Instead, considerable sums were spent on areas where technical efficiencies could be achieved, and in fact over time there was an almost total re-equipment of the company's spinning, winding and warp preparation machines.

Yet Dons' post-1963 survival in jute required more than this. On 1 March 1963, for example, the board agreed that it was unlikely that they would be able to withstand competition from abroad unless they could find 'some way of weaving cloth without using so much labour in the process'.[15] There was a limit, though, to how much additional labour could be shed.

Not only did costs have to be reduced. In spite of the re-equipment which had taken place at Strang Street in the late 1950s, there were times during the early 1960s when yarn output was insufficient to meet the needs of the company's factories, and in December 1965, for example, yarn had to be imported from Eire and Spain in order to maintain cloth production.[16]

It was production costs, however, which were proving to be the greater problem. Up until 1963 it had still been possible to reduce weaving costs by adapting existing machinery and thus

Jute cloth being loaded one on of the company's lorries for dispatch. St James' Works, Forfar, 1960s

shave labour costs. By the start of 1962, for example, all of Dons' medium-width looms (62 to 86 inches) had been converted to automatic working. Indeed, in January 1962, rather than buy new broad looms at a cost of £2,500 each, the directors decided to purchase 24 second-hand four-yard-wide looms for making hessian backing, from Nairns of Kirkcaldy, for only £90 each. The board was 'willing to gamble' on the strength of their technical capabilities that these machines could be altered to meet their requirements.[17] This proved to be the case, the modified machines performing well when compared with the new (but not 'modern') wide looms currently available.

Nevertheless, the question during 1963 was still what sort of new looms should be purchased. Numbers of them were coming on to the market and indeed, in 1963 alone, three new shuttle-less looms appeared, and were scrutinised by Dons' representatives. That which first impressed Dons was the 'Onemack', made by James Mackie & Son Ltd of Belfast. It offered continuous weaving, smoother mechanical performance and thus fewer breaks of the warp threads, and was twice as fast as the 68-inch automatic looms currently in use at St James'.[18]

Its other advantage was that the weft was inserted by two long rapiers or spears, one at each side of the machines, so that it could weave continuously without the weavers having to stop to load and unload cops. The French 'MAV' had the advantage of being compact and economical to run.[19] A Spanish machine, the 'Iwer', was also considered.

There were disadvantages with each of these, however. The 'Onemack', for which Dons placed a provisional order of 12 in March 1963, was better suited for 'continuous runs of mass production type', rather than the shorter runs which Dons required for their speciality products. By June the order had been reduced to two, as it was discovered that customers disliked the kinds of selvedges produced by the 'Onemack'. Ultimately, none was purchased. The 'MAV', which during the course of the year had begun to look more promising than the 'Onemack', required substantial modification before it could be used to weave jute. None was ordered.

Given the uncertainties about the new technology then available, and the fact that the company had a solid foundation in lightweight hessians and scrims, and indeed that they had extended their commitment to hessian backing for tufted and needleweave carpets, the longer-serving members of the board considered that it was both unnecessary and unwise to embark on substantial new expenditure. In 1964 D. L. Urquhart, then chairman of the AJSM, pronounced the outlook for jute in floor covering as being reasonably good. His fellow directors appeared willing to share his equanimity: their collective state of mind is reflected in a minute of May 1965, when it was agreed that the company's 'future policy', would be to consolidate their current position, bring their various units up to 'acceptable profitability', and in general to develop only within the limits of their cash resources.[20]

Further Acquisitions, Diversification – and Polypropylene

The 1960s saw numerous mergers and acquisitions in the jute industry, the most notable example of which was the creation of the Scott & Robertson group, with total assets of £5 million.[21]

Dons had, in fact, bought a controlling interest in 1958 in Moffat & Son Ltd, a small Forfar manufacturing firm, the managing directors of which had decided to give up the trade following the reduction in protection for hessians in 1957. As Moffats, whose Haugh Works were located in South Street, Forfar, near Strang Street Mill, were manufacturers of fine hessians, it was anticipated that the acquisition would 'give the group a wider field of activity'.[22]

Of much greater importance was their acquisition, through share exchange, of the innovative firm of J. & J. Smart (Brechin) Ltd, founded in 1838, when their Valley Works had housed over 200 hand-looms. The possibility of a merger had been discussed informally in 1960, although final negotiations did not take place until the winter of 1962–63. Ultimately it was agreed that Dons should give Smarts 25,858 of their ordinary shares, which at the time were together worth £34,908. John B. Smart, son of the firm's then chairman, G. Beveridge Smart, also joined Dons' board. Although considerably smaller than Dons (making only one-sixth as much cloth, for instance, and with a total labour force of only 160), Smarts had much to offer.

Firstly, they made not only (fine) jute cloth, which accounted for 36.7 per cent of the company's output in 1960–61, but also cotton (14.7 per cent), viscose (10.2 per cent) and flax (38.4 per cent).[23] Secondly, although Smarts had not had the capital resources to finance any large-scale expenditure – average annual net profits for the seven years from 1956–57 to 1962–63 were only £1,039 – they had been trying out new fabrics and did have considerable technical expertise. John D. B. Smart (b.1932), educated at Harrow, but who was given weaving lessons at the age of eight or nine, and who was eventually to become the joint managing director at Dons responsible for production (with Peter S. Low in charge of sales), played a major role in this regard, taking his managers to international machinery trade fairs to search out new ideas,[24] a tradition to which the company still adheres. And thirdly, the move made sense from the marketing point of view, as Smarts sold around a third of their output through Lows. Indeed, a strengthening of the sales organisations of the two companies was given as the principal aim of the merger.

As the take-over of Smarts indicates, the other major feature of the first half of the 1960s was a limited form of diversification – the search for profitable business activities, preferably textile-related, which would help to compensate for the declining opportunities in jute and provide a sounder basis for the company's future. Although as was seen in the previous section, the company was to some extent marking time in the early 1960s, the directors were kept informed of, and were always prepared (some more enthusiastically than others) to look at new possibilities. That at the end of 1963 they had bought no shuttle-less looms, for instance, was not because the directors were unaware of the latest developments in machine technology; shuttle-less looms, they agreed in 1963, were coming 'more quickly than many people recognise'. They still had to find new products, though.

Dons had begun this process in 1949, when, along with Ballantynes of Peebles, the directors had established a subsidiary company, Strathmore Woollen Co Ltd, in which they were the major shareholders. In large part this company was set up in response to the uncertainties then current in the raw jute trade. Although when demand was buoyant and jute supplies assured labour was in short supply, there were occasions when jute could not be obtained, or only at a high price. Accordingly, production had to be curtailed; by providing employment, however, it was hoped that the existence of Strathmore would persuade workers not to leave the textile industry and thereby reduce further the pool of available labour. Weaving, on 42 looms, was carried on at Forfar, in Canmore Works, the first time they had been used for production purposes since Dons acquired the site, with the cloth being sent to the Borders for finishing, although later machinery for this purpose was installed at St James'. The partnership, however, was unsuccessful and high wool prices in 1951 led to orders drying up. In February 1952 Ballantynes withdrew. Within a year though, Strathmore was again in business, solely in Dons' hands, and became a source of some satisfaction, its 'quality fabric equal to the best of its kind' winning accolades at both the Brussels Universal & International Exhibition and the Canadian National Exhibition in 1957.[25]

As this example suggests, the company's attempts to diversify in the first half of the 1960s met with mixed success. Perhaps the most unlikely departure for a jute-spinning and manufacturing company such as Dons was its involvement, in 1963, with Dobbie McInnes (Electronics) Ltd, of Hillington, Glasgow, which later became D-Mac Ltd.[26] Their main interest was in the design and development of graphics equipment for the publishing industry. However, it soon became clear to Dons that the venture was going to require large capital advances from them, and in December 1964 they gladly accepted an offer of £50,000 for the business from the Thomson Organisation Ltd.[27]

A more obvious departure for Dons was the production of flocked material (used for car seats, for example) where thousands of short fibres are electrostatically fixed to an adhesive-coated backing, and trials in this area began in 1963. By November 1965 sales of the product had begun, but unsatisfactory performance on the part of the West German machinery caused production delays and led to orders being cancelled. It was entirely out of keeping with the new image the company was in the process of building, and accordingly, the venture was abandoned in October 1968.[28]

Even more logical – or so it seemed at the time – was the directors' decision in June 1964 to approve expenditure of £40,000 on the establishment of a package dyeing plant in Forfar.

Not only did this promise savings of between £20 and £40 per ton in dyeing costs, but it also provided Dons with an opportunity to start a 'speciality business' in dyed and treated yarns (and the cloth made from them, notably striped backing for the hearth rug trade). Furthermore, it had the great advantage that even if the jute trade disappeared Dons would 'still have a modern and efficient dyeing plant' which could be used 'for a great variety of different processes on yarns of various kinds'.[29]

Also of potential longer-term significance for Dons (though again, not necessarily to the company's benefit) was their involvement with Daniel Buchanan & Sons of Preston Works, Prestonpans, manufacturers of leathercloth and polyvinyl chloride (PVC) coated paper. The firm was struggling to survive and in 1965 had become insolvent. Dons were reluctant to see the works close as they were a major supplier for Low Brothers, who were able to sell some 20,000 yards of coated fabric a week. The failure of other possible suppliers in December 1965 forced Dons to take over the 'supervision' of Buchanans.[30] By 1969 though, with D. Murray Low in charge at Prestonpans, and aided by the late 1960s fashion for PVC coated fabrics, sales of Buchanans' products had risen to 'unprecedented levels'.[31] In January 1971 a double day shift was introduced (as opposed to a single day and an evening shift), which, it was anticipated, would make it possible to manufacture 60,000 lineal yards per week.[32]

More promising initially, at least on paper, was Dons' decision to join forces with the Chaspec Manufacturing Co of Greenwich, Connecticut, USA, to form a package-making business in Scotland, and after inspecting a number of possible manufacturing locations in central Scotland, it was decided to purchase the Abbey Works in Arbroath in February 1964.[33] The level of orders, principally for boxes for the US whisky trade, and packages for long-playing records marketed by the *Reader's Digest* magazine, was lower than anticipated, however, and in May 1966 Dons bought out the Americans for a modest sum. The venture, which was renamed Don & Low Ltd, continued to stagger on well below its potential level of operation, and indeed was saved by the arrival of an order from the *Reader's Digest* on the very day that it was scheduled for closure, in October 1968.[34] Don & Low at Arbroath, however, simply failed to fulfil its initial promise, and by April 1975 only 18 people were employed at Abbey Works,[35] although the number rose later.

The recollection of those who lived through this period is that these were not the happiest of times. Only great vigilance and determination on the part of some board members had prevented what was perceived to be an attempt by one of their number to acquire a controlling interest in the firm, the shares of which in spite of the uncertain future had in the opinion of at least one contemporary board member been deliberately (and mistakenly) undervalued.[36]

The company's search for a successful new product drew to a close at the end of 1965. Polypropylene, a derivative of petroleum, which is made by polymerizing propene or propylene, had first been developed in 1954. As far as textile manufacture was concerned, it took two forms, either as multifilament yarns or as flat tape, which is slit from sheets or extruded polypropylene, wound on to spools and subsequently woven. In the USA, it was increasingly used as a backing for tufted carpets. It was an adequate substitute for jute, it was cheaper, and its price was falling (from 45 pence to 24 pence per lb between 1959–65).[37]

Although individuals within the company had been aware of these developments from the early 1960s at least, in November 1965 the first reference to polypropylene appears in the company minute-books. While memories have blurred with the passage of time, and there is some confusion about the precise chronology of events, it appears that it was J. Gavin Don who urged the board to look formally at polypropylene. A London-based stockbroker with his eye on the wider world, Don had noted a brief report in the *Financial Times* that Jute Industries had developed an interest in polypropylene in the USA. Dons' board, he insisted, should look at the new material too.

At this initial stage, although the directors recognised that they were dealing with a potent new raw material, they were unsure about 'the extent to which polypropylene will replace jute'. Changes, they anticipated, would be 'gradual rather than catastrophic'.[38] As it happened, for Dons, they were neither. As will be seen in the next chapter they were at the forefront of the move to introduce polypropylene to Tayside, and were involved in the first attempts to weave with it. Within a year of their first trials with multifilament yarns, with which the company had anticipated (wrongly) that they would be able to weave polypropylene scrim, they had taken options on new polypropylene tape-weaving looms worth more than £200,000. These were to produce tufted carpet backing. Dons had found their future.

Chapter Ten: Low Brothers and Diversification

1 Yearly Accounts, 1953–54 – 1959–60, St James' Works.
2 Howe, *Dundee Textiles*, p20.
3 Ibid, 30.
4 Ibid, 41.
5 Minute Book No 4, 1961–65, 17 February 1961, p216.
6 Minute Book No 4, 1961–65, p216, p324.
7 Bartlett, *Carpeting the Millions*, p199.
8 Ibid, 192; Minute Book No 2, 1946–55, 18 November 1954, p218.
9 *Dundee Courier*, 27 December 1955; 3 October 1957.
10 Information provided by Michael Hill in interview with J. Stewart; internal document provided at time of public flotation, 1981–82, p118.
11 Ibid, p173.
12 Minute Book No 4, 1961–65, 14 April 1961, p222.
13 P. H. Grinyer, D. G. Mayes, P. McKiernan, *Sharpbenders: The Secrets of Unleashing Corporate Potential* (London, 1988), p125.
14 Minute Book No 4, 1961–65, 14 September 1962, p260.
15 Ibid, 1 March 1963, p278.
16 Ibid, 17 December 1965, p405.
17 Ibid, 19 January 1962, p243.
18 Ibid, 1 March 1963, p278.
19 Ibid, 18 October 1963, p302.
20 Ibid, 14 May 1965, p371.
21 Howe, *Dundee Textiles*, pp40–41.
22 *Forfar Dispatch*, 30 January 1958.
23 Auditor's Report for Don Bros, Buist & Co Ltd, 1962.
24 Grinyer *et al*, *Sharpbenders*, p209.
25 *Forfar Dispatch*, 9 January 1958; see too *The Scotsman*, 27 December 1967; for further information on Ballantynes, see C. Gulvin, *The Scottish Hosiery and Knitwear Industry 1680–1980* (Edinburgh, 1984), pp126–7.
26 Minute Book No 4, 1961–65, 19 November 1963, p306.
27 Ibid, 18 December 1964.
28 Ibid, 9 August 1963, p293; 19 November 1965, p400; Minute Book No 5, 1966–74, 19 January 1968, p505; 18 October 1968, p522.
29 Minute Book No 4, 1961–65, 19 June 1964, p329.
30 Ibid, 17 November 1961, p237; 19 February 1965, p360; 5 April 1965, p368; 18 June 1965, p381; 17 December 1965, p405.
31 Minute Book No 5, 1966–74, 17 October 1969, p548.
32 Ibid, 15 January 1971, p588.
33 Minute Book No 4, 1961–65, 21 February 1964, p310.
34 Minute Book No 5, 1966–74, 18 October 1968, p522.
35 Minute Book No 6, 1975–80, 18 April 1975, p719.
36 I have benefited greatly from discussions with J. Gavin Don, John D. B. Smart and William Low about this period in the company's history.
37 Howe, *Dundee Textiles*, p32.
38 Minute Book No 4, 1961–65, 19 November 1965, p400.

Chapter Eleven

Changing Focus: From Jute to Polypropylene, 1966–75

The period 1966 to 1975 was as momentous as any in the company's history. In the autumn of 1966, as has been seen, Dons took what at first were tentative steps into polypropylene. By Christmas the company had made a major commitment to the new material. The circumstances in which this occurred form an important part of this chapter.

It was a remarkable period for the company in other ways too. For one thing the board lost its last direct descendent of the Don founding fathers, when following a bitter boardroom battle over the future status of the company, J. Gavin Don, a well-meaning man but one whose manner and idiosyncracies had made him few friends amongst his fellow-directors, had been forced to stand down in 1973. Shortly afterwards, in March 1975, David L. Urquhart, Lord Tayside, died. In a sense his death was symbolic, for both within the company, and from the point of view of outsiders, Urquhart represented the jute interest. It was more than that, though: he had been Dons' chief jute buyer at a time of increasing instability in the raw jute market. No one else was capable of dealing so effectively in raw jute, and indeed, in 1970 when he had been ill, Dons simply bought no jute, preferring instead to utilise the stocks he had built up before going into hospital.[1] Yet even before Lord Tayside's death, profits from polypropylene tufted carpet backing had begun to overtake those of jute.

The transfer from jute to polypropylene, however, was not effected without considerable cost, as well as numerous technical trials and tribulations. At first sight, compared to jute, polypropylene appeared to be a markedly less troublesome raw material to work with. In terms of cost and predictability of supply this was partly true, though in other respects the reality was rather different.

POLYPROPYLENE: GETTING STARTED

Dons' immediate response to the appearance of polypropylene on Tayside was cautious, publicly at least. Indeed, in his last statement to the shareholders as chairman, in August 1966, F. J. Buist, made no reference to the material, and after reporting a year of mixed results, he dwelt instead on the generally depressing outlook for jute.

Nevertheless, having decided in October 1966 not to pursue their interest in multifilament yarns, Dons placed their first order for polypropylene tape, in order to make sample rolls woven on conventional jute looms, adding a twist to the tape in order to prevent 'pull off' from the cop. Some modest investment followed, in the form of an order for an Italian SMIT shuttleless loom, priced around £6,500.[2] At this point Dons' interests in polypropylene were developing in tandem with at least three other Dundee textile firms, who also placed orders for SMIT looms, which were the only viable machines readily available which were capable of weaving cloth wide enough to be heat set, tufted, latexed and finally yield the requisite four-yard-wide tufted carpet.

In December, however, the situation changed dramatically. Whilst in the USA on business connected with Strathmore Woollens, by then 'one of the most vigorous and vital members of the production group',[3] William Low had taken the opportunity of visiting Dalton, in Georgia, the centre of the US tufted carpet industry. Noting that something like 30 per cent of the primary carpet backing in the US tufting trade was made of polypropylene, Low became convinced that there was a similar market potential in the UK, which was still using jute carpet backing.[4] Also in December, whilst in London in connection with his work with the British Standards Institution, Michael Hill took the opportunity (at the suggestion of Low) of meeting Peter Johnstone, European representative of the US chemical

Michael H. J. Hill (b.1929), Col L. E. Hill's son. He joined Dons in 1954 before becoming a director in 1958. Heavily involved in the company's transfer into and development of polypropylene, Hill was the last relation of the Don family to take an active part in the company. He retired early when Shell took over in 1986

and textile company, W. R. Grace of New York. What Hill learned was that two Dundee companies, H. & A. Scott and Scott & Robertson, were to attend trials in Switzerland of a new kind of weaving machine built by Sulzer Brothers of Winterthur. Recognising the possible importance of the new technology, Michael Hill and John Smart arranged to be present at the trials too. Of immense significance, as will be seen below, was the fact that Hill and Smart asked that a beam of Grace's tape be flown over to Switzerland for the trial.

Although these trials were to be carried out on Sulzer's standard 130-inch machine, it was learned that a 153-inch version was to be made in the foreseeable future. And while this was too narrow for use with state-of-the-art, non-heat-set tape, the two men recognised its potential for use with heat-set tape.

Such was the enthusiasm of Hill and Smart for the Sulzer weaving machines, which were twice as fast as the SMITs, as well as being cheaper to operate (and, with minor modifications, also capable of weaving jute), that a special board meeting was convened on 22 December, at which approval was given for the purchase of 12 Sulzer broad-looms of 153 inches, as well as one narrower loom of 130 inches, to be used for experimental purposes. On 23 December Hill visited Sulzer's head office both to confirm the order and obtain assurances that Dons would receive their machines, which were then little more than prototypes, before anyone else in the trade. Other companies such as Low & Bonar had held back, evidently because of the width problem with non-heat-set tape (see below), and were perhaps reluctant to abandon their commitment to recently purchased wide jute looms. Delivery of the narrow machine was promised for July 1967, with the main order following in mid-1969. The cost of the machines, including erection, electrification and a boiler for heating, was £110,000, which could be met from the company's reserves, and state investment grants of 40 per cent.[5]

Adopting the new technology successfully was far from straightforward and the new venture represented a massive gamble on Dons' part. Although the machines from Sulzer Brothers arrived early (all were in Forfar by October 1968), the intervening period gave Dons a much-needed – indeed critical – breathing space in which they had, first, and most importantly, to organise their supplies of suitable polypropylene tape, and secondly, to provide factory space for the new looms. Thirdly, they had to acquire suitable beaming machinery.

Polypropylene tape was available, but not without difficulty. For instance, the Dundee combines, Jute Industries Ltd and Low & Bonar had established an extrusion business by the name of Polytape, but in an understandable attempt to corner the market, refused to heat-set any cloth which was not made entirely of their product. Indeed they also set up a manufacturing arm, Synthetic Fabrics (Scotland) Ltd, on Dons' doorstep, in Forfar.[6]

To some extent all this is incidental, for as has been seen, the immensely successful Sulzer trials in Switzerland had been conducted with a beam of polypropylene tape made by W. R. Grace, and indeed it had been the conjunction and compatibility of Sulzer looms and Grace tape that had in large part persuaded Dons to move so quickly into polypropylene weaving. Unusually, Grace's tape was made using a spinerette system rather than the slit-film one. Ultimately, successful experiments were made to heat-set the tape by their 'Dawbarn process' prior to weaving which would make it less liable to shrink than conventional tape.

It was this factor, initially at least, which enabled Dons to make optimal use of the Sulzer looms. With Grace's tape, Dons' gamble could pay off, and vitally, give the company an invaluable lead over their local rivals. The standard width for finished carpets at this time was 144 inches, backing for which Dons could provide – just – with their 153-inch-wide Sulzers, their first customers being advised that they needed to allow only five inches shrinkage in the stentors in which the cloth was heat-set. Only at temperatures above 132°C did adverse effects take place. Owing to the problem of shrinkage of other tapes, however, a number of Dundee firms, including their principal rivals in the field, Low & Bonar and Jute Industries Ltd, purchased SMIT looms, which were 163 inches wide. As has been observed, these were slower and far less efficient than the Sulzers, and required greater inputs of tape.

Sulzer looms weaving jute, St James', early 1980s. Dons' acquisition of Sulzer looms from 1967 was a vital factor in the lead they established as weavers of polypropylene. The first Sulzers were located at Canmore Works

Clearly it was out of the question for Dons to obtain their supplies from the US. W. R. Grace, however, did have plans to establish an extrusion and weaving plant within the UK. Building upon the relationship which had developed between the two companies from the end of 1966, Dons managed to persuade Grace's to locate not at Skelmersdale, Lancashire, which had been their original intention, but in Forfar. They were encouraged by Michael Hill and John D. B. Smart to drop their plans for weaving in Britain, while Forfar, the Americans were persuaded by William Low and others, offered them a great deal: proximity to Dundee, where many potential users of polypropylene tape were based, and local knowledge; more importantly, Dons guaranteed to consume their tape, at 3s 6d per pound if less than 750 tons per annum, and 3s 5d if over that figure. In addition Dons provided the American company with 15,000 square feet of factory space at Canmore Works for their extrusion lines, at an annual rent of £3,750.[7] Apart from the obvious advantage of this arrangement for Dons, they were also permitted to buy up to 50 tons of tape a year from other sources for experimental purposes. Only one other firm, Scott & Fyfe of Tayport, Fife, showed any serious interest in Grace's tape.

The space required both for the extrusion lines and the Sulzers could not be found either at St James' or Strang Street. Indeed, with so much of their plant devoted to jute, unless they were to build from scratch, Dons had little option but to adapt Canmore Works, which they had purchased in 1936, to accommodate the Sulzers. Although Strathmore Woollens were based there, considerable space remained free both for the company's requirements and those of W. R. Grace. Substantial rebuilding work was necessary, however, before the Sulzers could be accommodated – a hard acrylic floor had to be laid in order to take their weight, for example – and by the time the factory was officially opened, more than £500,000 had been invested in it,[8] and this was only the start.

Grace's extrusion lines at Canmore began working in April 1968, with the intention of supplying Dons with six million miles of polypropylene tape per annum, more than sufficient to meet Dons' production target of 12 million square yards of tufted carpet backing. Grace's did not remain in Forfar for long, however, and in June 1969 their extrusion business in Forfar was purchased by the Thiokol Chemical Corporation of Virginia, USA,[9] who in 1971 developed a green-field site at Newfordpark on the western edge of the burgh of Forfar for their extrusion plant. As with Grace's, Dons maintained good and close working relations with Thiokol, who in the early 1970s were persuaded by Dons to produce coloured tapes, which they had not done previously.

Although Dons could not begin to use their Sulzers until 1968, in the previous year they had begun weaving flat polypropylene tape on a commercial basis on their traditional jute looms. An AJSM investigation in the autumn of 1968 into the progress of polypropylene in the Tayside textile industry revealed that even in this respect Dons were amongst the local leaders. Although some firms were anxious to play their cards close to their chests, it seems that of their fellow spinners and weavers, only Jute Industries Ltd had made the same progress; others were still at the experimental stage. Some declared that they were not interested even in going that far.[10]

Before large-scale production of satisfactory material could begin though, other technical problems had to be overcome by the men most closely involved with the new machinery, namely Michael Hill, John Smart, David Petrie, Ed Stewart, and a fitter from Sulzer. There were considerable initial difficulties with the selvedge, for example, while the roll-up mechanism which the company had earlier so successfully developed could not be used with the Sulzers, the operation of which became (and remained for the next two decades and more) the responsibility of David Petrie. The beaming machinery used for jute was unsuitable for polypropylene, and custom-built equipment had to be developed. Fortuitously for Dons, this was done – in a remarkably short time – by Hamish Tough of the Tayport-based firm of Scott & Fyfe, who were also in the vanguard as far as the installation of the new Sulzer technology was concerned, in conjunction with Leesona Ltd of Heywood in Lancashire. Furthermore, the speed at which the Sulzers worked, and the requirement of large quantities of tape which could be fed into the looms regularly and smoothly, necessitated the manufacture, by WHK Products of Wilmslow, Cheshire, of creels which were 74 feet long, capable of holding 1,200 'extra large' packages of Grace's tape, the equivalent of 100,000 yards. Even this only allowed half-width beams to be produced, which led to distortion of the fabric. During the first year of large-scale production, considerable problems were experienced in obtaining material of a high enough standard and indeed, as late as October 1969, the directors noted that they were 'still not supplying a fabric which is entirely satisfactory for all purposes'.[11] A partial solution was the purchase of a full-width beamer and a double-sized creel.

Of concern too was intense competition from two rival companies, Synthetic Fabrics, and especially Patchogue-Plymouth (later Amoco), an American company, who it was noted in October 1969, were 'making very considerable strides in the woven polypropylene field' – information which spurred Dons' directors to even greater technical efforts at a time when it was noted that 'Every few months something else is being produced to help the tufters.'[12] The market-place in polypropylene cloth for tufted carpet backing was not unlike a battlefield, upon which only the most vigorous combatants survived: 'an active and aggressive policy is essential at this time . . . a policy of caution will mean that we are left behind our competitors', the directors rightly observed in November 1970.[13]

To some extent, the market for polypropylene backing for tufted carpets was constrained by the fact that if the carpet pile was badly spaced, the white backing tended to show through – 'grinning'. As polypropylene was non-absorbant, it could not accept dyes. Dons, of course, were not alone in having to face up to this; they were, however, at the forefront when it came to dealing with the problem.

Early in 1971 Dons, represented by William Low, Michael Hill, and George Guild (the exceptionally able head of Dons' development department, which had been set up in 1966), visited an Austrian factory which produced equipment for making 'needleweave' fabrics.[14] Essentially this is a method of inserting nylon fibre in the form of a fleece into primary backing cloth. The process has two favourable results: first, the production of a material which does not fray when cut; and secondly and more importantly, because nylon can be easily dyed, the problem of 'grinning' is eliminated. Convinced of the commercial potential of needleweave, by May 1972 Dons had installed at Canmore Works a Fehrer needleweave machine, five metres wide, and although there were considerable teething problems with it, even at 70 per cent efficiency, operated on a four-shift system, the Fehrer was capable of processing the output of 20 Sulzers.[15]

Further investment in needleweave units followed, with a £150,000 Menzel rolling machine, for example, which enabled the firm to produce rolls 5,000 metres long, a five-fold increase over what had been possible beforehand.[16]

By November 1975, in which month alone Dons sold one million square metres of needleweave cloth, they were well ahead of their rivals in this field, and the purchase of another (narrow) needleweave machine for Canmore Works was announced.[17]

The late 1960s and early 1970s were years of continuous technical change and adaptation for the company, who, despite their investment in the first Sulzer looms for polypropylene weaving which had appeared on the market, had been anxious for Sulzer Brothers to develop looms which were capable of weaving rolls of cloth in four or five-metre widths (or 157.6 and 197 inches respectively). Early forays into Europe had made it patently clear to Dons that Continental demand was for these widths, wider than could be made on the first batch of Sulzers. When the wider machines did become available in prototype form in the early 1970s the narrower models were moved to Brechin and St James' to weave jute, with 32 of the wide Sulzers being installed at Canmore, which had become the jewel in Dons' manufacturing crown. By the end of 1972, a total of 40 of the wide looms had been purchased.

The introduction of polypropylene weaving, and later needleweave, involved major upheaval for the workforce too. With the appearance of the Sulzers, the rows of tightly packed looms which had so long been typical of the jute factory disappeared. So too did many weavers' jobs: when production at Canmore Works began in 1968 it was anticipated that three weavers would be able to operate 15 Sulzers at 90 per cent efficiency (running for 54 out of 60 minutes), while ancillary work such as beaming, drawing, loading and unloading was to be carried on by a further eight workers. Later, as many as 20 or more Sulzers could be looked after by one operator.

Whereas weaving on the 'orthodox' looms had been done exclusively by females, Sulzers were operated by both men and women. New skills too were required, and supervisory staff had to be trained to manage the new machinery, in Switzerland, on five-week courses. For the operator, less skill was required than had been the case on the older machinery where the best (usually most experienced) weavers who could look after four looms had continuously to repair ends and change the shuttles every two or three minutes. Training for 'orthodox' loom work lasted around six weeks, under the guidance of a 'weaving mistress'. A Sulzer operator, who still required close observational skills and the ability to respond immediately if things went wrong, could be trained in two weeks.[18]

Initially the company managed to obtain sufficient workers who were prepared to adopt the new 24-hour four-shift system which polypropylene production demanded. Yet as in the immediate post-war years, labour shortages began to appear in key areas and in June 1973, for example, needleweave production was reduced as some units could not be manned.

Two factors were thought to be discouraging suitable workers: low wages – comparable rates in England were 'considerably higher' than in Forfar; and the new shift system.[19] Improvements in the working environment had been accomplished by consulting the British Colour Council during the reconstruction of Canmore Works.[20] Cosmetic change, however, was clearly not enough, and in 1973 Dons decided to make a radical change in their pension arrangements. Beforehand, on marriage, women had had to leave the pension scheme and could only rejoin after working for a further five years. Henceforth marriage was to make no difference to Dons as far as women's conditions of employment were concerned.[21] The wage rates of key personnel were raised beyond the current rate of inflation in an attempt to make working in the 'new' textile trade more attractive.[22] Throughout, Dons – pushed in this direction by the Lows – placed a premium on maintaining good labour relations, and indeed were rewarded by the cooperation of their workers in both Forfar and Brechin in adapting to the four-shift system. Without this, it is doubtful if the company could have achieved its early lead in large-scale polypropylene weaving.

Markets and Marketing

It is equally true that new markets had to be found and more aggressive marketing methods employed if Dons were to succeed in their polypropylene venture. If the company's investment in the Sulzers was to pay off, they had to be run more or less continuously. By 1972 each of the 40 Sulzers weaving polypropylene at Canmore Works was capable of producing 700,000 yards per annum.

In one respect the omens were good, in that even before Dons began to send out their first samples of polypropylene cloth, domestic sales of tufted carpets had overtaken those of woven carpets.[23] Their sales efforts, under the leadership of Peter S. Low, were rewarded in August 1968 when Dons received their first 'substantial' order, of 1.6 million square yards, for polypropylene tufted carpet backing.[24] By October the directors could reflect with some satisfaction that they could sell all the polypropylene cloth they could make until the end of the year. Yet within the UK, Dons were dependent from 1968 until 1970 on orders from only a small number of carpet manufacturers – Cyril Lord of Donaghadee was a principal buyer – and indeed in November 1969, after losing a substantial order due to sub-standard tape and poor weaving, the directors considered it a matter of great concern that the company was 'now very dependent on the continued goodwill of two or three customers'.[25]

Accordingly, no effort was spared by Dons in strengthening their sales' performance, improving their products and attracting new customers. Perhaps their greatest success in the last regard resulted from the company's presence from November 1971 at the Northern Floor Coverings annual fairs held at Harrogate, Yorkshire. The cost of a stand, which, fortuitously, had been located near one of the busiest parts of the hall, was £6,500. Following the 1972 fair, only one year after their first appearance at Harrogate, Dons had to turn away orders for seven million square yards of cloth as they simply did not have the capacity to meet this additional demand.[26] As major manufacturers of polypropylene cloth, Dons had arrived.

Within the home market, sales income (including that from jute, which it is unfortunately not possible to distinguish from polypropylene) almost doubled from £5.3 million in 1971–72 to

£10.4 million in 1975–76. Even during the industrial troubles of 1974, and the accompanying three-day week, Dons were able to maintain output (though not fully) of polypropylene at Canmore and at Brechin, using specially purchased generators.[27]

It was a time of considerable dynamism and corporate aggression. From the outset it had been anticipated by the directors that if the full economic benefit of the Sulzers and allied investment was to be achieved, they would manufacture much more cloth than they could sell within the UK, even though returns per unit of cloth were lower overseas. As early as October 1968, William Low had visited tufted carpet manufacturers in three of Britain's fellow EFTA members, Austria, Denmark and Switzerland, in the hope of obtaining buyers. A problem at this stage was that Continental demand was for cloth in metric widths, which, as has been seen, Dons were unable to make until the early 1970s. Even so, contacts were made and, later, Denmark (nurtured by William Low) became an important market.

Agencies too worked on Dons' behalf; remarkably early on, while on a European visit in October 1972, William Low and George Guild found their reputation had preceded them and that they had accepted 'that our quality had already proved itself'.[28] By itself, however, this was not enough in what was an increasingly competitive market.

Dons' own sales team was strengthened too. Around 1974, for example, Peter S. Low began the process of tempting Louis T. Smith to transfer his allegiance from Low & Bonar to Dons. Much respected in the trade, Smith, who had extensive experience not only in jute but also more recently in 'Propafleece' (Synthetic Industries' rival to Dons' needleweave), eventually joined Dons in 1976 as sales director. One of the attractions of Dons for Smith was the company's attitude to Europe. Indeed, from 1975, after six years on the waiting list for space at the Frankfurt Fair, the biggest of its kind, Dons were from their stand there more able to convince customers of the quality of their output.

They could not do it all on their own though, and also in 1975, with the assistance of Tata and Framco Barkotex of London, agencies with which Peter S. Low had been anxious to develop closer relations (partly because of the linguistic skills of their staff), Dons began to spread their net even more widely, and made their first moves in central and eastern Europe. For a company in an industry which had since the 1930s enjoyed a high level of protection and directed its attention first and foremost to the home market, this was a remarkable turn-around. Indeed, between 1971–72 and 1975–76, the value of Dons' export sales almost quadrupled, from £700,000 to £2.7 million.

JUTE: DOWN BUT NOT OUT

Jute spinners and weavers during the second half of the 1960s and first half of the 1970s were faced with an extremely difficult situation. Not only was demand for jute cloth declining, but for long periods supply side conditions posed major problems.

This was due principally to two factors. First, with the waning of Dundee's importance in the world jute trade, its impact on the raw jute market was marginal. The price was increasingly being set by the buying policies of China and a number of East European states. As many of these countries preferred to barter goods with Pakistan rather than pay cash, Dundee buyers were left to face high prices which were set by the Pakistani jute authorities. Inflated raw material costs, of course, simply made matters worse as far as their marketing of jute cloth was concerned.[29]

Secondly, after a period of relative stability in raw jute prices between 1962 and the autumn of 1965, there followed a decade of frequent skirmishes and two outbreaks of full-scale war between India and Pakistan, as well as the Bengali Rising of 1971 which led to the formation of the new state of Bangladesh. As a result there were great fluctuations in the price of raw jute, and occasions too when supplies were difficult to obtain. Thus, for example, at the start of the civil war in East Pakistan, raw jute, which had already risen to a premium on the spot market, sold for £134 a ton. A month later in April, it had risen by a further £30. As a result, all prices for Dundee and imported hessians were withdrawn. Although Dons had stocks for six months, as the war went on they were forced to turn to inferior Siamese and Burmese jute, not only because of its lower price (£106 a ton in June 1971), but also as insurgent guerrillas had announced that anyone caught selling raw jute would be killed.[30] In spite of this, and due in large part to the prudence and foresight of the ailing D. L. Urquhart, Dons were not so badly hit as other Dundee firms such as Sidlaw Industries, where a three-day week was introduced in December in order to preserve stocks.[31]

Indeed, even though the situation in Bangladesh did not improve as far as the jute trade in general was concerned, Dons managed – in 1974, for instance – to purchase sufficient jute at the right time, just before a price rise of £20 a ton was effected owing to the realisation that flooding had halved that year's jute crop. This enabled Dons to choose between selling finished goods at lower prices than their competitors could bear, or wait until a general price rise enabled them to make 'good profits'. They chose the latter course.[32]

As this indicates, demand for jute goods was on occasion bouyant, and it should not be forgotten that until 1973 jute made a greater contribution to Dons' profitability than polypropylene. In the first quarter of 1966, for example (admittedly at a time of stability in the raw jute trade), Dons sold all the jute they could make and turned away business as they did not have sufficient production capacity.[33] And as has already been noted, some of the narrower Sulzer looms had in 1970 been adapted for jute production.

Nevertheless, the brutal fact was that the market for jute cloth was narrowing. Jute hessians had few buyers, although the Arab-Israeli conflict in 1967 brought a flurry of orders for this type of cloth. On the other hand, two years later the prices obtainable for jute hessians were described as 'ridiculous' and 'unrealistic'.[34] In order to make profits in jute, Dons were increasingly being forced back on their speciality, jute scrims.[35] Demand for these could be intense, as during August 1972 when it rose to 'unprecedented' levels, particularly for narrow loom scrim, which necessitated the introduction of an evening shift.[36] Ironically, the other important end use for jute was dependent on the success of polypropylene, with which a jute weft had been woven by Dons into a 'union fabric' since 1968.

However, if the end for jute was not quite in sight, with the ascendancy of polypropylene there was nothing on the horizon which could justify the company devoting much creative energy to it. Conditions in Bangladesh continued to be unsatisfactory, and in December 1973 it was decided to reduce working to a single day shift at Strang Street, where 'less and less' was being produced.[37] The Sulzers at Valley Works, Brechin, were devoted once more to polypropylene. During 1975, following Lord Tayside's death, most of the company's old four and five-yard looms at St James' were scrapped, as too were a number of Northrops, the newer wide jute-weaving machines.[38] Instead, a single 213 inch Sulzer loom, which could do the work of six Northrops, was installed for weaving jute 160 inches wide.[39]

Chapter Eleven: Changing Focus

1 Minute Book No 5, 1966–74, 15 May 1970, p567; see too entry for 18 December 1970.
2 Ibid, 14 October 1966, p454.
3 *The Scotsman*, 27 December 1967.
4 Minute Book No 5, 1966–74, 22 December 1966, p469.
5 ibid, 17 February 1967, p474; 14 April 1967, p482; information too was obtained from Louis T. Smith, who was at this time employed by Low & Bonar.
6 Ibid.
7 Ibid, 15 December 1967, p503.
8 *Forfar Dispatch*, 3 April 1969.
9 Minute Book No 5, 1966–74, 14 February 1969, p532; 13 June 1969, p541.
10 DUA, MS 84/27/4, Association of Jute Spinners and Manufacturers, see File 'Polypropylene Enquiries', September 1968.
11 Ibid, 17 October 1969, p548.
12 Ibid.
13 Ibid, 20 November 1970, p583.
14 Ibid, 19 February 1971, p590.
15 Ibid, 17 November 1972, p640.
16 Minute Book No 6, 1975–80, 14 March 1975, p715.
17 Ibid, 14 November 1975, 735; 17 December 1975, p738.
18 *Cordage, Canvas and Jute World*, May 1969. From file of cuttings, MS 100, Dundee University Archives; information derived also from discussions with Ed Stewart and Alister Wilson.
19 Minute Book No 5, 1966–74, 15 June 1973, p663.
20 *Cordage, Canvas and Jute World*, op cit.
21 Minute Book No 5, 1966–74, 16 November 1973, p675.
22 Minute Book No 6, 1975–80, 11 July 1975, p726.
23 Howe, *Dundee Textiles*, p30.
24 Minute Book No 5, 1966–74, 16 August 1968, p521.
25 Ibid, 21 November 1969, p526.
26 Ibid, 13 October 1972, p638.
27 Ibid, 18 January 1974, p680; 15 February 1974, p681.
28 Ibid, 13 October 1972, p638.
29 Ibid, 19 December 1969, p555.
30 Ibid, 16 July 1971, p610.
31 Ibid, 17 December 1971, p619.
32 Ibid, 15 November 1974, p705.
33 Ibid, 18 March 1966, p424.
34 Ibid, 21 November 1969, p552; 20 March 1970, p563.
35 Minute Book No 6, 1966–74, 15 August 1975, p729.
36 Minute Book No 5, 1966–74, 25 August 1972, p636.
37 Ibid, 14 June 1974, p692.
38 Minute Book No 6, 1975–80, 17 January 1975, p709; 14 November 1975, p735.
39 Ibid, 14 November 1975, p735.

Peter S. Low, William Low and John D. B. Smart at St James' with the Sulzer weaving machines in the background, c. 1983

Acquiring Newfordpark from Thiokol in 1977 was a major step for Dons, and allowed the company to manufacture its own polypropylene tape

Chapter Twelve

Growth and Consolidation, 1975–86

During the later 1970s Dons reaped the rewards of their early lead in polymer-based textile manufacture. Pre-tax profits soared from £413,000 in 1971–72 to £1.3 million in 1976–77, the first time ever they had surpassed £1 million. As Table 12.1 shows, they almost reached £4 million in 1978–79, a 'Klondyke' year according to William Low, who took over as chairman in 1975, as well as becoming chief executive.

Table 12.1 *Don Bros, Buist & Co Ltd, Turnover and Pre-tax Profits (£000), 1975–76 to 1985–86*

Year	Turnover	Pre-tax Profits
1975–76	13,179	732
1976–77	16,802	1,306
1977–78	22,281	2,645
1978–79	26,976	3,987
1979–80	28,567	1,874
1980–81	24,998	188
1981–82	26,634	1,415
1982–83	28,156	1,219
1983–84	39,226	2,859
1984–85	51,577	4,559
1985–86	48,240	2,506

Source: Company annual accounts, St James' Rd

Although Dons had been able to increase both their turnover and profits against the background of depressed economic conditions of 1975 and 1976, this was not possible during 1980 when markets were described as 'extremely low' in Western Europe, 'bad' in Eastern Europe and 'disastrous' at home. With many of the company's customers either closing down or on short-time, the board decided that they should accept business 'even at ridiculously low prices' in an attempt to keep the various factories in operation. Even so, short-time working was introduced in some parts of the group.[1]

Yet neither the record year of 1978–79 nor the bleak months of 1980–81 were typical of the period as a whole. Indeed it should be noted that the figures for 1978–79 were inflated by the inclusion for the first time of Thiokol's turnover and earnings in the accounts (see below). This chapter is concerned not so much with the short-term fluctuations in the company's fortunes but rather with the principal themes and developments in a decade which culminated with the take-over of Dons by Shell. It was a period of substantial corporate expansion and major structural and financial reorganisation.

Polypropylene: maintaining the lead

In volume terms, the European market, in which, as has been seen in the previous chapter, Dons had begun to make a serious challenge in the early 1970s, became increasingly important. By 1977, following a massive 69 per cent rise in sales between 1975 and 1976, Europe had become the company's main outlet for polypropylene carpet backing.[2] Much of this was the result of the company's efforts at the Frankfurt Fairs, as well as through the agency of Tata AG, who did much to smooth Dons' path into both EFTA and EEC markets. In 1979 Dons made their first appearance at the Paris Fair.

Expanding sales, of course, necessitated further investment in plant and machinery, and between 1974 and 1976 some £2 million was spent by Dons.[3] In January 1976, for example, following the company's second appearance at the Frankfurt Fair, an order was placed for an additional eight 213-inch Sulzers, capable of weaving some five million square yards of polypropylene annually. Eight more were ordered in March, again with a view to satisfying European demand.[4] By 1982 there were 92 Sulzer looms at St James'. In needleweave too, where George Guild was making considerable progress, capacity was expanded with the arrival of a third Fehrer machine at Canmore Works in January 1977.[5] This increased the firm's potential output of this fabric to 50 million square metres per annum, which made Dons the biggest manufacturer of needleweave cloth in Europe.

Not surprisingly, the company was running out of space. Sidlaw Industries' (formerly Jute Industries Ltd) decision in 1976 to close down their Den Burn Works in Brechin appeared to provide a partial solution, though, and Dons purchased the factory for £100,000. By August 1977 it had been fitted up with 12 Sulzers, and with a pool of skilled labour to draw from, was ready to join the highly efficient Valley Works and underline Brechin's role as the company's main source of polypropylene for the UK market. By the end of the year Den Burn was producing the equivalent of 16 million square metres of polypropylene per annum. Although Den Burn was closed down as a result of rationalisation after the reverse of 1981, in the following September Dons acquired, for around £700,000, the machinery from Low & Bonar's Victoria Works. It was anticipated that this purchase would give the company a greater hold over the polypropylene trade, not least because it secured for them 32 more Sulzers, some of which were newer than those at St James', as well as 16 Dornier looms, for weaving jute.[6]

In order for Dons to maintain their place at the front of the region's polypropylene manufacturers though, more was required than simply additional productive capacity. Secure supplies of polypropylene tape were essential, as was strict quality control. Dons went a long way towards meeting these requirements when the company embarked on what was by far their most ambitious undertaking during the period under review, namely the acquisition of Thiokol's Newfordpark factory. This they did, at an eventual cost of £5.3 million, in December 1977. The massive investment, which was funded by a combination of bank loans and overdrafts (most previous financing had been from within), gave Dons for the first time complete control over all polypropylene production from the polymer stage onwards, and indeed the ability to sell tape themselves, while the Thiokol management were able to redirect their energies into 'speciality' chemicals.[7] A further bonus for Dons was that Thiokol's Robert C. Naylor joined them as a director.

Since the establishment of a laboratory at Canmore Works when the company had first begun to weave polypropylene tape, Dons had placed a high premium on research, and the results of this made major contributions to their fortunes. New techniques, such as 'open end' or dref spinning, were introduced, using polypropylene fibres from Newfordpark. Ultimately the yarn made by this process replaced jute weft in the company's secondary carpet backing, thereby further weakening jute's status within the group. New lines were developed, notably in geotextiles, one of the most notable products of which was 'Lotrak'. This was the outcome of a collaborative effort involving Dons, the Lambeg Industrial Research Association and the University of Edinburgh, which had been directed towards ways of discovering civil engineering applications for needled and woven polypropylene. Unusually in an industry which still had a strong attachment to its heritage and rather too much respect for manufacturing and selling skills learned through a lifetime in the trade (although these could still be invaluable), Dons were beginning to employ graduates such as civil engineers (as they had employed carpet technicians in the early days of polypropylene) as 'technical sales' staff in order to develop products which were precisely matched to their end uses. Sales of Lotrak, which could be used for a variety of civil engineering and building functions, stabilising earth embankments for example, began on a small scale in 1976, but as its success was proven, within two years sales had risen to over one million square metres per annum.[8]

Near the end of the 1970s, however, there were signs that the polypropylene market was becoming glutted. In 1978–79 Dons achieved no increase in export sales, partly because Amoco (formerly Patchogue-Plymouth) offered very generous terms to prospective buyers, and in June 1978, for instance, obtained orders from one of Dons' customers by offering extended credit facilities.[9] Early in 1980, as the sterling exchange rate was rising, it was noted with some discomfort that the same company (Amoco) was 'taking business at any price in order to maintain 5-day working'.[10] Dons adopted a similar strategy, accepting large unprofitable orders of 3.4 million square metres of polypropylene cloth from Poland and the USSR, in order to maintain production and reduce overheads, and, of course, to

Dref Spinning,
Canmore Works

Shot which vividly demonstrates the extent of Dons' commitment to Sulzers, St James', early 1980s

ensure their continued presence in the market. In the longer run, however, the appearance in the lower end of the market of polypropylene-backed carpeting made in Ulster, the Continent (especially Belgium) and the US, as well as the so-called underdeveloped countries, was interpreted as a warning that the search for new 'niche' products, preferably in the quality end of the trade, had to be maintained. Another period of diversification was begun, but this time – with one exception – within the textile industry.

A major step in this direction was taken in June 1983 when negotiations were opened with Scott and Robertson PLC regarding the possible purchase by Dons of Tay Textiles, which employed 450 people in two plants, in Dundee and Perth. The attraction of Tay Textiles to Dons, for which they paid £350,000, was that they made a specialist polypropylene tape which was used to make FIBCs (Flexible Intermediate Bulk Containers). Remarkably strong, these products, marketed under the name 'Taybags', could carry weights of up to two tonnes.[11]

Dons' aim, which was to make make Tay Textiles an efficient and profitable part of the group (Tay Textiles was encumbered with debt when Dons bought it), was not easily achieved though. Reorganisation and refitting at Perth alone cost £412,720,[12] while in Dundee production of FIBCs was shifted from Bower Works into National Cash Registers' former Camperdown factory in May 1986, following refurbishment and the siting of Don and Low's sales division there, at a cost of £1.25 million. This was part of a wider process of rationalisation of Dons' production, extrusion being halted at Tay Textiles' Stobswell Works and concentrated instead at Newfordpark.

In January 1986 a five-shift system was introduced into all of the company's factories. The benefit of this to Dons was that the machine working time was raised from 46.3 weeks per annum to 50.7, with the only break occurring at Christmas and New Year. Continuous production was vital if the company was to obtain a return from the £4 million which had been earmarked for investment in new machinery. Although the employees' traditional holiday pattern was broken, there were considerable advantages for them too from the new system in that working hours were reduced from 42 to 39, while over a year the new shifts were the equivalent of only 44 weeks of five days.[13]

Thus far, the impression may have been given that the reorganisation of the firm's activities took place on a rather haphazard basis. Of course, there were times when this was true, as potential opportunities were seized as they arose, as in November 1979, when Dons took a majority shareholding in a computer firm, Gate Microsystems of Dundee. Of only marginal relevance to Dons though, the firm was sold within a year.[14]

Between 1976 and the time of the Shell take-over, however, some formal reorganisation was undertaken. The first step was in the spring of 1979, when six administrative divisions were created: Don Textiles Ltd, the most important, which controlled all the company's weaving production in Forfar and Brechin; Don Fibres Ltd, which was concerned with polypropylene extrusion; Don Coatings Ltd, which was the new name for Buchanans of Prestonpans; Don and Low Ltd, the packaging plant in Arbroath; Strathmore Woollens and Low Brothers. Shortly thereafter a seventh division was created, Don (Forfar) Ltd, to act as a central administrative unit.[15] This organisational structure was modified in the following year when an Industrial Textiles Production Division (ITPD) was established, incorporating the Forfar and Brechin factories as well as Don Coatings and Low Bros, along with an Industrial Textiles Sales Division (ITSD).

Reorganisation brought closures too, of the less successful components within the group. Production at Don Coatings, for instance, was stopped in July 1982, even though a Menscher coating machine had been purchased and installed at a cost of £535,000 in 1980. In spite of its cost it had rarely performed at more than 50 per cent capacity. The operation at Prestonpans had not been as successful as had been anticipated, partly due to inadequate market research and what some judged to be poor industrial relations. In March 1983, on the recommendation of Alister Wilson, then the director in charge there, it was decided to abandon production at Strathmore Woollens, which was taken over by David D. Cowley, Strathmore's Scottish sales manager. Don & Low Ltd, the packaging subsidiary at Arbroath, had actually done better in the second half of the

Dons' new raw material. Polymer extrusion line at Newfordpark, 1980s

1970s than the poor first half. Even so, although the Royal Wedding in 1981 had provided a temporary fillip, 1980 had been a difficult year and in 1982–83 the company sustained a trading loss of £115,000. Don & Low (Packaging) Ltd, as the company was renamed in May 1983, continued to make losses and in November 1985 was sold to Low & Bonar.[16]

Reorganisation of a vastly different sort (which had been unsuccessfully urged on the Board a decade earlier), had occurred in May 1982 when with some trepidation the company went public and became known as Don Bros, Buist PLC. A year later Dons were given a full Stock Exchange listing (the first Scottish company to obtain this since 1979). The 6.5 million shares, which were expected to sell for between 63p and 65p, actually rose to 83p during the first day's trading, but eventually settled back at around 70p, giving Dons a valuation of some £5 million.[17]

With their financial basis looking more secure, the directors could plan for the future in a way which had hardly been possible beforehand. One of their first moves was to acquire the aforementioned Tay Textiles. At the same time, as has been seen, Dons continued to divest themselves of the less successful parts of the group. Further restructuring occurred in January 1984, when in an attempt to consolidate and co-ordinate the group's activities J. & J. Smart, Low Bros and Don Fibres, along with the trading activities of Don Bros, Buist & Co were merged into Don & Low Ltd, the name being launched in May. The holding company, however, continued as Don Bros, Buist PLC.[18]

JUTE: FURTHER RATIONALISATION

Although jute sales had been maintained during the second half of the 1970s, the supply of raw materials continued to be unpredictable, making it necessary for Dons to hold large stocks. Despite this background, as has been noted already, a number of Dornier looms were purchased, underlining the company's continued commitment to jute, even at this late stage – although the acquisition of the Dorniers did have the advantage of releasing Sulzer weaving machines for use in poly-

The former NCR site at Camperdown, Dundee, which was acquired by the Don & Low Group in 1985 and officially opened by the Secretary of State for Scotland, Malcolm Rifkind, in May 1986. The complex was used both by Tay Textiles Ltd and the sales organisation of Don & Low.

propylene, for which they were better suited. For jute, however, the way the wind was blowing was becoming increasingly obvious, and in June 1978 the news broke that H. & A. Scott, the Dundee-based firm of jute spinners and polypropylene weavers, were to cease spinning jute.[19] Dons determined to continue, although there was some further rationalisation, with jute production being concentrated solely in Strang Street. Indeed, there was still some life in the company's traditional trade: although output was 'modest' in the middle of 1981, jute was still making a profit.[20] Even so, in the longer term, as far as jute spinning was concerned, Dons were on the retreat, with 14 of the company's 24 Mackie Apron Draft spinning machines being sold off between 1979 and 1981. By the spring of 1983 the quantity being spun had fallen to an uneconomic level of 22 tonnes a week and, as a result, the board decided to abandon jute spinning altogether. Henceforth jute yarns were purchased from Sidlaw Industries, and increasingly, from abroad.

Chapter Twelve: Growth and Consolidation

1 Minute Book No 6, 1975–80, 4 July 1980, p1065.
2 Ibid, 26 January 1978, p821.
3 *Forfar Times*, 18 June 1986.
4 Minute Book No 6, 19 March 1976, p745.
5 The enforced departure of Guild from the company in March 1981 is much regretted by the current management.
6 *Forfar Dispatch*, 3 March 1977; Minute Book No 7,1981–84, 3 September 1982, p1206.
7 Minute Book No 6, 1975–80, 23 December 1977, p816.
8 Ibid, 13 February 1976, p743; 24 February 1978, p826.
9 Ibid, 16 June 1978, p843.
10 Ibid, 29 February, 1980, p1043.
11 Minute Book No 7, 1981–84, 21 October 1983, p1308; *Forfar Dispatch*, 27 October 1983.
12 Ibid.
13 *Forfar Dispatch*, 19 September, 1985.
14 Minute Book No 6, 1975–80, 23 November 1979;3 October 1980, p1075.
15 Ibid, 19 April 1979, p889.
16 Minute Book No 8, 1985–88, 22 November 1985, p1454.
17 *Forfar Dispatch*, 19 May, 1983.
18 Minute Book No 7, 1981–84, 28 May 1984, p1362.
19 Minute Book No 6, 1975–80, 16 June 1978, p843.
20 Chairman's statement, 1980–81.

Don & Low's newest factory, Orchardpark, Forfar, opened in 1988

Chapter Thirteen

Shell: The End of an Era and a New Beginning, 1986–92

By any standards Don Bros, Buist PLC was an immensely successful company by the mid-1980s. After the poor financial year of 1980–81, profits rose to a peak of just over £4.5 million in 1984–85. Turnover was £51.6 million, almost twice the 1978–79 level and more than six times that of 1974–75, when for the first time polypropylene had become more important for Dons than jute. Although home sales continued to bring greater returns to the company – which had captured 60 per cent of the UK domestic market in polypropylene carpet backing – Dons managed to extend their market-share abroad, partly by being prepared to accept slimmer profit margins, and even to endure losses in some areas (e.g. Greece). As a result, export turnover was increased from £5.5 million in 1979 to £16.7 million in 1985. The company was the UK's biggest polypropylene extrusion and weaving unit; in Western Europe, only one polypropylene company was doing better. The esteem in which Dons were held in Europe is in part reflected in the re-election for the third time of William Low as chairman of the European Association for Textile Polyolefins in 1984, a post which his son W. Barclay Low (currently Dons' personnel director) has held since 1989.[1]

Beneath the surface though, there was considerable unease. Much of this was due to what can best be described as the succession problem, which by the middle of the decade had become a damaging distraction. From the mid-1960s executive control of Dons had in effect been in the hands of five directors, Ernest Gourlay, Michael Hill (the largest individual shareholder on the board), Peter S. Low, William Low and John Smart. Chief amongst them, however, in both rank (i.e. as chairman and chief executive) and demeanour, was William Low. The others, of course, had reasonably clearly designated roles, although Hill felt uneasy with his strategic development remit. Each too, in their various ways, had made valuable contributions to the company. Three of them, Hill, Low and Smart, could legitimately lay claim to higher things (although John Smart's health was failing) – and in the early 1980s it became apparent that an opportunity for advancement would soon open up.

William Low was approaching retirement age, and accordingly increasing attention was given to the question of who was to succeed him. Such was his stature within and when acting on behalf of the company that it would clearly take quite a remarkable individual to satisfy Low – as well as other 'non-combatants' on the board – that his successor was both worthy and capable of stepping into his shoes. Unhappily, in the short term, none of the potential heirs (of which the most anxious to replace Low looked to those around him to be Michael Hill) could obtain sufficient support from their fellow directors. Earlier, signs that Robert Naylor was being groomed as the heir-apparent had produced strong opposition from individuals on the boards of Don Bros, Buist & Co and the subsidiary companies. Bruised but not bowed, Naylor left the company in 1982.

Clearly the impasse had to be broken, as a divided board would not be in the best condition to deal with a series of challenges which the company faced. The most immediate was what was soon acknowledged to be an 'alarming' number of difficulties at Tay Textiles, while there were also worries about poor production figures at Newfordpark and Wallace Works in Perth, and high jute stocks. Canmore Works' dref spinning operation was much less than satisfactory too. In the longer run there were worries about the variability of polymer prices – and over the growing competitive threat of their major rivals in Europe, Amoco and TTC. There were signs too that Dons may have lost something of the edge they had had earlier in the development of new products. (Very soon after the takeover, for example, it was reported that Amoco's CLW was attracting customers away from Dons formerly innovative needleweave products.) The appointment of Peter S. Low and John Smart as joint managing directors in March 1985 gave both men a taste of greater responsibility within their separate spheres (marketing and production respectively), but in the longer run may not have been the best solution to a situation which required single-minded leadership.

With the benefit of hindsight, the logic of a takeover of Dons by a multinational petrochemical company like Shell can be readily understood. As early as 1979, when Dons (through Don Fibres Ltd) had become Shell's biggest polymer customer in Europe, Shell had suggested that the two companies might collaborate on research into new products and equipment in the polypropylene field. Although Dons' board turned down the proposal, it was agreed that Shell would supply 60 per cent of Dons' polymer requirements.

Yet at the very time that the conditions of the takeover were being finalised (during the summer of 1986) Dons were conducting acrimonious discussions with Shell about the poor quality of the polymer they were delivering at Forfar, a situation which was ultimately considered by William Low to be so serious that he ordered a reduction in the quantity of Shell polymer being purchased. This was the sort of problem which could be resolved through the closer but informal technical contacts which had developed between the two companies prior to 1986. Indeed, anything other than an arm's length understanding of this sort had looked most unlikely as late as 1984 – at least publicly – when William Low had assured Dons' customers and staff that despite the restructuring which was then taking place within the group (and specifically the transfer of the marketing and selling functions of Low Brothers & Co Ltd to Don & Low PLC), 'we are still very much the same family firm we have always been'.

It was this fact and the culture, traditions and fierce loyalties which were bound up with what had been a remarkably long-lived locally-owned family firm which caused many people within the company, from director-level down to the office and shop-floor, to treat the possibility of a takeover by Shell Chemicals UK with some apprehension. In some quarters the reaction was outright hostility when in the early months of 1986 the first news began to trickle out that an approach had been made to Shell and that a deal was in the offing. Despite the considerable reservations of some members of the board, however, discussions continued and at the end of May the directors and the vast majority of the shareholders accepted Shell's offer of 175p per ordinary share. This was 41 per cent above the prevailing market value, and gave the company a capital value of just under £23 million. As a result, large shareholders such as the Dons and their relations, as well as the Buists (who between them accounted for over half of the company's shares) made considerable financial gains. At the same time though, they lost control of a company with which the forebears of the former had been involved for the best part of two centuries. Henceforth, Dons was to be a wholly-owned subsidiary of Shell.

Both Shell and those members of Dons' board who had been the strongest advocates of the move were convinced that the new arrangement would bring substantial advantages. Dons would have access to Shell's research and development facilities. Shell's capital resources would be a major benefit if Dons were to maintain their heavy investment programme, which in the pre-Shell years had been in the region of £2 million to £3 million per annum. The multinational's 'international facilities' and overseas links would make it easier for Dons to expand their sales in the Third World, a developing market which they wanted to be in from the start. There was the security too of the support of a petrochemicals giant, which would make it far less likely that Amoco or any other major rival would embark on a price-cutting war with Dons. For its part, Shell hoped to benefit from Dons' technical and marketing expertise in polypropylene.

The takeover also settled the thorny matter of the succession. On the same day that Shell's appointees, John A. Collins (who had been mooted in some circles as a possible successor to Low) and C. N. C. Haslam joined Dons' board, Michael Hill retired, and so severed the last ties which the Don family had with the firm. He was followed out in September by the Buist's representative on the board, John B. Watson. Ill-health forced the resignation of John Smart at the end of January 1987.

Part of the agreement with Shell was that William Low should remain as executive chairman for a year in order to ease the transition process (although in fact Low did not finally relinquish the post of non-executive chairman until the autumn of 1989). Further continuity at board-level was provided by Ernest Gourlay, the company's director of finance, company secretary S. L. Howie, Peter S. Low, Donald B. Grant (a highly respected accountant brought in by William Low) and Professor P. H. Grinyer of the University of St Andrews, who had been invited by Low (with the support of Michael Hill) to bring his considerable expertise in management theory and practice to Dons shortly before the Shell takeover.

Altogether new to the board – and indeed to textiles – was the new chief executive Alasdair N. MacCallum, who took up his post in November. MacCallum was a chemistry graduate from the University of Glasgow who, after gaining management experience with a number of companies, had engineered a remarkable turnaround in the fortunes of Devro Ltd in Glasgow. His appointment with Dons (made following a recommendation to Shell by the British Linen Bank), which was at first greeted with some scepticism by some of the company's older staff who were suspicious of the fact that MacCallum was not a dyed-in-jute 'textile man', proved to be of immense importance.

STIFFER WINDS – BATTENING DOWN AND CHANGING TACK

By 1986 the period of more of less continuous expansion which had characterised the polypropylene industry in its earlier years was well and truly over. Although the textile trade had always been cyclical in nature – and continued to be – the longer term outlook was much less comfortable than it had been in the 1970s. Ominously, in April 1987, it was reported to the board that 'Over-capacity looks like being a problem in our industry for some time'. This was to prove to be a painfully accurate forecast, and a theme which was to emerge time and time again over the next four years. There were moments of optimism (as in February 1989) when it looked as though a new equilibrium in the market-place would be established within a reasonable period. Such hopes, however, always proved to be ill-founded.

The problem was most acute in Europe; it still is. That this was not a temporary phenomenon but an instance of serious structural dislocation in the market first became obvious in 1987 when the Belgium-based Beaulieu Group, the world's largest manufacturer of tufted carpets, began to make significant quantities of primary backing of their own. A fact-finding visit to Beaulieu by Alasdair MacCallum and Peter S. Low in the second half of 1987 revealed that they were also laying plans to extrude their own polypropylene – as a result of frustrations they had encountered in obtaining sufficient volume at acceptable prices from producers already in the field. This was a major blow to suppliers such as Dons, who faced the prospect of selling in a European market for tufted carpet backing which, as a consequence of Beaulieu's actions, would in 1987 terms be at least one-fifth smaller. With polymer prices in the autumn of 1987 being 25 per cent higher than they had been a year earlier, a fall in export prices of between five and 15 per cent and a rise in home market prices which was not greater than the retail price index, the outlook was far from promising.

Despite this, 1987 and 1988 were moderately successful years for Dons. As Table 13.1 reveals, export turnover did rise between 1986–87 and the year ending December 1988, while at home the increase in business was even bigger. Together these results made for a pre-tax profit-level for 1988 which 'comfortably' exceeded the budget forecast.

Table 13.1 *Home and Export Turnover, and Consolidated Pre-tax Profits (£m), 1986–7 – 1990*

Year	Turnover (home)	Turnover (export)	Pre-tax Profit
1986–87	25.9	17.4	3.7
1987 (7 mths to Dec)	15.0	10.2	2.1
1988 (to December)	28.1	18.0	3.7
1989 (to December)	27.0	19.3	4.0
1990 (to December)	25.3	19.2	4.6

The board could also take considerable comfort from the performance of some of their rivals.[2] In Dundee, for example, William Halley's profits from their textile business were reported to have dropped sharply while in Northern Ireland, Synthetic Industries saw a fall in profits from around £1 million in 1985 to £156,000 in 1987. And long before these figures were reported to the board (in April 1988) the directors had noted with some satisfaction that while their Sulzers were still busy, some 100 of Amoco's looms in Europe and 70 of those belonging to

Holland's TTC were idle. A similar situation was observed in the first half of 1989.

In large part, the fact that Dons were able to operate at more or less full capacity was due to the success of their marketing efforts (although a weakening of sterling against the currencies of their major European competitors at the end of 1986 was also advantageous in the short-term). Under the direction of Peter S. Low, the company's sales staff had conquered markets throughout Europe. Unlike some of their competitors, who were restricted geographically by their parent companies, Dons were able – indeed encouraged by theirs – to search for additional outlets in the first years of the Shell era, with markets being established both in the Middle and Far East, entry into which was often eased by the contacts Shell could provide. For a time in the late 1980s it looked as though Dons would establish, with Shell's assistance, joint manufacturing operations with producers in countries such as China, India and Saudi Arabia.

Although these did not materialise – in China because the political situation destabilised in 1989, for example – the company's intensified sales efforts did produce measurable results. One estimate suggested that at the peak of the company's sales drive in the Middle East, Don & Low had captured between 80 and 90 per cent of the market for carpet backing. In a sense, though, the most remarkable achievement was to be seen in Australia where, by 1987, after several years' work, Dons had secured some 17 per cent of the market for Forfar-made carpet backing – despite unsubstantiated claims by Amoco that the company had been operating a 'dumping' policy. By the end of 1988 Peter S. Low was able to report that Dons had managed to achieve a highly impressive 14 per cent of the world market for their products.

This should not detract from the company's relatively strong performance nearer home, especially from the end of the 1980s when the recession, exacerbated in the UK by high interest rates, sharply reduced consumer demand in the company's traditional carpet, upholstery and house-building markets. Yet while sales of and returns from carpet backing fell as companies such as Lowndes Queensway, Coloroll and B&Q ran into difficulties in 1990, Dons were able to increase their market share, from around 42 per cent in 1988 to some 50 per cent in

1990, when, significantly, agreement was reached with Coats Viyella (the UK's biggest carpet manufacturer) that Dons would in future supply half of their tufted carpet backing requirements. (Shaw Carpets, however, are currently Dons' biggest single customer for tufted carpet backing.) Sales of other products on the other hand – notably geotextiles with their immensely successful products such as Lotrak – strengthened consistently, both at home and abroad, although these too began to be adversely hit by the downturn in construction industry activity in 1990.

Impressive as they are, however, volumes and market-share alone provide an inadequate measure of performance, and in this regard there was a marked change of emphasis within the company. Traditionally, Dons' directors had been inclined to judge the achievement of their sales personnel by the volume of cloth they sold – the greater the number of square metres of orders the better. In order to secure these, and to squeeze out competitors, Dons had long been prepared to accept low prices or even sell at a loss – high tariff barriers, for instance, meant that their Australian trade was unprofitable. In addition (and echoing the situation as it had been in Victorian and Edwardian times) the company prided itself on the range of its products – which as late as 1988 was seen to be giving it an edge over some of its rivals who had rather less to offer. In the sense that Dons made and sold carpet backing and geotextiles, this was indeed beneficial. This, however, was not the problem.

The fact that Shell is a more demanding shareholder, combined with the much more rigorous market conditions of the late 1980s, when prices were low virtually everywhere, had led to a major rethink, with Alasdair MacCallum in October 1991 urging the sales force to consider the volume of money rather than the volume of cloth. Earlier, in 1990, as had happened when a similar problem had emerged in the difficult 1920s, the first steps had been taken to rationalise production by reducing the range of qualities of cloth on offer (over 1,000 were identified by Derrick G. Mitchell shortly after his appointment as Sales and Marketing Director in October 1989) and concentrate instead on those which offered the best profit margins.[3] Alister Wilson, who had left the Boase Spinning Co in 1969 to join Dons as factory manager at St James' (which was then devoted solely to the manufacture of jute), and risen through the ranks to become manufacturing director, successfully urged the board that the company's long-established sales philosophy should be altered from one driven by customer wants to one which was geared to customer needs. Wilson's appointment late in 1991 as Operations Director, a new post created to co-ordinate sales and production is both testimony to his ability and an indication of Dons' determination to improve their competitive position in the market-place.

Greater attention was also to be paid to the size of orders: the operating costs of Nonwovens (see below), for instance, had exceeded their budget forecast partly because they had (necessarily) accepted too many small orders, a practice which throughout the group reduced margins not least because of the costs involved in employing the administrative, clerical and supervisory staff who were required to process the orders. In addition, and nudged in this direction by Shell, Don & Low Ltd's sales strategy was given a sharper focus in the amended 'Country Plan' for 1990–95 (a Shell-led innovation), with the emphasis being placed on the Middle East and Europe rather than in the more distant territories which had been developed in the previous four or five years. Significantly, a few months beforehand in January 1990, the board of Don & Low Ltd had decided to conduct market research in Germany, where formerly Amoco had been given virtually a free hand. By the end of 1991 the campaign had got under way, with the recruitment of the German-born Klaus Gersabeck as European sales executive in Don & Low's new Dusseldorf office. Further appointments are to follow as Dons strive to sharpen their sales drive in Germany, France and the Benelux countries. These are very recent developments, and although the first signs are promising, at this stage it is simply too soon to judge how effective they will be. Other weaknesses which were identified after 1986 have been tackled, with varying degrees of success.

Very early on (in the winter of 1987), during a review of the company's marketing and development operations, it was recognised by the board that in order to improve its position vis-à-vis its rivals (notably Amoco) and satisfy its new owners, the company would have to rediscover its earlier enthusiasm for product innovation. Such products, the board agreed, also had to be of an acceptable quality and price. Although they were satisfied that they were doing well enough in keeping the company's existing products up to date, it was also felt that despite the successes of the 1970s and early 1980s, sales performance could be improved, in particular by penetrating new markets. As has just been seen, considerable advances in this direction were made during the subsequent years.

As far as new products were concerned, agreement was quickly reached that the company would embark on an entirely new venture – appropriately enough in chemical-based non-woven fabrics, which are currently used for a variety of purposes such as agricultural crop covers ('GroShield'), membranes for the construction industry ('FrameShield'), and protective clothing ('Daltex'). They also have medical applications. During the spring and summer of 1987 a proposal was put together for capital investment from Shell (who strongly supported the project) of £4.9 million for plant and equipment to produce spun-bonded cloth. In July 1988, less than a year after the foundation stone was laid, Don & Low Nonwovens was launched at the company's new factory – 'the best modern building in Angus' – at Orchardpark, Forfar. The total investment was to be £6 million, a sum which emphasises the importance to Dons of Shell's capital resources. It was an important milestone in the company's history for less obvious reasons too: since the appearance of Shell, there had been understandable fears in Forfar about the extent to which the multinational would remain committed to the area. The investment at Orchardpark made it clear what Shell's position was, and that Don & Low's future was secure.

The first omens were good, with a £1 million order from Europe announced shortly after the plant was opened. Recession and a variety of problems within Nonwovens itself, however, dampened the early enthusiasm, and although turnover in 1989 was £6 million and the quality of their innovative products favourably commented on by customers, production costs were too high, not only because of short runs and frequent colour changes but also due to much higher than forecast waste levels from the Reicofil non-woven machines. Price cutting abroad simply compounded Nonwovens' difficulties. Attempts to resolve some of these by tightening up accounting pro-

John Collins in St James Works, Forfar, shortly after he joined Don & Low (Holdings) Board in his position as Chief Executive of Shell Chemicals UK. (John Collins has since been appointed Chief Executive of Shell UK)

cedures with the appointment of a new finance manager, reducing waste and stock levels and appointing a fresh managing director, were not enough to avert a loss in 1991 of some £0.5 million, although substantial progress had been made.

As this suggests, new technology and new products have played a prominent role in Dons' recent history. Vital too, though, has been continued investment in up-to-date technology in the core business, tufted carpet backing. Thus, in 1990 £2 million was invested in 20 new high-speed Sulzers for St James' Works. Costing £80,000 each, the new machines were capable of running at 280 picks per minute, compared to their predecessors' 220 ppm.

The obvious need for a high degree of technical know-how has resulted in a discernible difference in the type of personnel employed by the company at management level. In the 1950s and 1960s Dundee's Technical Institute was the region's main provider of vocational training in textiles and it was unusual to find university graduates or diploma holders from higher education at Dons, or indeed in the jute industry as a whole. In this respect, Michael Hill's educational background and training were unusual, although also highly advantageous. It is now commonplace for the company to recruit graduates and highly trained technicians for senior positions, as in the cases of Dr Andrew Ferrar, a Cambridge graduate who joined the company as strategic development director at the end of 1987, and Les Squires, with a PhD from the University of Leeds, who became Nonwovens' technical manager in 1990. More recently Alison Gambling, a Cambridge graduate, has been appointed as marketing manager. Where universities have had something to offer, Dons have been prepared to utilise it. Thus, following a marketing course at the University of Strathclyde in 1987, which was attended by most of the directors of both Don & Low and Tay Textiles, it was decided to conduct an internal reorganisation of the company's sales division by establishing business centres which would be separately responsible for floor-coverings, industrials and, later, geotextiles.

More had to be done, however, if Dons were to achieve the competitive position to which the management aspired. Almost from the very first post-takeover board meeting it became apparent that Shell's representatives would be scrutinising the company's performance much more closely than anyone in Dons had been used to before. Profit margins, the rate of return on investment – cost efficiencies – replaced the share price as the measure of corporate achievement.

Clearing the decks

Prudently, according to those who worked with him, the new chief executive Alasdair MacCallum spent his first few months at Dons watching and learning, acquiring the language and know-how of the textile trade both in the UK and overseas and discovering what made Dons tick. Along with other newcomers on the board, he soon recognised that there was room for improvements, some of which have already been discussed.

In addition to these it was becoming increasingly obvious in 1986 and 1987 that as Dons were not then in a position to distance themselves from their rivals in terms of quality or price, not only would new markets have to be opened up but in order to improve the company's competitiveness and attract further investment from Shell, ways would have to be found to cut costs and increase productivity.

This meant looking closely at the less successful parts of the group. Easily the most notable of these was Tay Textiles Ltd, acquired as part of the diversification strategy which had been commenced prior to the Shell takeover. From the time of its acquisition by Dons, the venture had promised much but despite considerable investment (notably at Camperdown in Dundee) and spirited efforts on the part of those involved, it never realised its potential. With the appointment of a new management team in 1987 the subsidiary seemed to have turned the corner but bad luck (the bankruptcy of a major customer) and a downturn in export sales in the second part of 1988 and early in 1989 led the board of the holding company to reconsider Tay Textiles' position within the group. Throughout, it had either made losses, or profits which were lower than anticipated, and despite a last-minute cost-cutting exercise which involved redundancies at both staff and shop-floor levels, in August 1989 it was agreed to sell Tay Textiles to Van Leer (UK) Holdings Ltd. Although Dons carried the considerable burden of Tay Textiles' debt, the elimination of the accumulated losses improved the holding company's revenues by over £950,000. With plans in hand to dispose of the Camperdown site, Dons were in the final stages of their second withdrawal from Dundee this century, which had begun with the sale of Bower Works and Henderson's Warehouse, the functions of the last being replaced in Forfar by the Broadcroft warehouse and loading bays over the road from St James' works. Further disinvestment took place when, at the end of 1987, the board decided that they should abandon the loss-making multifilament yarns sector where, in technical terms, Dons had fallen behind and which was diverting managerial energies away from more profitable activities. Viewed in the long term though, the biggest departure for Dons was the decision to retire from jute.

JUTE: DOWN – AND FINALLY OUT

As has been seen, Dons' commitment to jute had been waning for some time, and by the second half of the 1980s its position within the group – with spinning having been given up in 1983 – was extremely vulnerable. Not only was the trade at the mercy of the pricing policies of India and Bangladesh, but it also became apparent that the jute business was suffering due to the company's lack of a 'jute expert'. Sales and profit levels were also dropping off. As a result, early in 1990, with the number of rolls being sold well below half those manufactured at Strang Street, it was decided to conduct a review of the company's jute operation, though in the short term to make a spirited effort to increase sales to the ailing building industry.

Although a new manager of the jute department was found, his period in office was to be extremely short. Losses continued as prices remained low and stocks accumulated as attempts to obtain new orders failed. There was only one realistic course of action and in May 1990 the board of Don & Low decided to 'withdraw from jute'. What in historical terms was a momentous decision was rapidly executed, although for a time it appeared as though their manager, Ron Murray, might head a group which would purchase Strang Street from Dons. Any lingering hopes amongst those jute workers who had a strong emotional attachment to the old fibre that Dons could be persuaded to change their mind were dashed in December when the number of shifts at Strang Street were cut from two to one, leading to 30 redundancies. In January 1991 the board put a stop to all production and ordered their agent to have all jute stocks cleared out before the end of June. Another link with the company's past – forged a century and a half beforehand – had been broken.

The executive directors of Don and Low in June 1982.
Back: *Andrew Ferrar, Allan Hall, Barclay Low, Tim Ward*
Front: *David Petrie, Alasdair MacCallum (Chief Executive), Alister Wilson*

Management, men (and women)

As part of the programme of rationalisation and reform, Alasdair MacCallum initiated dramatic changes in the nature and ethos of the company. Although part of a deliberate strategy, this was necessitated too by the disappearance from the firm of key figures: company secretary Stuart L. Howie retired early, in 1989; tragically, two sales directors, David Smith and Louis Smith, died while on company business. New men (including those mentioned previously) were brought in at middle-management level and above. Women too began to make an appearance in more elevated posts than ever before – the aforementioned Alison Gambling who took up her position in marketing in 1991, for example, and Dorothy Johnston, Dons' pensions manager from 1984. This was a revolutionary departure for a firm in an industry which has traditionally only employed women in subordinate positions.

Delegation of responsibility has been very much part of the new strategy, the result of which has been the tapping of latent talent at various levels of management. The business centres which were established in 1987 in an effort to make each unit within the group more accountable and profit-conscious were part of this process. Earlier in the same year the 'BS 5750' philosophy – a quality-control management system which it is increasingly necessary for businesses to qualify for if suppliers such as Dons are to remain on their customers' lists – was introduced to the group. Such were the cost savings and other efficiencies achieved as certification spread – to Valley Works in Brechin and Wallace Works in Perth in 1989, for example – that in 1991, after an investigation revealed that further improvement was possible, a Total Quality Management (TQM) programme, co-ordinated by W. Barclay Low, personnel director, was instigated throughout the group. Although this has created a very different culture within the company compared to that which had prevailed up to 1986 – 'a happy ship' is how one contemporary described it – discussion with those involved indicates that motivation at all levels has increased significantly. Through TQM and its emphasis on personal development within the company, it is anticipated that further gains will be forthcoming.

This is despite a considerable cut in numbers and the departure of some senior staff. In 1985 Don Bros, Buist & Co employed in the region of 1,500 people; the figure in 1991 was nearer 800. By a combination of careful planning, sensitive management and good fortune, the numbers involved at any one time have invariably been small, alternative employment has often been offered to those affected and, as a result, the company has been able to maintain good relations within those communities which provide the bulk of the labour force.

In his efforts to root out inefficiency, MacCallum was strongly supported by Shell, whose priorities and concerns have over a remarkably short time been absorbed by Dons. The need to improve working conditions and safety was emphasised from the outset (and is now a priority within the group), with John A. Collins, managing director of Shell UK and chief executive of Shell Chemicals, expressing concern at his first board meeting in Forfar about the level of noise within some of Dons' factories. In 1987 an enhanced programme was introduced involving programmes such as Unsafe Act auditing techniques and forklift-truck driving skills courses, which have cut considerably the number of lost-time accidents: in the first part of 1990 one million man-hours (a period of almost six months) were worked without a single lost-time accident. The discussions on safety matters which have taken place between management and shop-floor workers have helped to develop a company-wide rapport which in its turn is making for more productive relationships within the company.

Shell's influence has been felt in other ways too. It was from that quarter that the most penetrating questions about Dons' business strategy and cost controls came in the early post-takeover period, when Shell were represented by John Collins and C. N. C. Haslam, Shell UK's finance director, who in the same capacity was succeeded on the Scottish company's board in 1989 by M. L. Raiser. The appointment of K. D. Ward, a chartered accountant who had worked for Shell for 12 years, to succeed Dons' long-serving finance director Ernest Gourlay who retired in 1989, represented another break with past practice, tightened the Shell connection and provided the board of Don & Low with an opportunity to look afresh at the company's financial procedures. Significantly it was Ward who produced the fateful graphs early in 1990 which revealed so starkly the steady decline in jute profits. With Stuart Howie, he had also been responsible for urging the board of Don & Low to tighten their credit controls, which had slackened towards the end of the 1980s, and for pointing to the need for a reduction in stock levels – objectives which are now shared by the group as a whole.

It was, however, William Low's retiral from the position of non-executive chairman of the group at the end of 1989, and his replacement by Shell's Evert Henkes, which effectively marked the end of the old era and declared beyond doubt that a new partnership had been forged.[4]

So far, the indications are that it has been highly successful. On a personal level, recognition of this came in 1990 when it was announced that in 1991 Alasdair MacCallum would become chairman of the CBI in Scotland. The group's figures tell an impressive tale too. As has been seen, turnover of Don & Low (Holdings) Ltd had remained static over the three years to December 1990. At first sight the changes which have been discussed in this chapter appear to have produced only modest improvements in pre-tax profits (see Table 13.1). Yet Dons has a record which compares well with other Scottish-based textile companies during what has been the bleakest period the industry has experienced since the early 1930s.[5] The figures for consolidated profit before tax have risen every year since 1987; so too have dividends. Now the European challenge is under way. Much preparation has been done to ensure that Don & Low is ready for it. As the company enters its third century, the historical record indicates that it will be met.

Chapter Thirteen: Shell

1 Most of the material for this chapter is taken from current minute-books and related papers. These have been supplemented by interviews with serving and past directors and other senior members of Dons'staff. In order to respect confidentiality, precise references to sources are not provided.

2 Unless otherwise stated, references to 'the board' mean that of the holding company, which until the spring of 1987 was Don Brothers, Buist PLC. At that time the name was changed: after more than a century 'Buist' was dropped and 'Dons' was registered as a private company, Don & Low (Holdings) Ltd. At the time of writing there are two subsidiaries within the group, Don & Low and Don & Low Nonwovens.

3 Mitchell left the company in 1991.

4 Henkes is chief executive of Shell Chemicals and managing director of Shell UK. The company's current personnel director, W. Barclay Low, one of Low's sons (and a graduate of the University of Ulster), who joined Dons in 1973, now maintains the sole formal link with the Low family.

5 See, for example, *The Scotsman* 'Business 300' supplement, 11 December 1991.

Index